Living A Dream:
the education of a duck hunter

by Norman Seymour

Artwork by John House

Preface by Tony Dean

Foreword by Harvey K. Nelson

Published by Minnesota Waterfowl Association

Table of Contents

Acknowledgements/Dedication i

Preface...iii

Foreword ix

Introduction xiii

My First Duck Hunt 1

My Apprenticeship..7

Duck Hunting Along the St. Lawrence...15

Getting My Act Together 23

Delta Days 31

My Introduction to Waterfowl Management....................................41

Black Ducks Down East 51

Atlantic Sea Ducks...69

The Prairie "Duck Factory" 83

The Wintering Grounds: California Dreaming 99

The Grass Roots Hunter 111

Does the Gun Really Matter? 123

Can We Learn from the British? 141

Europe and the Anti-Hunting Movement.......................................159

My Wild Goose Chase...169

Atlantic Traditions 187

Waterfowl Conservation at the Millennium...................................201

Waterfowling Tomorrow?..217

Epilogue 228

Bibliography 229

Acknowledgements

I am indebted to the many people who helped me with comments and advice. Some persisted through several drafts. Without the following people, I'm certain this book would not have been completed: Alan Afton, Ray Arnett, Bob Bailey, Bob Bancroft, Bill Barrow, Wayne Cowan, Harold Duebbert, Eric Frasier, Ray Lewis, Frank McKinney, Dan Nelson, Gerry Parker, Gary Pearson, Mark Pulsifer, Bill Ready, Greg Soulliere, Bob Stuck, Rodger Titman, Greg Yarris, Dave Wielicki, Steve Wilds, and many others.

Special thanks go to Tony Dean and Harvey Nelson for providing the preface and foreword, as well as helpful comments, and to Tony Erskine, Jim Phillips and Reynold Stone for editorial assistance. Over the years, Tony Erskine, Jim Phillips and George Reiger helped me to refine my thinking on many issues. Only my typist, Bonnie McIsaac, can herself tell you the role she played in getting this book into shape.

Thanks also to the Minnesota Waterfowl Association for its support. I'm pleased to be associated with this fine advocate for duck hunting.

Dedication

I dedicate this book to the many people who have contributed to my education, and to my wife and family who have always supported and encouraged me in the pursuit of my dreams.

Preface

I grew up on the prairies of central North Dakota. I lived on a farm for several years and each spring snow melts formed a seasonal wetland perhaps a half-mile from our house. Each day, I'd scurry home from school and crawl on my belly to get an up-close look at the ducks. I remember my heart thumping as I crawled through the vegetation and discovered I was eye-to-eye with a mallard drake. From that moment forward, I've enjoyed a life-long love affair and fascination with ducks.

I've hunted ducks since the 1950s and from then until now, have witnessed a continual population decline. Hunting was excellent throughout the 1950s and 1970s but I saw a dramatic decline during the 1980s. That decade marked an extended drought on the prairies and I was less than optimistic about the future of ducks and duck hunting. However, in the early 1990s, moisture arrived. Cold winters with heavy snow followed by quick spring thaws had floods rolling across the Dakota prairies. In a lifetime on these prairies, I'd never seen better habitat conditions. With the Conservation Reserve Program (CRP) in place, my pessimism turned to optimism, but then, though populations increased, they didn't match expectations. The numbers of ducks I'd see each autumn in the best breeding habitat on the continent, fell far short of what I'd witnessed in the 1950s and 1970s. Like many duck hunters who'd heard projections of record flights, I experienced their disappointments. I called duck hunting friends in all four flyways. The story was the same everywhere. The ducks were always, "somewhere else." In 1999, Minnesota, a state with more active duck hunters than any other, suffered through their poorest duck season ever. Ironically, waterfowl managers had predicted the best fall flight on record.

What happened? What circumstances combined to produce such meager fall flights in so many areas when habitat conditions appeared to be better than at any other point in the previous 60 years?

The reasons are complex. The solutions, I fear, are elusive.

In March, 1998, I attended the Minnesota Waterfowl Association's Waterfowl Seminar at Fergus Falls, MN and there, heard Norman Seymour deliver a talk on the future of waterfowl hunting. As I listened, I realized he was saying the same things I'd been saying about ducks and the problems they face. I interviewed him the following day and we became instant friends.

I'd see Norm two more times over the next two years. We appeared together on a panel discussion at the famed Delta Marsh station at Portage La Prairie, Manitoba, the following year. That evening, Norm and I gathered with a group of bright young waterfowl student-researchers and talked ducks. Norm and myself were the last ones to call it a night, so engrossed in duck talk that when we finally did, it was already early morning.

We were concerned about ducks. We'd seen the rosy forecasts and, as a former Ducks Unlimited volunteer, I once believed they were doing a great job on the Canadian prairies. My illusions were shattered a year earlier when I traveled to Manitoba to fish. Instead of a myriad of wetlands, I saw endless wheat fields and little evidence of Ducks Unlimited's presence on the prairies. As scarce as water was, grass was an even scarcer commodity. Where, I wondered, would ducks nest?

When I returned home, I talked with an outdoor writer colleague, Dan Nelson, who had been touring Saskatchewan at the same time I was in Manitoba. His report echoed mine. And since we'd both grown up in the duck-rich Dakotas, we were under no illusions that there would be a big fall flight from prairie Canada. And we both realized that if we were to lose the CRP program on the prairies, the Dakotas would look a lot like prairie Canada.

It was time for straight talk about ducks, about wetlands and about the prairies. Unfortunately, none of it was coming from the waterfowl management establishment. For a lifetime, I'd heard, "When the water returns, so will the ducks." The water came, of course, but duck production lagged far behind what that habitat should have produced.

I remember the day I walked a CRP field with Carl Madsen, one of the best and most innovative waterfowl biologists I've known, and soaked in the information he passed along.

"If someone were to advocate cutting what remains of the old growth forests," he said, "the public outcry would be instant and forceful. Yet, that's exactly what we've done on the prairies. We've eliminated millions of acres of old growth prairie and with it has gone the diversity we need to raise ducks and all other kinds of prairie-dependent wildlife."

Problem is, as duck hunters, we've been vigilant about maintaining wetlands but have paid scant attention to that all important grass component that is equally important to breeding ducks, songbirds and a host of other prairie inhabitants. And while it's easy to place the blame on farmers, the fact is, they only respond to the hands they're dealt. I believe it's going to take fundamental change in government agricultural programs; change that can help farmers make a decent living and provide a home for wildlife. Interestingly, while some agricultural organizations pooh-pooh those who seek to protect wetlands and grass, the drainage and plowing hasn't done much for farmers. The problems today are no different than they were when I was a kid on a Dakota farm. It's never been the ability of a farmer to raise crops productively that's in question. Rather, it's his ability to get a fair price for what he produces.

There's another problem that's been plaguing ducks. The predator community on the breeding grounds has been so altered, it's become a prime reason ducks haven't recovered. Predator management is far from the only thing that needs to be done, but more and more biologists who spend time in the field have come to the conclusion that in an altered landscape, it should be another tool in the manager's kit.

Finally, there's the management community. They've rarely reached out to hunters to make them a part of the duck recovery effort. Some shroud waterfowl management in a veil of secrecy and reject any participation from the hunting community. Yet, without hunters, they'll be without jobs. Fortunately, there are still good waterfowl managers out there who recognize that this is not rocket science. Provide the birds with adequate water and grass nesting cover, manage predators where necessary, regulate harvest and ducks should do well.

What's lacking, of course, is accountability. If a private business were to predict record sales and then fall far short of expectations, you can imagine the management shake-ups. Stockholders demand accountability. I've held the opinion for some time that those of us who hunt ducks are, in fact, stockholders. When I read about Ducks Unlimited's Prairie Care initiative but see little evidence on the ground, I wonder why we haven't questioned them. And, I was cha-grined when I asked one of their top scientists how many ducks DU's prairie Canada projects produce. He responded by saying, "I don't know." We need to demand accountability from DU. But we also should demand the same from our state and federal agencies.

There has been one significant change. The computer, a technological tool, has largely replaced what duck men once did; and that is to observe, record and deduce. Today, a population model is built via computer and all of the data factored in. There are few Jerry Stoudts, Art Hawkins, Al Hochbaums or Harold Duebberts out there, pioneer waterfowl men who'd dedicated their lives to ducks. And seemingly, they all retired within a 20-year period, replaced by younger, computer-age biologists, none of whom are old enough to remember when we had many more ducks. There have been more changes. The U.S. Fish & Wildlife Service doesn't seem to be in the duck business these days, at least not in the way they once were. The Canadian Wildlife Service lets Ducks Unlimited run the Canada show. And finally, I think waterfowl managers have misjudged those of us who hunt ducks. They think we want to kill more ducks. What they've failed to grasp is that what we really want is to see more ducks.

Ironically, while ducks have floundered, geese have pros-pered. Though they have provided hunting recreation during a peri-od when ducks were in short supply, once a duck hunter, always a duck hunter. Almost everywhere that giant Canada goose restoration projects have taken place, it's usually only a matter of time before populations increase to nuisance levels. And certainly, no population increase has puzzled waterfowl managers more than the burgeoning mid-continent snow goose flock.

As that flock grew, the birds became warier and in an effort to curb the growth managers resorted to extreme measures, all of them involving hunters. They instituted a spring season, allowed the use of unplugged shotguns, electronic calls and increased bag limits. And, in the finest tradition of doublespeak, they called it a "conser-vation season." The message sent: shoot as many geese as you can without the normal restraints. The season hasn't appreciably reduced populations but it's certainly lowered hunting ethics. Snows are wary, you won't find arctic birds around metro golf courses. If anything, that wild trait should have more value in a hunting world gradually going the way of stocked birds and shooting preserves. The management effort has accomplished little beyond reducing the value of these birds in the eyes of managers and hunters. I get a pain in the pit of my stomach when I hear waterfowl managers refer to snows as "sky carp." Equally important, this effort has removed a huge chip from something called hunting ethics.

It is against this backdrop that Norm Seymour has authored the most important work on waterfowl to date. He brings a unique perspective to this endeavor. He's a well-traveled duck hunter, having hunted in his native Canada, the U.S. and even in European nations. He is a researcher, considered one of the top authorities on black ducks. And, he is a teacher, a man who helps turn young minds into inquiring ones.

Norm began hunting under the watchful eye of a favorite uncle. He later studied under Al Hochbaum at the Delta Waterfowl Research Station in Manitoba, and he currently teaches waterfowl biology and management to eager young students at St. Francis Xavier University in Antigonish, Nova Scotia. With teachers like Norm, I know there's hope for a new generation of young waterfowl managers. Young men and women who won't be constricted to the rote-like "but we've always done it this way," mold.

Most important, he brings passion and his no-nonsense, inquiring mind to the issue of ducks. Like most of his colleagues, he recognizes habitat as the first requirement, but questions that we have enough ducks to fill the habitat that remains. He wonders about the impact of the gun, questioning the liberal limits that follow minor spikes in the duck population. And mostly, he questions his own profession. Have they done enough? Have they done it right? Have they involved hunters, their main constituency, in the effort to restore ducks?

Whether you're a waterfowl manager, a student, or like me, a passionate duck hunter who wonders if we'll ever again see sky-blackening flocks riding a north wind south, this book will give you much to ponder.

Tony Dean
Tony Dean Outdoors, Inc.
Pierre, South Dakota

Foreword

The waterfowl resource and related habitats constitute a treasure important to all North Americans. The welfare of most waterfowl species and their environs is being threatened increasingly, and the complex task of managing North American waterfowl is never-ending. The continued existence of healthy populations and habitats will depend on more sophisticated management programs with adequate funding support, and dedicated people to carry them out, professionals and laypeople alike. It is now more important than ever that the waterfowl hunting fraternity and other waterfowl enthusiasts, step forward to defend this valuable resource that stirs their blood and refreshes their souls.

This book is for waterfowl hunters, written by a knowledgeable and avid hunter. It also was written by a professional waterfowl scientist and educator to stimulate deeper thought by wildlife managers and administrators. The author speculates on the future of the sport of waterfowl hunting in North America and the ability to cope with new challenges confronting waterfowl management. He relies on his personal and professional experiences to weave a fascinating treatise, in simple but precise language, that will quickly grab the attention of all hunters and waterfowl enthusiasts. Once they read the first few chapters they will find it difficult to put the book down.

Norm Seymour grew up in a "wildfowling environment" among family and friends in rural Ontario and Québec. They cherished the time spent in nearby marshes observing migratory birds and calling black ducks into their decoys. These early outdoor experiences triggered Norm's interest in pursuing a career in zoology and wildlife management. His interests in waterfowl and wetlands on the Canadian prairies led to the opportunity to conduct graduate studies on the breeding ecology of the shoveler at the Delta Waterfowl and Wetlands Research Station in Manitoba. He later returned to Nova Scotia, where he began his formal education to complete his doctoral research on black ducks. He joined the faculty at St. Francis Xavier University as a Professor of Biology where he helped expose young minds to natural resource issues. He also continued to work on black ducks and became a recognized authority on that species and their habitat requirements.

The author's strong interest in waterfowl hunting has prevailed throughout his academic career. In describing his passion for ducks, he relates fascinating accounts of his hunting excursions in many parts of North America. He refers to these experiences as "living a dream." These experiences also caused him to reflect on the drastic changes that have occurred over the past 40 years and their effects on waterfowl population levels, distribution and hunting opportunity.

As a scientist, he presents his perspectives on population and distribution changes, habitat deterioration and fragmentation, the important role of private lands and agricultural programs in maintaining wetland and grasslands in the landscape, problems concerning hunting opportunities on public versus private lands, and the implications of more complicated and restrictive hunting regulations. He recognizes that many uncontrollable environmental influences, such as climatic changes and precipitation cycles, often have more direct effects on waterfowl populations than intensive management practices. Serious questions are raised about certain federal and state/provincial policies, programs and biopolitical actions that have far-reaching impacts on water and habitat quality and quantity, especially on private lands. He speculates about the real effects of hunting on current duck populations and raises the unanswered question about mortality from hunting being additive or compensatory. Deep concern is expressed about the inability of present day managers and researchers to fully understand what is causing the decline in black ducks, pintails and scaup, contrasted to the present overabundance of snow geese. The final chapters represent the author's philosophical views on the future of waterfowl hunting and what must be done to maintain strong public support for future waterfowl, wetland and grassland management programs. He recognizes that much has been accomplished in the past through habitat protection and development, but speculates that present population management strategies for setting annual hunting regulations for ducks tend to be too liberal. The current focus on habitat protection and enhancement under the joint venture concept of the North American Waterfowl Management Plan (NAWMP) has been highly successful. Many other partnership efforts launched in recent years have produced great dividends for the waterfowl resource. He expresses concern, however, that continued success is dependent on retaining adequate breeding, migration and wintering habitats on private lands. He also expresses the belief that the NAWMP does not go far enough in addressing population distribution objectives and hunting opportunity.

Hunter recruitment needs careful consideration, with special efforts to encourage greater youth participation and to provide hunting opportunities. The increasing anti-hunting sentiment must be dealt with directly. The question remains, How can the spirit of wildfowling be instilled in this and future generations during the next millennium? Present day hunters, wildlife managers and researchers, other waterfowl enthusiasts and the general public must collectively join forces to help mold these attitudes and decisions. Norm Seymour presents some unique perspectives on these current, critical issues. For these reasons, *all waterfowl hunters must read this book!*

Harvey K. Nelson
U.S. Fish & Wildlife Service (Retired)
Special Consultant to the Minnesota Waterfowl Association

Introduction

Ducks have been an integral part of my life since childhood. In fact, I can't remember a day when I haven't thought about ducks. Studying their biology and management sustains my intellectual curiosity, but it's my passion for duck hunting that emotionally bonds me to them. Although the intense thrill that I experienced in my youth has diminished, hunting waterfowl is the most satisfying activity I pursue and I suspect there are few things grown men do with such enthusiasm. I believe it is important to perpetuate this exciting part of our outdoor heritage not only because I know what it has meant to me, but because I believe it has social value.

As the sub-title suggests, this book is about my education as a duck hunter. It is about the development of my thinking-my perspective-on waterfowl management and hunting, and in this I had a lot of learning to do. Although I call upon my training and experience as a biologist, I'm writing the book as a duck hunter. And I'm writing it for duck hunters who want to become better informed. It's my interpretation of and my opinion on issues of waterfowl management and hunting.

I'm writing this book out of concern. I'm concerned about the loss of interest in waterfowling by young people and I wonder what can be done about it. This problem is acute in Canada. But I'm also concerned about how we hunt and manage waterfowl. I'm saying to hunters that we need to be *ethical* and *conservative* in our hunting, and I am saying to professional waterfowl management that it should promote this perspective. I believe that some hunters and professionals have lost perspective in this regard.

I'm saying that there are issues in waterfowl management that may impact negatively on the future of waterfowling and that these issues need attention. I'm asking professional management whether or not it could be doing some things better. I believe ducks and duck hunting would be better off had management done some things differently. For example, even if biological evidence suggests waterfowl can sustain liberal harvests, I'm saying there are good reasons not to support this approach. There are dimensions to killing animals that go beyond statistics and utilitarian science. I'm encouraging hunters to take the conservative approach and to personally show restraint, try to better see waterfowl hunting as the privilege it is.

This is my point of view and, as I reveal, I didn't always think this way. I still wrestle with doing the right thing every time I go hunting. I think the way hunting continually challenges us to try to do what is ethically right is one of its important values. I'm not telling the reader what to think, but I'm encouraging a "healthy" skepticism. I'm raising questions about how we hunt and manage waterfowl. I think they are worthwhile questions that need answers.

The two chapters on management in Europe are included to show that there are different perspectives and other ways of doing things. If there are worthwhile elements that would improve our system of management, then perhaps we should adopt them. Also, there are events happening elsewhere that will affect North American hunting, and we should be aware of them.

Finally, I believe that individuals can make a difference. This book is a plea to get involved with protecting the future of waterfowling. Nobody but hunters can ensure that waterfowling will remain part of North America's outdoor heritage.

My First Duck Hunt

In the darkness of my bedroom I lay awake listening for big trucks gearing down as they slowed for the curving highway in front of my aunt and uncle's house. I would hold the alarm clock up to the window to read the face in the headlight glare. Rarely had more than 10 minutes passed since the last truck. I was too excited to sleep. In the middle of the night I heard my uncle get up to check his barking foxhounds. He moved quietly through the kitchen toward the kennel. But I had already gotten out of bed and peeked through my window. I saw the raccoon that started the ruckus disappear into the blackness. I lay back down on the bed waiting for another truck to roar past and wondered if daylight would ever arrive. My young mind raced in overdrive because the dawn would bring the realization of my childhood dream—my first duck hunt. I was 13 years old.

Since age nine I had accompanied my uncle, Harold (Lal) Linnett, as he hunted, fished and trapped along the north shore of the St. Lawrence River near my home in Cornwall, Ontario. A man of average height, he had a stocky physique and was exceptionally strong. His most noticeable physical characteristic was his premature baldness. He always wore a baseball cap outdoors, but removed it when he came indoors causing his deeply tanned face to exaggerate the glowing whiteness of his pate. He had returned home from World War II, borrowed enough money from my grandmother to buy a car, taken a job in a nearby textile mill where shift work gave him lots of time for himself, and settled beside the river to resume his passion for the outdoors. There were many uncertainties in his life but they didn't extend to hunting and fishing.

I idolized Uncle Lal. I felt excitement whenever I returned home from elementary school to see his old blue Chevy parked in our driveway. Once he arrived to show off his new double-barrelled Browning shotgun which he had been eyeing for weeks in a local sporting-goods store. I watched transfixed as he stripped down and reassembled the firearm in our kitchen. When he let me hold it, I cradled it in my arms. It was too heavy and long for me to shoulder. Later that fall he brought six blue-winged teal to the house. I wouldn't let my grandmother prepare them for the pot until I'd enjoyed manipulating the teal into what I imagined to be life-like postures and creating my conception of a duck hunt. Since my father didn't hunt, I dreamed of the time when I'd be able to go afield with Uncle Lal.

I attempted to satisfy my curiosity about the natural world by exploring the local countryside. I recall the thrill of discovering my first blue-winged teal on the marshy margins of Hamilton Island, 12 miles east of Cornwall, where since age five I'd spent the summer with my parents, sister and grandmother. I watched as three drakes bobbed their heads and uttered high-pitched peeps in an effort to woo a nearby hen. The drakes were resplendent in their breeding plumage-steel-blue heads with large white crescents between their eye and bill. The sombre brown hen rarely reacted to their courtship rituals. She seemed more interested in eating. But several weeks later I found her down-lined nest hidden in the dry grass along a pasture fencerow, and on several occasions I saw the hen with her brood of ducklings.

I collected insects and bird eggs which I kept in carefully labelled shoe boxes. My mother nurtured my interest by buying me field guides which I would pore over for hours. She never seemed to tire of testing my growing ability to identify birds I'd never seen. Inevitably, one of my Christmas gifts would be a subscription to a hunting and fishing magazine. My father, who worked his way up from gang laborer to assistant manager of the company that supplied electrical power, freight haulage and public transportation for the city of Cornwall, spent hours indulging my passion by driving me over country roads to look for wildlife. Often, we would stop and explore on foot. One morning we flushed a black duck from her nest on an island beside the Long Sault Rapids, a narrow section of the river where the current seethed and boiled. The rapids were later inundated by Lake St. Lawrence, a massive hydro-electric project that drowned everything for miles around, including the village where my grandfather had been a black-smith and my father had been born. I took one pale olive egg from the hen's nest; it remains in my collection to this day.

On my first trips afield with Uncle Lal I simply tagged along. I watched when he stood to bring down a high-flying black duck, deftly pull a walleye from the river's depths or lift a muskrat from a steel trap. I felt an emotional rush when he set loose his baying pack of Walker and blue-tick hounds to chase a fox across the snow-covered hills. He never was reticent on these outings and I listened to every word with a raptness that would have astounded my school teachers. He talked about his time in the navy and being adrift in a lifeboat for days in the cold North Atlantic after his corvette, the *Snowberry*, had been torpedoed by a German U-Boat. He talked about the St. Lawrence River in all its moods and seasons. He talked about ducks, which were plentiful in local marshes, and duck hunting. From carefully listening and closely observing I learned many of nature's secrets, but mostly he taught me to love and embrace everything about the natural world. He had time to spend outdoors and he had time for me.

Bits and pieces of all this raced through my young brain as I lay in bed that night in September, 1954. Tomorrow was opening day of Ontario's duck-hunting season. I had practised shooting that summer with Uncle Lal's 410-bore single-shot. In August, we spent several evenings cutting and hauling basswood poles and cedar boughs to build our blind. We completed construction weeks before opening day. The five days of school leading up to the big day passed with agonizing slowness. When Friday finally arrived and the four o'clock bell signalled the end of class, I dashed to the factory parking lot where we'd arranged to meet. I was to spend the night at my aunt and uncle's house.

When I finally heard my uncle awaken, I jumped from bed and began dressing. After a quick breakfast we walked down to the boathouse in the predawn blackness. I felt so proud, so mature. I was carrying my new 12-gauge shotgun under my arm. Several days earlier my Dad had given me the Stevens pump-action shotgun. I was expecting a single-shot. The repeating action surprised and delighted me.

Our blind was built on a small bulrush clump bordering a pocket of protected, open water. It was in the middle of a two-mile long bulrush bank and a favorite gathering spot for locally raised waterfowl. Our blind was so near to my uncle's house that Aunt Bessie could watch us from the front porch. Uncle Lal had no need to stake a claim to the blind site; everyone knew that he hunted there on opening day.

Night sounds filled the air as my uncle rowed us out in his old wooden punt. On the open water he carefully arranged three ancient canvas teal decoys and a dozen new mail-order *papier-mâché* black ducks. Roosting blackbirds flushed with a clamor when we tucked the boat into a clump of rushes, climbed into the blind and began gazing out into the blackness. The hunt had begun.

I sat on an old wooden butter box and waited for the first faint wash of pink and gray on the eastern horizon that would enable me to see the ducks that we could hear winging through the air and splashing among the decoys. Scores of hunters had invaded the river's marshes and distant guns began booming long before I made out the silhouette of a duck swimming in the decoys. My uncle whispered a reminder to brace my feet as I poked the barrel of my shotgun through a gap in the cedars. I pointed at the bird and pulled the trigger. A great flash of light shot toward the unsuspecting teal. After the commotion subsided I could see the small blue-wing motionless on the water. I had killed my first duck. I was elated.

The graying light brought the sound of gunfire to a high, virtually continuous pitch. The cannonade echoed all along the river. Flocks of ducks milled about the sky in confusion. After the first half-hour of shooting I began to see black ducks flying high overhead, winging inland across the blue September sky to find refuge on small, secluded wetlands where they would wait until dark before returning to roost. But flocks of blue-wings continued to flit about the marshes. Hunters took a high toll, particularly during the first two hours of daylight. This was no time for a birdwatcher to visit the river, although that was of no concern to me in those days.

I killed four more teal that morning and watched my uncle display his extraordinary wing-shooting skill. I can still see three black ducks that descended toward our rig. They flared as my uncle stood to shoot and then splashed dead among the decoys. My uncle rowed the punt when we retrieved the birds, but I got to pick them from the water. I held them and smoothed their feathers before carefully arranging them on the floor of the boat. We talked about ducks and duck hunting while waiting for another flight. We shot until noon, then went ashore for lunch. We would gun in the evening, and I could hardly wait for our hunt to resume. Why did we have to go in for lunch, I wondered.

I had to be the happiest kid in Ontario as we sat on the lawn behind the house under a warm Indian Summer sun and cleaned the birds. My only nagging doubt concerned the legal bag limit. We had retrieved 15 teal and three black ducks that morning. I knew my uncle's lawful limit was eight ducks. I was underage and not legally allowed to hunt or carry a gun. Earlier, we had visited "Old Man" Leduc, who lived down the road. He had just returned from his blind on a small pond deep in the marsh where teal and black ducks raised broods during the summer. He sat in his punt that September afternoon surrounded by small brown bodies. He had killed 60 teal, every one pot-shot. He never hunted ducks after opening day despite a three-month-long season. It would take a dozen female blue-wings to produce enough young to equal his kill. I was too intimidated to ask my uncle about the high kills. Clearly, bag limits were not part of our local waterfowl hunting tradition.

The evening hunt brought another six teal and five black ducks to our bag. I accounted for four of the teal. As we came ashore under a dark, star-lit sky, I began to question my shooting skills. My uncle allowed the teal to land among the decoys and encouraged me to shoot them on the water. He fired only at flying ducks. I had missed every one. I began to suspect there was a right and wrong way to kill ducks. I vowed to improve my shooting. I was learning.

The long day's end found me exhausted from a lack of sleep, but in an upbeat mood. As I lay in bed that night, before I closed my eyes and fell asleep, my mind was a kaleidoscope of beating wings. I had never experienced such intense emotions and I wanted to experience those feelings again and again. I knew, as only a young boy can know, that I would hunt ducks for the remainder of my life.

Living a Dream

My Apprenticeship

The St. Lawrence River cast a spell over me. Its waters provided high adventure. The river was more than three miles wide near my home and dotted with scores of small islands-the beginning of the Thousand Islands chain. I could look across the water and see New York's Adirondack Mountains. On a clear day I could make out in the northeast the faint outlines of Quebéc's Laurentian Mountains.

The valley landscape consisted mostly of flat farmland interspersed with stands of hardwoods. The main crop was corn. Numerous creeks wound through the valley. The small streams drained into the river to create thousands of acres of shallow-water marsh where I spent untold hours exploring the bays, backwaters and channels. It was ideal for a young duckhunter and budding naturalist.

My parents had leased land and built a cottage on Hamilton Island, part of the Akwesasne Indian Reserve. After it was winterized I lived beside the river from April to November. The shipping channel was only 200 yards from our front porch.

The three month hunting season provided almost continuous gunning. After the opening day cannonade, which sent our locally raised ducks fleeing inland to find refuge on hidden wetlands, a brief lull occurred before migrants began arriving. The first big flight in early October consisted of ring-necked ducks. The "marsh bluebills," as local hunters called them, came out of the forested bogs of the northeast. They were followed in mid-October by lesser and greater scaup-the "true bluebills" which rafted by the thousands on three wide expanses of the river known as Lake St. Francis, Lake St. Louis and Lake St. Pierre. Goldeneyes, the "whistler" of the hunter, usually arrived in good numbers by mid-November. And when late-season weather conditions were right, and small inland waters were frozen, local and migrant black ducks provided extraordinary shooting.

My obsession with hunting did not halt my off-season curiosity. One warm spring day I decided to climb a willow on a nearby island hoping to find a woodpecker egg in an old tree cavity. I was startled by a hen goldeneye bursting from the entrance. I reached in and brought out a beautiful olive-green egg, which is still in my collection. I thought this tree nesting hen was unique, but a few years later I discovered Francis Kortright's book, *The Ducks, Geese, and Swans of North America*, and learned that goldeneyes are one of several duck species that nest in tree cavities. The book also told me why all blue-winged teal we shot early in the season appeared to be females. The drakes which had moulted and lost their colorful mating plumage after breeding had not yet replaced their drab feathers with new finery.

The most spectacular off-season event occurred each spring when northbound flocks of lesser and greater scaup temporarily gathered on the river. I was astonished to see so many ducks. Individual rafts of more than 10,000 scaup were common in April. Their mass departure always began in late afternoon and continued into the night. Flocks of 100 or more would skitter across the water, circle to gain altitude (often over our cottage) and then head west. I would watch flock after flock follow the same route and vanish into the western sky. The next morning the water would be nearly barren of scaup. I longed to follow them to their prairie and tundra breeding grounds.

At first I hunted almost exclusively with my cousin George, who was Uncle Lal's stepson. My uncle kept a careful watch over us. He was fanatical about gun safety, but his shooting instructions today would be considered highly suspect. He began by teaching us the dubious art of shooting sitting ducks. With blue-wings, he said, we should rise and quickly fire at a single duck because the skittish teal would instantly take wing. Bluebills, however, would at first swim toward one another. We should hesitate and allow them to form a huddle, and then fire into densest part of the flock. Despite these instructions, I noticed he only fired at flying ducks.

Black ducks created a different problem because these wary birds seldom landed in the decoys. The key was knowing when they were in range, when to rise and begin firing as the ducks approached the decoys. My uncle would say, "Now!" and we would leap to our feet and start shooting at incoming blacks, which always were in close range over the decoys. But when my cousin and I were left to our own devices one of us would invariably jump up too soon, fearing the other would get the first shot, and fire at ducks that were still too far away.

This was followed by the difficult task of actually hitting a flying duck, either those we allowed to approach within range or, more likely, those which left in haste after we potshot their companions. My uncle stressed the need to aim ahead of the duck and "keep swinging!" as we pulled the trigger. He must have despaired at times that we would ever learn to shoot, but he never let our competitive zeal interfere with our enjoyment. He reined us in gently and we longed for his praise.

We hunted teal, black ducks and ring-necks from the blind in front of his home, but killed relatively few. Each weekend we would hear via the local hunter's grapevine of big kills on other parts of the river and, like all young hunters, began longing to gun distant waters, especially the numerous islands across the commercial shipping channel where goldeneyes gathered in significant number. During summer fishing trips I gazed with envy at stone blinds erected on rocky promontories. My first opportunity to gun whistlers came after two years of supervised hunting. My uncle had decreed my cousin and I were sufficiently mature and skilled enough to hunt on our own. This was followed by an invitation from Mr. Guy Smith, a man in his 60s who was both a friend and colleague of my father. He had built a cabin on Smith Island where he spent every spare moment. He owned the only cottage on the half-acre island which he leased from the Mohawks. Over the years he had constructed several stone blinds around the shoreline that allowed him to gun under all weather conditions.

My cousin and I motored over from Hamilton Island in my punt in late afternoon. Our timing was perfect. A November storm was brewing. The wind was swinging to the east and gaining strength. A hard blow would cause the ducks to fly at dawn from their roost on Lake St. Francis, perhaps into our spread of decoys. We could hear the rising wind while sitting in the warmth of the cabin listening to Mr. Smith's tales of waterfowling. He talked late into the night.

Dawn greeted us with a heavily overcast sky as we entered our stone blind. It had been constructed with Mr. Smith's keen eye for detail. It included a ledge to hold our boxes of shells. Heavy burlap lined the inside of the rock walls to break the wind. We had rigged a small flock of decoys that bobbed on the cold, steel-gray water in front of us, and awaited the first flight. Mr. Smith did not accompany us; he stayed behind to busy himself around the cabin.

Our wait was not long. A gale was building. The driving wind made the whistlers fly. They winged past in threes and fours, and in small flocks of as many as eight or ten birds. Very early a lone whistler broke away from a passing flock, banked into the wind and sailed in a tight arc straight for our rig. As it started across the decoys, I stood and swung through like my uncle had instructed. The bird, a hen, crumpled at my shot. I had killed my first whistler. I gazed at the duck for several minutes before my cousin alerted me to the approach of another flock.

I fired many more times that morning before downing my second bird. My shot struck a brown-headed female at almost the same instant my cousin killed a green-headed, white-plumaged drake. I can close my eyes after all these years and see them cart-wheeling through the air together to splash in the decoys. It has always reminded me of Winslow Homer's painting *Right and Left.* The painting depicts a mortally wounded male and female whistler tumbling from the air. Only careful investigation of the painting reveals the gunner in the background, his double-barrelled shotgun against his shoulder.

Periodically during the morning we returned to the warm cabin to get the chill out of our bones. At noon we feasted on a delicious fish chowder which Mr. Smith had prepared from perch and walleyes he'd caught a few days earlier. We returned to our island in mid-afternoon. Our hunt was over. Our 16 ducks were lined up across the front seat of my punt. I still can visualize the smudge of oil on the breast feathers of the second goldeneye I'd killed.

Yet it was not my limit of goldeneyes that made this hunt so memorable. I didn't realize it immediately, but it was Mr. Smith himself. It involved more than his wonderful hospitality. It went beyond the fact we were legally underage. "That isn't important," Mr. Smith explained, "because you are physically able and responsible enough to handle guns and enjoy the hunt." What made this hunt stand out was Mr. Smith's insistence that we kill no more than our legal limit. I'd never before met anyone who cared about limits. Most local water-fowlers took whatever came across their decoys, and on days when big shoots were possible, bragged about how many "limits" they'd killed. Mr. Smith left no doubt that he believed hunting involved more than killing as many ducks as possible. We were expected to respect the limit while hunting as his guest. Mr. Smith was the first real sportsman I'd ever met.

Although I was gaining confidence with each hunt and had earned the right to go afield without adult supervision, I didn't feel I'd yet graduated from my duck-hunting apprenticeship. There is no way to explain this nagging doubt. It comes from deep inside. Then one November I drove to my uncle's house before dawn. We planned to hunt on the Québec side of the river where he had constructed a blind for late-season shooting. My uncle had just finished working a double shift at the mill and explained that he was too tired to hunt. "You go on your own," he said. "You know what to do."

I vowed to be especially careful as I walked down to the boat house. My uncle was very particular about his boat, motor and decoys. Mist rising from the river obscured my view as I headed out into the shipping channel. Visibility was limited to a few yards; I would never be able to see a passing ship in time to avoid a mishap. Since the main channel of the St. Lawrence had been widened and deepened in the mid-1950s, every hunter's fear was being run over or capsized by one of the 700-foot vessels that plied the river. My cousin and I had once rescued a fellow whose boat had been overturned by a laker.

As I crossed the channel I shut down the motor occasionally to listen for the warning throb of diesel engines. Fortunately, I heard none and I felt a rush of relief when Quesnel Island loomed darkly out of the mist. I'd navigated the mile-long run perfectly. I silently congratulated myself. I knew the remainder of the way through the marsh like the back of my hand and soon could make out the black silhouette of the blind.

The blind was framed with basswood poles and brushed with cedar boughs. It was built along the edge of a dense stand of bulrush and cattail that stretched for a quarter-mile between two islands. A 100 yard-wide channel of open water snaked through the rushes, creating a thoroughfare for ducks moving between two open-water feeding areas. I quickly rigged my decoys-two dozen bluebills in a fishhook pattern directly in front of the blind, six whistler blocks in a small clump about 30-feet downwind from the hook, and a dozen blacks scattered close to the blind in a sparse stand of rushes. I guided the boat to the blind and stepped onto the platform. Shooting light was still 20 minutes away.

The first pink streaks of light tinged the eastern horizon as I stood in the blind peering over the tops of the cedars. A sudden rush of bluebills heading downwind as if jet-propelled, caught me by surprise. In an instant, they banked tightly into the wind, flew along the shank of the fishhook and pitched in the water in front of me. As I reached for my shotgun, I remembered my uncle's instructions. I stomped my foot on the wooden floor of the blind. The alarmed birds swam together in a tight clump and held their heads high, looking back at the blind as they paddled slowly out of the decoys. I raised my gun and fired. My first shot went over their heads, but my second killed two birds. My third shot stopped a duck as it skittered across the surface.

A few minutes later a single whistler made me shoulder my

gun. I pushed the safety off and swung on the duck as it approached in perfect range. Click! Pump! Click! I had failed to reload! I was thankful Uncle Lal wasn't alongside to witness my oversight. But within minutes four goldeneyes swung toward the blind. Three landed among the decoys, but the fourth stayed high and presented a perfect right-to-left shot. I killed it cleanly. The duck fell not more than 10 feet in front of the blind. I swelled with pride at my shot.

A lull developed after the first hour, but then I glimpsed out of the corner of my eye a flock of ducks wheeling low over the marsh behind the blind. I crouched down and looked back. They were blacks! They flew toward me and then suddenly dropped into the decoys without so much as a preliminary inspection. I felt a strong urge to grab my shotgun and immediately fire. Instead, I remained kneeling and watched them through the cedars. I counted 33 as they washed and drank. Two had already tucked their bills under their wings, preparing to sleep. The flock probably had just returned to the river from feeding in a nearby cornfield. They were so close together I could have killed a dozen with one potshot.

But something within me had changed. I stood up, causing the ducks to erupt frantically from the water. My first shot brought down two as they towered upwards. I missed cleanly with my second shot, but killed another with my third round. When I fired, it was climbing and drifting away on the wind, more than 30 yards from the blind.

Three black ducks killed on the wing! I was elated. My mind raced. What if I hadn't come out this morning? Look what I would have missed!

It was still early and plenty of birds were on the move, but I knew nothing could match, much less beat, the black ducks. I decided to call it a day. I could hardly wait to get back, show my seven ducks to my uncle and recount every detail of the morning. I gathered my gear, picked up the decoys and soon was on my way. As I passed Quesnel Island I saw Basil, an Indian fisherman, cleaning his catch. I slowed the boat to wave and then held up my three blacks. Basil broke into a broad smile. I revved up the engine and headed out across the shipping channel. I knew my uncle would be surprised and pleased.

Although I did not immediately realize it, my duck-hunting apprenticeship was ending and that morning was pivotal. After that I began to feel increasingly confident about *all* my waterfowling skills. I was 17 years old and, thereafter, rarely shot a sitting duck.

Duck Hunting Along the St. Lawrence

As idyllic as my childhood had been, my teenage years were difficult. I challenged authority at every turn and usually met considerable resistance. Hunting and fishing were in a sense my salvation, an escape from my difficulties which provided some peaceful moments.

My adolescent rebellion expressed itself in many ways, but the most significant involved education. I began to view high school as something that had to be endured. This was especially true after I turned 16 years of age and I got my driver's license. My dad bought me a 1941 Plymouth, probably to keep me from asking for his car, and I already owned a wooden punt and 7.5-horsepower Scott-Atwater outboard. I began escaping to the St. Lawrence's marshes and islands, especially on those autumn and early winter days when scudding gray clouds and rising winds meant the ducks would fly. School authorities raised eyebrows over my increasing absences, but this was only part of the problem. On those days I attended class my mind was elsewhere. I rarely completed homework assignments. The result caused my parents a great deal of anguish. School officials recommended against me returning for my senior year. Complete it, they suggested, when I was ready to apply myself. I wonder how many of my teachers thought that would ever happen? So, at age 17 I became a high school drop-out.

However, I did not view dropping out as the end of my intellectual development. I continued to read, but only what I wanted to read-sporting magazines, field guides and books such as *The Ducks, Geese and Swans of North America*. In fact, I pored over anything to do with the habits of wildlife and fish, subjects not taught in school. This, I believed, was knowledge worth acquiring.

My belief was reinforced by visiting business executives who hired me each summer as a fishing guide. To a man they told me how much they valued my skills at finding fish. In their eyes I was successful. They told me how lucky I was to live on the St. Lawrence, adding that they sometimes wished they could trade places with me. Curiously, none suggested I get my high school diploma and go to college. Their comments fostered my conviction that a formal education was unnecessary for the outdoor life I wanted to lead, and this made me dismissive of anyone who suggested I return to school.

Sometimes I did wonder about myself and my future, especially when I met friends of my parents who'd tell me that I was "crazy" for dropping out. But I usually found comfort in comparing myself to two individuals. Wasn't I better off than my cousin George, who around that time suddenly vanished? He left no note when he left home. He simply walked off, devastating my aunt and uncle. To this day no one knows what prompted his disappearance, but I know his teenage years were troubling for him. Ten years passed before he called home. The other was a friend of my father whom I guided each summer. I got to know him well, and learned that he maintained two houses. His aged mother lived in one and his wife in another. Apparently neither woman was aware of the other. I never figured out why he kept two homes, but I could see that for him fishing was an escape from the complexities of his life. He cherished every moment of his interludes from reality. And people thought *I* was crazy??!!

Like the recreational cocaine user who risks his life but rationalizes his drug-taking by saying, "I don't take heroin," life's outrageous individuals provided me with justification to continue my immature obstinacy. I loved my hunting and fishing, but I suppose I knew even then that they weren't going to give me much direction in life. However, in the meantime, I took a job reading electric meters in Cornwall. I worked alone and no one criticized me as I walked from house to house. I got to know every resident along the river who owned a rig of decoys. I often spent so much time talking "ducks" with them that I had to work overtime to complete my rounds.

And then I discovered Montréal's nightlife. This sophisticated bilingual city, about 60 miles east of Cornwall, enticed me with its siren song. At age 20 I moved to the city, rented an apartment and worked as a laboratory assistant for a paper company. I investigated ways to convert wood chips into pulp by day and spent my nights in the crowded bistros along *Rue Ste. Catherine.* I have to admit, drinking a Molson ale in the company of an attractive young woman sometimes made me put hunting and fishing to the back of my mind!

The only real anchor in my life involved the St. Lawrence River. Each autumn the waterfowl migrations followed their ancient schedule and arrived at the appointed time. I found peace of mind when afield, and went duck hunting at every opportunity. My growing self-confidence allowed me to look on each outing as an effort to fine-tune my skills.

Sadly, soon after cousin George disappeared, my Uncle Lal developed heart trouble which made outdoor activity too strenuous. He rarely went hunting and lost much of his enthusiasm for life. This forced me to find new hunting companions. Before long I found Robin Casgrain, who lived beside the river in the nearby village of Summerstown, and Ted Lavigne, a schoolmate. Both took their hunting seriously and were skilled outdoorsmen.

Robin had inherited a blind site on the east end of Spanner's Point on Lake St. Francis. It was built along a 300-yard strip of bulrush that was locally famous for its diving duck shooting. We purchased a large rig of beautifully carved and painted bluebill decoys from a fellow who believed diving-duck hunting had deteriorated to the point where it was no longer worth the trouble to set up for them.

One hunt from Robin's blind remains fresh in my memory. It began on a calm morning with good numbers of bluebills rafted on the open water of the lake. Although initially most flights stayed too far away for good shooting, a freshening west wind got the birds moving along the rush bed. We had killed four or five and were sitting patiently when a passing flock turned into the wind and headed for our decoys. They approached from my side. When they came in range, I stood and killed a duck with each of my first two shots. A third shuddered and skipped a wingbeat when I fired my last round, only to glide into a nearby hunter's spread of decoys to be "finished off." Robin dropped three with three shots, all of which fell dead into the decoys. Six bluebills (more or less) with six shots! When we returned to the blind in mid-afternoon a pair of canvasbacks swung across our rig. I dropped the female and Robin killed the drake. My hen was only the second canvasback I shot in my youth; my first was a drake I shot with George. These big, highly prized ducks were once common along the St. Lawrence, but by then were rare. I had never before handled a duck with such a thick neck. On the return trip home that evening we struck a partially submerged log, knocking out our motor. We had to row the remaining three miles. But we were under a full moon and clear, starry sky and we were still energized by the day's hunt. We had plenty to talk about and we were in pretty good shape. The long row to the island passed quickly.

By this time I had enough experience and skill to gun selectively. I was no longer satisfied to kill whatever came along. I had learned the habits of different species and I preferred hunting for one particular kind when I went afield. I'd explored new areas of the river each year and now considered my "home water" to be a 150-mile stretch that began about 50 miles east of Montréal and ended 50 miles west of Cornwall. I hunted most frequently on the broad expanses of

Lake St. Francis and Lake St. Louis.

Late-season became my favorite time to go afield. It was the best time to gun drake goldeneyes, the wariest of diving ducks. Mature drakes don't acquire their striking black and white plumage until their second year. They have survived at least one gunning season and make few mistakes in judgment. They're as wary as any black duck, which many view as the smartest duck. The best whistler shooting came in December when few hunters challenged the elements. The extreme cold often created dangerous conditions, but in my youth the risk made each hunt doubly exciting. Three times I found myself in serious trouble. Once it was entirely my fault.

Three of us had motored out to a pole blind in the middle of the river in late December. The temperature hovered near zero. We got out of the boat onto the shooting platform and within minutes had downed three goldeneyes. I turned to get into the boat to retrieve the birds and discovered it was 40-feet downstream, drifting with the current. I had failed to securely tie the boat to the piling. I took off my clothes and prepared to swim, but when I dipped my foot in the frigid water I nearly went into shock. We waited for hours before an Indian fisherman came upon our drifting craft. He tied it to his boat and headed upstream to look for its owner. He was far out in the river when we spotted him. Hypothermia had already begun to set in. We waved our arms, jumped up and down and fired shots to attract his attention. As he neared our blind he looked at us with a sad, knowing gaze, slowly shaking his head from side to side. He said nothing as he handed us the bow line. To this day Robin and Ted carefully watch when I tie a line to a dock or duck blind.

I also found time to hunt occasionally with new acquaintances. One day I went out on Quebéc's Lake St. Pierre with Paul-Emile and Robert, two fellows I worked with. They owned a sink-box, a form of floating blind that's used for gunning diving ducks. It provides a means of hiding on open water. The wooden sink-box is akin to a bathtub which is sunk in the water up to its rim. You sit below the surface in the dry tub and rise up to shoot. It's so deadly American authorities banned its use in the 1930s. Several Canadian provinces also have prohibited it. I'd never hunted from a sink-box.

We rigged the sink-box, which was designed to accommodate two gunners, two miles from shore. Paul-Emile and I took up our positions in the box while Robert motored about half a mile away and anchored. The bluebills flew almost continuously but when there was a lull in the flight, Robert rousted them from their resting areas by bearing down on them at high speed. There were only other hunters out on the lake and they too benefitted. Nobody was likely to object. Despite my concern about what I'd gotten myself into, I found it thrilling to look up at birds approaching the decoys only a foot or two above the water. I stopped after shooting what I considered a reasonable number of scaup, but my hosts continued. Our total bag that day consisted of more than 80 bluebills. They viewed a "good day" as one in which they killed between 150 to 200 ducks. I suppose I was concerned about getting "busted," unlikely though it was, but more importantly I think, their bloodlust offended my view of moderation. I rarely passed up an opportunity to hunt from a sink-box, but I never again hunted with them.

Ducks were not so plentiful along the St. Lawrence in the late 50s and early 60s that you could routinely kill your legal daily limit of eight ducks, plus the two bonus scaup or goldeneyes that were allowed after mid-October. My "old days" are not that old! Robin and I considered a day afield very successful if we retrieved our limits. On those days when large numbers could be killed we sometimes shot more, but these were exceptions. Game wardens did not deter widespread overshooting. I was never checked by the law in all the years I hunted along the river. My uncle, who knew the local warden, told me he never went out on the river to check hunters because he was afraid of the water. Nor did he wait at landings to check waterfowlers coming in from the marsh. There were few places along the river where there was any serious enforcement.

I should add that while most local waterfowl hunters ignored the lawful limit, they did not lack an ethical code. They frowned on excessive kills. One particular individual supplemented his income by illegally selling ducks, even though he had a good job at the mill where my uncle worked. One morning when my uncle and I stopped to visit his father, he came out of a shed where he had "breasted" his morning's bag. I stared at his unshaven, tobacco-stained face as he described his shoot. He told us he'd trespassed that morning on private land leased by a hunting club. He believed he had the right to hunt anywhere, even though several weeks earlier he'd torched a blind of a hunter who had the temerity to build "too close" to a site he planned to hunt. The unfortunate fellow didn't discover the arson until he arrived on the scene the night before the opener. The renegade was shunned by nearly everyone and was known to one and all as "Killer."

In a strange way this provided him with an identity and he worked to promote his outlaw image.

I was proud to be a member of the local duck-hunting community, as were Robin and Ted. This was an important part of our identities. I continued to work as a laboratory assistant, but after four years in Montréal my view of life was beginning to change. In my youth I looked on duck hunting as my sole route to manhood. But now I began to see that life consisted of more than duck hunting. I was slowly coming to the realization that at some point in the future, I'd likely want a good job, a wife, and a family. To achieve my goals, I knew that I probably needed a formal education. I'd have to get back into the system. At age 24, I decided to attend college.

Living a Dream

Getting My Act Together

In late summer of 1965, I packed my belongings into my VW Beetle and began the 800-mile drive eastward to Nova Scotia. My destination was St. Francis Xavier University, a small liberal arts school in the town of Antigonish.

Most of my friends had long since finished with school before I accepted the fact I would need a degree to keep chasing ducks the way I wanted to. My ambition was becoming focused. I wanted to become a waterfowl biologist, but I was in no hurry to actually resume my education. I didn't want to miss a single hunting season on the St. Lawrence River. Then I met Andrea, a recent immigrant from Liverpool, England, who would eventually become my wife. She was understanding but could see I needed a push. While I often talked about becoming a biologist, she pointed out that I appeared reluctant to take the necessary first step. It didn't take long to get the message that I could no longer just talk the talk if our relationship was to develop as I wanted it to.

My dismal performance in high school forced me to seek admission on the "mature student" plan. I wanted a university that not only would give me a chance to prove myself academically, but allow me to keep a shotgun and car in residence so I could continue to hunt. St. Francis Xavier accepted me as a "mature student" and had no problem allowing me to bring my shotgun. However, the Dean of Men adamantly opposed my request to bring my car, presumably fearing I would use it for illicit romances. My repeated pleas during the summer finally prompted the dean to agree to a compromise. I could bring my car provided I kept it on blocks during the school year. I privately vowed to ignore the up-on-blocks stipulation and made plans to rent a garage off campus to keep my car hidden from prying eyes when I was not hunting.

On the long drive east I felt the anxiety that faces every waterfowler who moves to a distant and unknown community. I wondered what duck hunting would be like in Nova Scotia and what difficulties I would face. As every experienced waterfowler knows, the drill is always the same when learning new country.

The first step is to determine the locally abundant species, when and where to hunt them. Local duck hunters, sporting-goods store proprietors and fish-and-game department personnel may provide the general information, but unless you can find someone to take you out and introduce you to the area, you have to work out the specifics yourself. This is very confusing to the beginning waterfowler or for someone new in an area.

In waterfowling, as in real estate, location is everything. Not all marshes attract puddle ducks and not all deep waters satisfy the needs of divers. The key to success is to find the precise location where ducks want to gather. This can be difficult because few waterfowlers will tell a stranger the location of their favorite slough, point of land or sheltered cove. Most often you are referred to waters that attract casual hunters who as likely as not drive away ducks with incessant, out-of-range shooting. Without assistance, it takes several seasons afield before you gain sufficient experience to discover hidden hotspots and know when to hunt them. This is an important part of hunting and it is so satisfying when what you have discovered starts to yield results.

Your options are also dependent on your equipment. A proper decoy rig is necessary to consistently attract ducks. As a general rule, ducks respond best to decoys of their own kind. The number of decoys you need is another matter. A dozen mallard or black duck decoys often is sufficient to attract most puddle-duck species on small waters. By comparison, a hundred or more scaup decoys may be too few if you are hunting a flock of 5,000 that is rafted on open water a half-mile from your blind. Also, a boat may be necessary if you're to get any shooting in some areas. As I headed east, I knew my hunting would be restricted. Once I had packed my clothes and other necessities, I only had room in my small car for my shotgun, a half-dozen black-duck decoys and a pair of hip boots.

All of this gave me plenty to think about on the long drive to northeastern Nova Scotia. Finally, I arrived in Antigonish, a community of some 5,000 people. I knew I was going to have to devote a lot of time to my studies. I'd never developed concentration and study skills. But soon after settling into the routine of classes I could see that I'd have time for hunting. I began exploring the nearby countryside to get a feel for the land and find places to toss out my decoys.

Early autumn was a glorious time to learn the rolling countryside. The foliage of the sugar maples, elms and poplars was beginning to turn fiery red, crimson and yellow. This blaze of color contrasted dramatically against the sombre darkness of the spruce and firs. Three rivers dominated the local landscape, winding through the dairy farms nestled in the shallow valleys. The rivers were rock-strewn streams that hosted good populations of sea-run brook trout and Atlantic salmon. Their depth fluctuated sharply, depending on autumn rains, and the water ran cold and clear. The rivers drained into a five-mile long estuary that emptied into Northumberland Strait.

I drove hundreds of miles over inland roads and along the North Atlantic coast. Ducks were hard to find, and predicting where they'd be from day to day was very difficult. I found myself limited to hunting the rivers and shallow marshes along the estuary. My primary targets were black ducks and green-winged teal. As the season progressed, I found myself watching longingly from shore as flocks of whistlers fed unmolested around the islands in the estuary. This reminded me of earlier days on the St. Lawrence. They were safe from me because I didn't have a boat. I also discovered a flock of about 300 Canada geese, but they rarely left the estuary to forage in nearby fields where I might get at them. Their behavior remained a mystery to me until I discovered that eelgrass beds provided them with plentiful food. They rarely left the open water for any reason.

I often found myself alone on the estuary, a pleasant change from the more crowded marshes back home. Many residents hunted deer, but ignored ducks even though the area had some of the best duck-hunting in the province. I finally met a couple of duck hunters who were very helpful, but the individual who had the greatest influence on me was Father Ernest M. Clarke, a sportsman so special he would have stood out in any company. He was not only an ordained priest, but he had a Ph.D. in physics and had achieved international scientific renown for his electron-scattering experiments.

I first encountered Father Clarke in freshman physics. He was the class instructor. A tall man with a swath of white hair combed over to the side, he always wore a black suit and roman collar. He also always wore a smile, as if he were perpetually happy. Naturally, the students had nicknamed him "Smiley." Early in the school year he told us that he sought truth in both science and philosophy, and his class was an extraordinary mixture of both. He was especially critical of what he called "the arrogance of modern scientists," a criticism I was later to hear made by duck hunters about some waterfowl biologists.

Father Clarke lived in a room in a student residence on campus. I visited him frequently, for he was a profound thinker and conversationalist, and I enjoyed his company. On my first visit I noticed a side-by-side shotgun leaning in a corner. "I'm a hunter," he explained. "I go out when time allows. I find grouse hunting very relaxing, and it's my exercise."

His view of hunting, however, was more than that of a man seeking to flush a few ruffed grouse or get some exercise. His private passion focused sharply on ethical behavior in all its forms, an issue he divorced from religion. "Ethics really has nothing to do with religion. It refers to right and wrong behavior in all our human endeavors. Doctors, lawyers, used-car salesmen and hunters should all behave according to a code of ethics. An atheist can have strong ethical principles. The fact I'm a Catholic priest talking about ethics is quite incidental."

Although he practiced tolerance and civility toward those whose views differed from his, he noted that every hunter faces the same ethical issues. "For example, you must decide *how* to kill. Do you shoot ducks sitting or flying? Do you become frustrated and fire at ducks at extreme range hoping to scratch down a bird but wounding more than you kill? Do you shoot over bait? Do you hunt ducks in extreme weather to take advantage of their momentary vulnerability?"

This was followed by the issue of bag limits. "Do you kill less than the legal limit, the limit or more than the limit? Do you restrain yourself? The choice is up to you. Your decision is more important than the law. How many ducks do you need to kill to have a good day? Do you judge success by whether you killed more than the next man?"

"Above all," he continued, "late at night when you are alone with your thoughts and only you pass judgment on your behavior, do you look back with contentment and view your killing as harmonious with nature? Or have you been selfish?" I'd never heard talk like this!

"Hunting," he concluded, "is a test of whether you can restrain your impulses and behave according to your principles of right and wrong. It challenges you every time you go afield."

Our ethical discussions often ranged far beyond hunting. It was rare that he didn't hand me a book to read, saying, "Here, take this. It should help to fill in a few gaps...."

His questions always posed food for thought. Many nights I would return to my room to think about my youthful excesses. He posed questions that I ponder to this day. Questions about both hunting and my profession of waterfowl biology. Father Clarke was truly an educator.

As for the local shooting, my hunts were never very productive. In the beginning weeks of my first season I sometimes failed to see a duck. But I slowly accumulated the knowledge necessary to successfully hunt ducks during the long three-month season, and by the end of my sophomore year I often killed two or three green-wings or black ducks before class. My roommate and I had a small hotplate in our room and the ducks provided relief from institutional cooking. And then I transferred to the University of Manitoba and had to start the learning process all over again.

My transfer was prompted by the fact I had gone to university to study ecology and wildlife biology. St. Francis Xavier provided me with a solid educational foundation, but did not offer the courses I needed and wanted. Also, late that summer Andrea and I got married. After loading up our old black Acadian the day after the wedding, we headed west to Winnipeg. Andrea had gotten a job teaching kindergarten. I looked forward to duck-hunting on the wind-swept prairies, the great breeding grounds of our migrant flocks and a place where each autumn ducks gathered in enormous number.

I found the flat prairies somewhat daunting. The endless miles of wheat stubble stretched to the horizon. I first focused on the Netley-Libau marshes at the south end of Lake Winnipeg, about a 45-minute drive from our apartment. I hunted the edges of the marsh and the surrounding sloughs, but quickly came up against the prairie paradox. I was seeing more ducks than I'd ever seen in my life, but killing very few. Often I'd look up to see flight after flight winging high across the sky. But most of my ducks were taken by jump-shooting small sloughs or pass shooting at birds leaving the marsh to feed in the stubble or returning to roost. I had no boat-only my hip boots and a dozen newly purchased mallard decoys-and I could not penetrate deep into the marsh where the flocks gathered. I decided to concentrate on stubblefields. I'd read plenty about shooting western mallards over stubble, and had killed black ducks over flooded buckwheat back east, but I found it difficult to locate landowners and obtain permission to hunt.

My growing frustration prompted me to strike up conversations about duck hunting with everyone I met in the hope of making a duck hunting contact. During the third week of October, shortly before freeze-up would end all waterfowl hunting, I chanced upon a stranger at a gas station who in the course of our conversation invited me to join him the following morning. He planned to hunt a field where several thousand mallards were feeding. Permission to hunt would be no problem, he assured me. Moreover, he had the decoys. All I had to do was meet him before dawn in an abandoned farmyard. It would mean skipping a chemistry lecture, but this was no deterrent. I was now a serious student, but I never gave chemistry class a second thought.

The weather was clear but it was cold and windy as Ray Worthington and I walked across the stubble in the predawn blackness. My companion told me it was the sort of weather he'd been waiting for and the raw, rising wind was ideal for where he wanted to hunt. We first set out two dozen oil-paper silhouette mallard decoys that were mounted on wooden stakes. Then we built a blind in a weedy ditch about 60 yards distant. The wind was blowing across the field toward us, so any decoying birds would fly over us. Dawn was still 20 minutes away when I heard the whisper of wings and calling of the vanguard flocks that circled the field. As I lay in the dank smelling grass waiting for shooting time, I stared into the velvet black sky, hoping to catch a glimpse of the mallards.

The dawn light revealed a sight I'd never before witnessed a phenomenon western hunters refer to as a duck tornado or cyclone. Out in the center of the field, far away from our waiting guns, a swirling mass of mallards formed a funnel that towered high in the sky. The ducks set their wings and spiralled down in ever tighter circles, until they touched down on stubble where the first ducks already were feeding. As soon as one group would land, an incoming flock would join the top of the funnel to begin their long spiralling descent. Soon birds were hanging in the air for several seconds a few feet above the stubble, facing into the wind, as they searched for unoccupied space to land. We could hear the chuckling calls of the birds on the ground. Every so often a small group would light, only to immediately get up and fly 50 or so feet before dropping down again. The field seemed alive with ducks, all of which were coming off the marshes of Lake Winnipeg. Every bird passed over us, but much too high to shoot. Our silhouette decoys were no competition for the hundreds of live ducks congregated in the middle of the golden field.

Then smaller numbers of mallards began coming in from a large slough where they'd roosted about a mile distant. They hadn't gained nearly as much altitude as the main flock, and they passed over us in good range. Within 45 minutes both of us had killed four drake mallards apiece. We then completed out our limits with drake pintails. I was thrilled when I looked down at the birds carefully lined up at the edge of the ditch. The green heads of the mallards glistened in the October sun and the brown heads and white neck spikes gave the slender pintails an air of elegance.

Our shooting did not bother the birds feeding in the middle

of the huge field. The high wind had muffled our shots. We were preparing to pack up the decoys when Ray suddenly motioned for me to get down, pointing to a thin line of geese in the distant blue sky. We crouched in the weeds as the giant Canadas drew closer on a flight path that would bring them directly over us. But I rose to shoot too soon and spooked the birds. They were still 50 yards out and frantically climbing when I fired my first shot. I saw the goose drop both feet. My second shot resulted in a puff of feathers, but my third had no apparent effect. I watched dejectedly as the goose flew downwind across the adjacent field. It began climbing to clear a stand of poplars when, to my surprise, it collapsed dead in flight. I ran most of the quarter-mile to where it lay at the edge of the stubble. I knelt down and gazed on the first goose I'd ever killed.

Ray forgave me for spooking the geese. Though not the shot he wanted, he'd scratched one down, too. After retrieving our big birds, we sat on the edge of the ditch and chatted. Ray told me he'd been raised on the Manitoba prairies and years earlier had moved to Toronto to find work. He made the return pilgrimage nearly every autumn to hunt ducks. The farm we were hunting, he said, was his uncle's.

I returned to Winnipeg in high spirits. I'd killed my first drakes-only limit, and it was a limit of choice prairie ducks-mallards and pintails. I also had the satisfaction of shooting my first goose. I savored the events of the morning and knew without doubt that I was going to enjoy duck hunting on the prairies.

I never saw Ray again.

Delta Days

At last, spring has arrived. Warm, soft breezes blow across the Manitoba prairies. The snow has melted and the black earth is beginning to turn green. After the cold, bleak winter each flight of ducks I see makes my spirits soar.

This late April morning I am hidden in a small blind alongside a flooded meadow near the Delta Marsh. In a nearby ditch that drains the surrounding fields are numerous pairs of breeding ducks, but I am interested only in 20 or so drake shovelers that come to this flooded meadow each day to feed. Their large, ponderous bills and muddling habits give them a humorous air, like funny old men with big noses. But these particular shovelers are probably young and virile. All are dressed in their courtship finery-iridescent green heads, chestnut flanks and white breasts. Yet none has found a mate. All the female shovelers in the area are paired, leaving these "frustrated" drakes to spend their days on this flooded meadow, commiserating with one another.

This morning, however, fate in the form of a young biologist will intervene. Before dawn I place a female shoveler in a chicken-wire trap in the meadow. The hen, obtained from the wild as an egg and raised in the Delta Research Station hatchery, will I hope attract these males and lure them into the trap. I want to learn why certain males obtain mates, and how they establish temporary dominance over part of a marsh that provides the necessary security for a female to construct a nest, lay eggs and begin incubation. I need identifiable birds to do this.

This effort marks the beginning of my master's degree research on territorial behavior. In the predawn darkness, as I await the shoveler drakes to arrive from the marsh, I think how much my life has changed in the past four years. My wife has recently given birth to our first daughter, Melani, who will be followed at two-year intervals by Sara and Emily. I have received my bachelor's degree from the University of Manitoba, and am enrolled in the university's graduate school. I'm associated with the Delta Waterfowl Research Station, the most distinguished waterfowl research facility in North America. I'm living a dream, doing what I always have wanted to do-studying the behavior of ducks.

The shoveler hen is confined to a small, protective cage placed in the center of a large, clover-leaf shaped duck-trap. Drakes cannot enter the female's cage but they can approach her closely by entering the trap through funnel-like entrances. The funnels enable drakes to easily enter, but it takes a while for them to learn how to exit.

At first light the drakes fly in from the nearby marsh. Soon they spot the four foot high chicken-wire duck trap (which was not there yesterday), but it doesn't spook them. They have eyes only for the hen, which they immediately spot. They quickly set their wings, splash down on the water and swim toward her. The drakes don't pause to feed. They're interested only in the female.

Slowly, they paddle around investigating the chicken-wire structure. Already they're jostling with one another, uttering low, guttural threatening calls. The female huddles in her cage, frightened by these males. Three drakes enter the trap through the funnels. By the time I stand up and walk toward them, there are eight in the trap. All the drakes flush, but the ones inside the pen fall back to the water after hitting the wire cover. I capture them and affix uniquely marked plastic disks to their bills. I want to be able to identify each drake. I set them free and they fly off. I return to my blind and within 30 minutes all the drakes have returned, including the tagged ones. Hormones are dominating their behavior. The drakes display and call to the female, perhaps a little like young men on *Rue Ste. Catherine*. It makes me wonder what duck hunting must've been like when spring-shooting and live decoys were allowed. One good hen, I think, could bring in a lot of drakes.

On the second day it becomes obvious the hen has chosen one drake over all others. He was one of the first to be tagged and quickly learns to enter and exit the trap. He spends hours inside the trap sitting beside her. The remainder of his time is spent chasing away other suitors that approach too closely. This is a remarkable change in the drake's behavior. Two days earlier he'd fed and loafed companionably with the other drakes on this very site. Now, he's claimed this part of the flooded meadow as his exclusive domain. He's established a territory.

Ian Newton, a visiting biologist from England who has accompanied me to watch the shovelers, suggests I might gain insight into how territories are established by manipulating the situation. "Why not," he asks, "move the female around the meadow to see how her mate responds? Will he follow her? Will he invade another drake's territory?" This seems worth trying.

Under cover of darkness I move the female in her small cage several hundred yards from the site. Her mate is unaware of the transfer.

He's been with her but all of the commotion I make scares him off. When I return the next morning he's sitting on his territory, chasing any shovelers that fly by. However, other drakes have already discovered the hen at her new site and are vigorously courting her and fighting among themselves. By late afternoon, one drake has established a territory around the female and is driving away the other suitors. The female's threatening postures and calls make it clear to me, and presumably to him, that she's not interested in his attention. He pays her no heed, behaving as if she'd chosen him as her mate. He flies to intercept in mid-air and chase away any incoming drakes, returning immediately to the female who, though constrained by her cage, tries to swim away.

Meantime, every hour or so the first male, the one the hen has chosen as her mate, leaves his territory and flies about the flooded meadow searching for her. He finds her the next day and immediately tries to join her. However, a fierce battle ensues, with the second drake, the pretender, emerging triumphant. The female's mate retreats to his territory, presumably to lick his psychological wounds. That night I return the hen to the original site, her mate's territory. When I arrive at first light next morning he's with her.

A few hours later, however, the second drake flies overhead and discovers the pair sitting beside each other. He immediately lands and swims toward the hen. This is the moment of truth for the female's mate. How has losing their earlier skirmish affected his confidence, I wonder? I quickly find out. The female's mate rushes across the water to attack. The males churn the water into a froth in furious battle. They grab and pull at each other's breast feathers. They slap one another with their wings. But within minutes, the pretender takes wing in defeat and returns to his territory. As the victor swims back to the hen, she bobs her head, presumably a signal of her approval. He's successfully defended his mate and territory against the intruder.

Later that day as I'm removing the female from the trap, I stumble and accidentally release my grip. She instantly flies and lands beside her mate who has been watching nearby. Moments later both take flight and vanish. I never see them again.

I felt privileged to be studying at Delta. I'd never heard of the institution until December of my first year at the University of Manitoba. Andrea had wrapped and placed under our Christmas tree a copy of *The Canvasback On A Prairie Marsh,* the classic work by H. Albert Hochbaum, the station's first director. When I read Hochbaum's description of the pioneering waterfowl research at Delta I was very excited and I remarked to Andrea that some day I'd like to be associated with such a man and institution. "Why don't you write him a letter," she suggested. I did, and a week later I was surprised to receive a reply. Delta had an opening for a student-trainee that spring, Hochbaum wrote, and the position was mine if I wanted it. Words cannot express my elation. I sent my letter of acceptance by return mail.

In April of 1967, just after final exams, I headed west across the unrelieved flatness of southern Manitoba to Portage la Prairie. I turned north for the final 17-mile drive to Delta, a distance that took me through fertile cropland that once formed the overflow lowlands of the Assiniboine River. Every so often, I stopped to watch flocks of Canada geese and snow geese in the stubble fields. It took me an hour to navigate the last mile of road which cut across the marsh. Not only was the road badly potholed, which slowed my speed to a crawl, but ducks were everywhere and I just had to stop to observe them. The many sounds of the marsh surrounded me and I could smell the decaying vegetation. Pairs of ducks and small flocks of drakes could be seen scattered across the shallow waters in nearly every direction. Flocks, perhaps arriving migrants, winged high across the sky. Elsewhere I could see courtship flights and males chasing intruders from their territories. One frantic female pintail raced low across the marsh to escape six drakes who were in hot pursuit of her. She barely cleared the tall rushes. She quacked and gabbled her disapproval during her frenzied flight and, in a final effort to escape, flung herself into the reeds and disappeared. I was amazed.

Eventually, I arrived at the station, located on the east edge of the village of Delta Beach, an enclave of about a dozen houses built on a narrow ridge of land that forms a barrier between the 25-mile long marsh and the open expanse of Lake Manitoba. The station consists of a small cluster of red wooden buildings whose centerpiece is Kirchoffer Lodge, the station's meeting place. Other structures house a library filled with scientific books and journals, a duck hatchery and a dormitory for single students. Small cottages are occupied by married students.

The station was the brainchild of James Ford Bell, who founded the corporate giant General Mills. Bell was an avid duck hunter who wanted to put back into the wild more ducks than he and his companions shot, so in 1911 he built a duck hatchery at Delta. The hatchery effort was abandoned as unsuccessful in the late 1930s. The station's focus then turned to basic biological research and training waterfowl biologists. By the late 1950s, it was well on its way to becoming the spiritual shrine of waterfowl biology. Many of today's waterfowl biologists cut their research teeth at Delta. And while the station is responsible for numerous technical papers, probably its greatest public fame has resulted from four books-Lyle Sowls' masterpiece, *Prairie Ducks*, and Hochbaum's three classics-*The Canvasback On A Prairie Marsh, Travels And Traditions Of Waterfowl,* and *To Ride the Wind.*

During my first two years, while still an undergraduate at the University of Manitoba, I assisted Rodger Titman, who was completing his Ph.D. work on mallard behavior. We spent part of our time on the Delta Marsh and the remainder in the Minnedosa pothole country, about a 50-mile drive to the west. Rodger was studying the dramatic aerial chases in which territorial males keep ducks of the same species away from their territories. This results in pairs being widely dispersed, nesting and raising broods far from one another.

It was working with Rodger that got me interested in territorial behavior, and this led to me deciding to study shovelers for my master's thesis. I spent two very busy field seasons doing my shoveler work. The northern prairie breeding season begins in early April with the arrival of mallards and pintails. Over the next three weeks, the other species arrive. By the time shovelers and blue-winged teal are ready to nest, mallards and pintails are well into incubation, and some females may even have broods.

My study area was the 30-foot wide ditch beside the road running through the marsh into Delta. This was a favorite breeding location for shovelers and blue-winged teal, but there were also gadwall, wigeon, mallard and pintail, along with the occasional redhead and dozens of coots.

I made observations from a beat-up, rented Datsun. Its maroon color was obscured by a permanent layer of mud that progressively thickened during the field season. I also used portable blinds, but most of my time was spent in a 20-foot tower anchored in the ooze of the marsh near the ditch. It gave me a panoramic view. I sometimes was there from dawn to dusk.

To the north, I could see the buildings of the village and research station dotted along the ridge. Southward stretched the flat expanse of the Portage plain, broken only by bluffs of oak and aspen. To the west and east, the marsh stretched to the horizon. On overcast days it had a heavy, sombre appearance, but on sunny days it came alive with color and brightness. Patches of blue water sparkled against the marsh grass that changed from golden brown to deepening shades of green as spring merged into summer.

I sometimes found my sojourns in the tower long, but I was never bored. How could I be? It was the breeding season and a myriad of birds made the marsh come alive. I spent hours listening to them and watching their courtship and territorial antics. There was always some drama being played out. The intrigues of the marsh were endless. And there were many memorable firsts for a young naturalist who was learning to be a scientist.

I saw my first white-fronted geese from the tower. A flock of eight came across the marsh so low they had to climb to avoid hitting the road-side power lines. It was their high-pitched, laughing call that alerted me to their approach. I watched them until they disappeared over the lake. A female mallard wasn't so lucky. In her desperate flight to avoid a pursuing drake, she hit a wire and broke her right wing. A few days later I found her carcass, picked clean by crows.

One day as I searched for duck nests, I identified a rare yellow rail. Although it never flew, many times earlier I'd seen the secretive little bird running only a few feet ahead of me through the grass. It was more like a mouse than a bird. But when I told people back at the station about this, they were skeptical. A few days later, I found it dead on the road. I must say it gave me great pleasure when I presented my prize to my doubting colleagues. It now resides in the Manitoba Museum of Natural History in Winnipeg.

Now as I look back, I have to force myself to remember the cold, wet, windy April days I spent in the tower. And also the sweltering hot days in June when the mosquitoes were almost unbearable. What I immediately recall is the excitement of being at Delta, and what I was learning. Every day held something new. Each morning before light I'd rush out to the tower, anxious to observe another chapter of the marsh saga.

Shovelers begin nesting soon after arrival at Delta. As with all dabbler species, shoveler hens are already paired when they arrive on the breeding grounds. Experienced females usually return to the same site where they've previously nested, while first-time breeders nest somewhere in the area where they were raised. Once the hen settles in, the drake establishes his territory along a nearby stretch of water. In my study, this was a 50 to 75 yard-long section of ditch. Hens built their nests in the previous year's dead grass, about 100 feet away. Although territorial males ignored other species, they chased away any intruding shoveler. Brief but intense fights would erupt between drakes, especially at boundaries between adjacent territories. However, these disputes ended after three or four days, and thereafter the males stayed away from each other. Territorial drakes also attacked intruding females, but unlike other dabblers which frequently attempt rape, these attacks were obviously hostile. A drake would peck and pull at a female's feathers until she departed.

A hen lays one egg a day, usually early in the morning, and a full clutch contains from eight to a dozen eggs. Incubation begins about the time the last egg is laid and lasts about three weeks. The shoveler drake remains with the hen until the third week of incubation, abandoning her just before the ducklings hatch. Mallard drakes, by comparison, abandon their hens much earlier in incubation, while pintail drakes rarely remain with a particular hen more than a few days.

Each morning I observed these events unfold. Around 10 o'clock I'd return to the station where the cooks, Dorothy and Margaret, would have saved breakfast for me. I got a little tired of rubbery eggs, but I wasn't about to complain. I usually checked the ditch every hour or so through midday, but I spent most of my afternoons reading in the station library. I found interesting the way scientists described behavior, even the words they used. Unlike naturalists and hunters who often personify wild animals, they never assumed they knew what the animal was thinking or feeling. This was something I had to learn, especially before trying to publish my research.

After a hurried supper, I usually returned to my observation blind, where I stayed until dark. I also spent time there at night, watching ducks through a special night-scope, recently declassified Vietnam war technology that had become available for field research. I maintained this pace from April into early August, the core of the breeding season.

When drakes abandon their females they gather with other drakes to moult, shedding their old, worn flight feathers (wing and tail) before growing new ones. The moult lasts about a month, rendering the drakes temporarily flightless. The hens, meanwhile, raise their broods of small yellow and brown ducklings on the ditch. They abandon them when they are about seven weeks of age. Females moult while they are raising their broods. The young begin flying at about eight weeks of age-around the end of July. Although some females were entirely unsuccessful, each year others fledged as many as eight or nine young.

My shoveler work built on earlier studies of other species. I found it very challenging and a little threatening in my student days when people unfamiliar with waterfowl biology asked me, "What is the purpose of territoriality?" My careful answer was that by providing a site for the exclusive use of himself and his mate, the drake insures his paternity of the ducklings. The female's reward is exclusive access to the resources of the territory-the nest site, food, loafing sites-for her and her ducklings. On a broader scale, territoriality causes pairs to widely disperse. In theory, this increases the hen's probability of reproductive success with obvious implication for the population. Not only does territorial spacing reduce competition for resources, but a predator would have to search long and hard to find widely dispersed nests. The costs of doing so would outweigh the benefits. It really isn't much more involved than that.

A second line of questioning which I frequently hear now comes from waterfowl hunters who are understandably sometimes skeptical of basic research. "What good has resulted from all this?" they ask. "What advantage do we gain by studying territorial behavior and knowing the territorial needs of each species?" My reply is it enables biologists to assess a wetland and determine whether it has the capacity to support more breeding ducks. These behavior studies shed light on one of the most critical issues in waterfowl management, that of carrying capacity. In other words, is there sometimes more breeding habitat available than there are ducks to occupy it?

Living a Dream

My Introduction to Waterfowl Management

L ate summer evenings are a delightful time to be on the
Canadian prairies. The days are growing shorter and the nights
are becoming cooler. Fields of wheat and barley wave in the
wind and glisten like gold. Young ducks are on the wing and gathering in large number on staging marshes. Blue-winged teal have begun
their southerly migration. A slough that yesterday teemed with blue-
wings is today suddenly and mysteriously barren. All of this activity
rekindles my hunting instincts, for it reminds me that the gunning
season is near at hand and it is time to begin removing from storage
my waterfowling paraphernalia decoys, calls, hip boots. A few decoys
will require attention.

Early one notable August evening in 1967, I was standing on
the edge of the Delta Marsh with Al Hochbaum. All my research for
the year had been completed and we were watching mallards rising
steadily from the marsh. They were flying out to feed in nearby wheat
fields. For more than half an hour we watched flock after flock wing
across the rose and gold sky. I'd never seen such a prolonged duck
flight. Each flock contained from 20 to 35 birds and we must have
seen more than 150 flocks. Later that night, Al estimated the total
flight exceeded 5,000 mallards. Nothing in my experience along the
St. Lawrence River or on the Nova Scotia estuaries could come close
to matching the procession of mallards that travelled across the
evening sky. To view so many ducks was like a dream come true,
another measure of how much my life had changed. And then I mentioned to Hochbaum in an offhand way that I was anxious for the
hunting season to begin.

Hochbaum possessed a notoriously short temper. He could be
curt to the point of rudeness, as I instantly discovered when he looked
me in the eye and snapped: "I watched evening feeding flights of
30,000 mallards when I first arrived at Delta. I believe the fall flight of
ducks over the Delta Marsh is down 30 to 40% since the 1950s, and
that's why I've stopped killing ducks. Ducks would be better off if you
didn't hunt them, either."

With that, he turned and walked away, leaving me emotionally stunned and intellectually confused, for I viewed Hochbaum as *the*
authority on all matters pertaining to waterfowl. I had no plans to stop
duck hunting, but how could I dismiss his acid rebuke? He'd observed
ducks on the prairies since the 1930s, and now he was saying that

ducks were in trouble and hunting was part of the reason. He wasn't an anti-hunter who had given up blood sports. Each autumn he hunted sharp-tailed and ruffed grouse. Could he be right about ducks, I wondered? I was too inexperienced to judge the truth of his words. His comments came at a time when I was watching the largest flight of ducks I'd ever seen. Certainly, to my mind there was no shortage. I could understand old-timers' complaints about thinning ranks of ducks, a decline I attributed to the drought which gripped the prairies during the decade of the 1960s. But periodic drought accompanied by declining numbers of ducks was to be expected. This was the natural cycle of the Great Plains, a cycle based on the availability of water.

Thus began my initiation into the bitter, divided world of waterfowl conservation. I'd arrived at the station believing that biologists sought the truth about ducks, including the role of hunting, and that the Canadian and American governments utilized this information to protect our migratory flocks. This quaint notion, I discovered, reflected my political naivete.

I wasn't in the dark about all threats facing waterfowl. At noontime students at Delta gathered for lunch in Kirchoffer Hall. The conversation almost always focused on one topic-ducks. I had fancied myself rather knowledgeable about ducks, but these noontime discussions often were as humbling as they were stimulating and enlightening, especially when we were joined by Hochbaum, station manager Peter Ward, or one of the many well-known biologists who frequently visited the station. I was amazed at their depth and breadth of knowledge. They could discuss mallards or canvasbacks, sago pondweed or hardstem bulrush, James Bay or Chesapeake Bay. All criticized the Canadian and American governments for subsidizing the drainage of tens of thousands of potholes across the northeastern Great Plains. This was viewed as the greatest threat to the long-term abundance of our continental flocks. As Hochbaum frequently stated, "This is a ridiculous case of one government agency (agriculture) working at cross-purposes with another (wildlife)." Wildlife managers were powerless to halt the wholesale drainage which agricultural spokesmen touted as beneficial to farmers. But the habitat problems facing ducks involved more than the permanent loss of wetlands, as I discovered on one of my first visits with Hochbaum to Minnedosa.

The Minnedosa region is famous for its innumerable small potholes. In places there are more than 100 per square mile. These nutrient-rich glacial sloughs produce as many ducks as any nesting habitat on the continent and a great deal more than most. A single slough no more than an acre in size can produce broods of 10 or more species of ducks. As we motored along rural section roads, I looked in awe on hundreds of breeding pairs scattered like confetti across countless small potholes. Then Hochbaum brought the car to a halt beside a slough where a pair of "lordly" canvasbacks, as he called them in his book, basked under the warm May sun atop a muskrat house. The female was in the egg-laying phase of her reproductive cycle. Her mate was keeping a watchful eye on her to insure he and not a carousing stranger would fertilize her eggs. The big canvasbacks looked enormous on the small pond. Hochbaum explained that diving ducks like 'cans have only a modest potential to increase their numbers compared to dabblers, but it's still impressive.

"The loss of prairie breeding habitat has been particularly devastating to 'cans, redheads and scaup," he said. "I believe in the Minnedosa region their numbers have fallen more than 50% since the 1950s. This is critical because 10% of the continental canvasback population breeds here."

And more was at stake than the draining of wetlands. Hochbaum decried the biological monotony of what he called the "wheat prairie." As we toured the countryside, he frequently directed me to observe examples of where the plow had reduced the once great expanse of biologically diverse grasslands to small, isolated islands of native vegetation. He noted that in dry years farmers could and often did plow right to the water's edge, thereby eradicating the pitifully narrow margin of vegetation surrounding each slough. This thin band of border vegetation often provided the only nesting cover available to puddle ducks.

"This area supports only a fraction of the broods it once did," he said. "A square mile of this habitat could produce as many as 800 ducks a year. How can we hope to replace such valuable habitat once it has been lost?"

Moreover, he discounted efforts to replace lost wetlands with artificial or manipulated sites, the type of projects advanced by fish and game agencies and Ducks Unlimited, the private waterfowl conservation organization I was becoming more familiar with now that I was living on the prairies. "How can we replace this biologically diverse habitat?" he asked rhetorically.

Then, Hochbaum said something that really shocked me. "We still face the problem of providing adequate breeding stock for the surviving remnants of native prairie. A wet prairie alone won't produce ducks. In many years, even relatively dry ones, there's still more habitat for use by ducks than there are breeding pairs to occupy it." He was the first person I ever heard make this contention.

Later that summer of 1968, I was confronted with a more insidious threat to ducks. Fellow student Mark Mattson and I were asked to accompany a group of visitors touring the station. All were veteran U.S. Fish and Wildlife Service (USFWS) biologists who knew ducks from decades of field work. They'd tramped through the rushes of a thousand potholes and they'd flown over the broad expanse of the northern prairies, as well as the wintering grounds farther south. They'd experienced breeding seasons when millions of shallow earthen basins glistened with water and the fall flight teemed with young ducks. They'd known drought-a time when few young were produced and the numbers of ducks flying southward declined precipitously. I recognized a few names such as John Lynch, Art Hawkins, Walt Crissey...I'd read some of what they'd written in the Delta library. We'd been told privately that these were "old men" the ones who'd pioneered modern waterfowl management in the 1950s. They were now on their way out, to be replaced by more academically qualified biologists.

These dedicated individuals had just completed the annual census of the North American breeding grounds. As we toured the station, they expressed alarm over the severity of the drought. They'd counted fewer than two million potholes on the Canadian prairies, compared to more than five million potholes in a wet year. They'd seen below normal numbers of breeding ducks across the prairies. They predicted a grim fall flight.

But after dinner, when the Scotch flowed liberally and we were sitting around Kirchoffer Lodge, their tongues loosened and the conversation went beyond basic biology and the prairie weather cycle of flood and drought. I sensed they knew their day was ending. They spoke with intensity, as if they wanted the students who'd gathered to remember their words, to bear witness to future generations of biologists about the causes for the problems confronting waterfowl management. For several hours they poured out their anger and frustration over the decline of ducks. I sat in silence, listening in horror to their descriptions of the problems facing ducks and the political maneuverings within the waterfowl conservation community. Over time, their voices have blended together as one, but I've never forgotten their insights:

• "Hunters will take responsibility for resident game like pheasants and deer, and accept, even promote, statewide season closures when populations plummet. But they resist severe restrictions on duck hunting, believing hunters in other states will kill the ducks preserved by their restraint."

• "Hunting regulations are too complicated and confusing. They also give hunters the false impression that waterfowl management can precisely control the numbers of ducks that return each spring to the breeding grounds."

• "Ducks Unlimited tells its members all problems can be solved by the acquisition of breeding habitat. It refuses to be bluntly honest about its limited ability to produce ducks."

• "Professional waterfowl management claims too much credit for the recovery of ducks that followed the drought of the 1930s."

• "The emphasis of the USFWS on the mallard as a barometer of the health of our duck stocks ignores perils facing other species."

• "The service has grown too big to be effective. Too many layers of bureaucracy separate decision-makers from men in the field, and too many employees are more concerned with career advancement and gaining political power than with ducks."

• "The service has lost sight of its goal to protect bountiful numbers of ducks. Instead, it has become too focussed on providing targets for hunters."

• "The USFWS and DU are unwilling to publicly acknowledge that the gun is partly responsible for our declining flocks."

• "In very dry years the duck season should be closed, or at least seriously curtailed."

Afterwards, Mark told me it had been difficult for him to hear such devastating criticism. He'd always lived on the prairie where waterfowl management, especially DU, found respect among hunters and the general public. He'd falsely believed, like so many hunters, that DU was a major reason there were enough ducks to shoot. I, too, had assumed somebody was looking out for ducks and the flights would always come down from the north. Now, I wasn't so sure. I was as disillusioned and upset as Mark. I wondered if these men were over-stating the issues, if their criticism involved more sour grapes than substance. I wondered if time would ultimately reveal the truth or falsehood of their beliefs. But whatever the eventual outcome, my eyes were opened that evening. I was no longer naive about "duck politics."

I found it interesting that all of these men planned to hunt ducks that autumn, even though some had suggested the season be closed. All vowed to restrict their kill. I, too, planned to go afield, as I had the previous season, despite Hochbaum's stop-shooting admonition. After all, the Delta Marsh was as famous a gunning marsh as any on the continent, particularly for canvasbacks, and I lived only a couple of hours away.

Still, I didn't go afield without some reservations. The warnings I'd heard about over-shooting haunted me. My thinking was changing slowly-very slowly, some would say. In fact, I'd changed in many ways. For example, I had quit killing more than my legal limit while still at school in Nova Scotia. However, I refused to believe my individual kill affected the survival of our continental flocks.

By the time I arrived on the Delta Marsh, the fabled canvasback gunning was history. The limit on both 'cans and redheads was two per day. I usually focused on bluebills and shot canvasbacks and redheads as incidentals. I sometimes avoided shooting them at all. Fortunately, bluebills still arrived on the marsh each autumn in enormous numbers. My first and last hunts during my four years in Manitoba are especially memorable. My first hunt came in early October when Mark Mattson and I drove out from Winnipeg. Long before dawn, we arrived at the research station where we loaded a canoe atop the car. We were soon launching at Portage Creek at the south end of the marsh.

Our destination was a reedy point on a shallow bay where a few days earlier we'd seen good numbers of scaup. The first gray streaks of light appeared on the eastern horizon as we tossed out our unpainted plastic decoys. We didn't build a blind. We simply stood in the tall reeds. Most of the ducks were new migrants, fresh arrivals that would be encountering hunters for the first time. They wouldn't be wary.

A hard breeze produced a chop on the water. The banks of marsh grass bent in the wind. The sky was overcast. And soon after it became light enough to shoot I heard Mark say, "Here they come." I looked up to see seven bluebills bearing down on us. They were no more than 10 feet above the water. Before I could get myself set for a decent shot, the little group scattered over the decoys as each bird looked for an opening to land. I was oblivious to Mark's shots, but I saw a duck fold up and splash down amid the blocks. My lone shot was nowhere near the fleeing bird I'd singled out. Within minutes another flock came flying downwind, but they had no intention of landing. I swung on a drake and killed it cleanly with my second shot. I watched spellbound as it bounced three times across the water. It must've been streaking along at 60 miles per hour. It marked my first "Delta" bluebill.

The dawn flight was spectacular. It seemed like every scaup in southern Manitoba wanted to come into our decoys. I'd never gunned diving ducks in such a setting, and I'd rarely shot so fast and furiously. We killed our 20-duck limit within 90 minutes.

We didn't immediately leave the marsh. We lingered awhile to watch the ducks, for the morning flight hadn't ended. And later as I was picking up our last decoy, something caught my eye. I glanced toward the western sky to see the vanguard of a new flight of migrant bluebills coming down from the northwest. They scaled down from the heights to land on the open waters of the bay. Flock after flock flew low over us. We could hear the rush of air in their wings. All massed in one big raft. We estimated it contained from 3,000 to 4,000 birds.

How, I wondered, could the few ducks I killed reduce to any measurable degree the numbers of scaup that migrated southward each autumn?

My last Delta hunt during my student days occurred three years later in the first week of November, just before the freeze-up would lock the marsh in ice for five months. My companion was Bill Milner, a tool salesman from Winnipeg. Snow had made travel across the prairie slow and hazardous. It was still falling when we arrived at the marsh, well after dawn. We slowly worked our way toward open water by pushing and pulling our canoe across a two-inch thick skin of ice that covered the shallow, protected parts of the marsh. When we neared our shooting point, I could see a three or four acre patch of open water. It looked ideal. We probably didn't need to rig any decoys, but we hurriedly threw out a dozen just to give the birds something to focus on.

Within minutes the first bluebills materialized out of the snow, appearing ghost-like over the decoys. At that distance, we could easily distinguish the strikingly beautiful black-headed drakes from the hens. We each killed a drake. Thereafter, the flight continued somewhat sporadically. We killed a duck here, a duck there. Finally, a flock of five came in. Bill dropped two. The remaining three circled and came back over the decoys. We downed all three. Bill canoed out to retrieve the birds. When he returned, he suggested it might be a good time to quit, especially since we had a long drive back to Winnipeg. We'd not yet shot our limits, but I didn't object. The wild conditions had made it a most exciting day.

After four years at Delta, my attitude was definitely changing. In prior years, I would have insisted we stay until we killed our limit or shooting time ended, whichever came first. Who cared what time of night we returned to Winnipeg? But the concerns of my mentors were beginning to influence my behavior, as was the fact I now had a wife and daughter! And though I wasn't yet ready to be the one to suggest prematurely ending a hunt, my lack of objection when others did so marked another step forward in my development as a waterfowler. I was making progress on the road to waterfowling maturity, but I still had a long distance to travel.

Black Ducks Down East

I would love to have stayed at Delta to do Ph.D. research, but Andrea put her foot down. She'd been working as a kindergarten teacher to support us but now she was pregnant with our second child. She felt it was time I got a job. Fair enough.

I had a couple of job prospects as a field biologist in remote northern locations but Andrea wasn't keen. Instead, she suggested I contact the head of Biology at St.F.X. about teaching positions. Teaching? Why not? A few days after I'd written to St.F.X., Professor Chiasson phoned me at home in the evening. "Yes," he said, "there is a two-year position available to teach introductory biology. We've just had an unexpected resignation," he explained. "Are you interested?" I was indeed interested, if a little apprehensive. What would it be like going from student to teacher, I wondered? But yes, I could do it. It wasn't working directly with ducks but it would be good experience. By late August, I had defended my thesis, sold our house in Winnipeg, packed up our belongings and was on the road to Nova Scotia. Andrea and Melani had gone ahead to Cornwall to be with family and wait for the baby. I stopped to visit them only briefly on my way through to Nova Scotia. I had to begin teaching later that week.

I had lots to think about on my drive to Antigonish. There was plenty happening in my life. Not long after arriving, I found a place for us to live and was soon settled at the university. Sara was born the day I gave my first lecture and a week later I picked up my family at Halifax airport. We were ready to start our new life in Nova Scotia.

Life was exciting, if hectic. I knew I'd be pushing it, but I didn't want to lose the 1971 hunting season if I could help it. I made a few phone calls to renew acquaintances and I visited some of my "old spots." Very little had changed. I had my course under control by mid-autumn and was finding time to hunt. I was also thinking about how I'd get some black duck research underway come spring. My experience at Delta and a memory from my youth were responsible for focusing my thoughts.

When I was about 10, I recall one early April evening standing in front of the cottage on Hamilton Island. I was casting a red and white spinner hoping a pike or walleye would grab it. It was almost too dark to fish when I was startled by a rush of wings and a staccato burst of calling overhead. I looked up. Three black ducks were silhouetted against the after-glow of the western sky. The first bird, the one that appeared to be uttering the strange chuckling call, had its head pulled over its back in a most unusual posture. Were my eyes playing tricks on me, or was the second bird grabbing the first bird's tail feathers? As I watched, the third bird, which had been lagging behind, caught up and forced itself between the other two. With that, all three scattered. The first and third birds then flew together and quickly disappeared into the darkness. The second bird circled and landed with a splash before me. All this took less than half a minute but the entire episode has remained indelibly imprinted in my mind.

It wasn't until I began working with Rodger Titman at Delta that I discovered what I'd witnessed. It had been a territorial chase. The second bird was the territorial male and he was trying to force the first bird, the female of an intruding pair, onto the water. Almost certainly, he would have attacked her, perhaps intending to rape her. The bird that flew between the two was the female's mate. He was trying to protect her. It was the territorial male that landed in front of me.

It didn't take me long to decide to study territorial behavior of black ducks. Little was known about it and there was a good population around Antigonish. I could see a future in this.

I soon discovered I enjoyed teaching, especially courses in my specialty, like wildlife ecology and management. However, after being at St.F.X. for three years, the Dean of Science made it perfectly clear that if I wanted to remain in academics, there or anywhere else, I'd need a Ph.D. degree. So, I started looking for a school immediately. I was delighted when McGill University not only accepted me into its Ph.D. program, but agreed to let me do my thesis research while teaching at St.F.X.

My main study area was and still is a 600 acre tidal marsh three miles from Antigonish. Two rivers meander through the marsh, forming myriad backwaters, gullies and mud flats. At low tide the marsh is all but dry but sometimes only the tallest vegetation breaks the surface. A diversity of small aquatic animal life abounds. This is the principal food of ducklings and it is what attracts female black ducks to the marsh to raise their young. Indeed, females bring their broods overland from smaller wetlands a mile or two away, while others bring their ducklings along the rivers from as far as 15 miles away.

Some black ducks only winter in the area, breeding farther north in Labrador. Others breed locally but winter farther south, principally along the New England coast. About 300 to 500 birds are permanent residents. Some of these females are already incubating their eggs by the time the northern birds depart for their breeding grounds. During December, there may be 600 to 800 black ducks on the marsh.

I monitor changes in the distribution and abundance of ducks and geese throughout the year. During the breeding season my students and I intensify our surveys, using vehicles and boats to locate birds. We also survey the area by helicopter two or three times during the breeding season. We know the location of almost every pair of breeding ducks. However, most of our time is spent observing the behavior of individual birds, many of which are marked so we can identify them.

My Ph.D. research was similar to what I did with shovelers at Delta. But in Nova Scotia I didn't have a support staff like I had at Delta. All I had to do there was watch ducks and try to be on time for meals. It was very hard work in the beginning but, in time, things got easier and collecting data for my thesis became a pleasure. However, there was more to getting my degree than doing research. I still had to satisfy McGill's residency requirement. I would have to take a leave of absence from St.F.X. This would be difficult because now, with the arrival of Emily, we had three young children. There would be no regular pay-check coming in, something we'd gotten used to. But we had saved some money and Andrea would work part time at the campus daycare centre. We felt sure that somehow everything would work out.

So once again we packed up the family car and this time we headed for Montréal. I didn't dare let myself even entertain the thought of hunting that fall. The St. Lawrence would beckon, I knew, but I would have to resist.

The year at McGill's Macdonald campus was incredibly busy. I managed a couple of hunts with Robin and Ted in our old haunts, but mostly I stayed close to the university. The time went by quickly, a blur in my mind, and soon I was back in Nova Scotia immersed in my black duck research. Unlike most researchers who live far from their work, my study area is only a few minutes drive from home or the university. I spend hours observing ducks throughout the year, without neglecting other duties.

Over the years, I've marked several hundred black ducks with colored and numbered plastic discs affixed to the bird's bill. Although marking them was easy, catching them wasn't. Fortunately my experience at Delta stood me in good stead. I used the same techniques, including the same wire mesh traps I used in my shoveler study.

In the winter when food was scarce and ice concentrated the

birds, I used corn to lure birds into the trap. One old female learned how to get in and out of the trap. She became so familiar with my assistant and me that she would stay in the trap scoffing corn when we approached. The other ducks would be hurling themselves against the mesh, frantically trying to escape. She sometimes ate so much she couldn't fly. Occasionally, we had to stop trapping because of great-horned owls. An owl would enter the trap at night and kill all the ducks. It'd rip off their heads with vice-like talons before eating the breast of only one or two birds. It'd be sitting on a carcass blinking when we arrived the following morning. Like the female black, these owls didn't try to escape once they knew we wouldn't harm them. However, on a couple of occasions they were really pushing the envelope.

During the breeding season, I used females to attract males into traps, but black ducks were much more difficult to catch than shovelers. Despite this, I eventually accumulated a large sample of marked birds. In fact, during the peak of my research I never visited my study area without seeing marked birds. Even after 30 years, I always learn something new when I visit the marsh.

I caught and marked many birds while they were still duck-lings. Sometimes their bills and legs were barely large enough to fit nasal discs and aluminum bands on them. I used an air boat at night to catch them, sometimes getting the entire family. The driver, sitting high atop a stool mounted ahead of an airplane propeller, would skill-fully maneuver the boat through the marsh, using a powerful, hand-held spot-light to locate the broods. The blinding light, the roar of the engine, and the high pitched whine of the propeller mesmerized the ducklings, which were usually accompanied by their frantic mother. As the boat bore down on the disoriented birds, two of us sitting in the front would reach out with long-handled dip-nets and scoop up the ducklings, but rarely the mother. We'd stop the boat, quickly band and mark the little birds, and return them together to the marsh. Usually within a day or two we'd see the mother and ducklings together again, apparently none the worse for their nighttime ordeal. I've been able to keep track of some of these marked birds for several years.

A female duckling which I marked (Yellow Five) one July returned to the marsh to breed with her mate, which was also marked (White Eight). She was 11 months old and he was three years old. They were both breeding for the first time. Yellow Five had returned to the same pond where she'd been raised with her siblings. Her mother took them there from where she'd built her nest in the soft ground under a clump of alders 100 feet from the pond.

As far as Yellow Five was concerned, this was a good place to nest and raise her first brood. After all, her mother had been successful. But her mother was already back in residence. In fact, she and her mate had been at the pond for two weeks-she was already incubating her dozen buff-colored eggs. This old female had nested there for three consecutive years and all three nests were within a few yards of one another. She fledged 14 ducklings during this period.

Yellow Five and her mate were now unwelcome intruders. Her mother undoubtedly recognized her, but the old female was preoccupied with her current reproductive effort. Her daughter was, in a sense, a competitor. Despite her success the year before with Yellow Five's father, she had chosen a new mate. The pond was now this male's territory. As far as he was concerned, no other black duck but his mate was welcome there. He repeatedly intercepted Yellow Five and her mate in mid-air as they tried to land on the pond. These aerial skirmishes were identical to what I'd watched so many years earlier on the St. Lawrence.

Yellow Five eventually nested next to a sterile pond about two miles away from her natal wetland. Although she hatched seven ducklings, she was forced to take her brood in search of a wetland with more food. Unfortunately, she'd nested too far from a suitable alternative and her ducklings died within days of hatching. This naive young female had chosen a "lethal site" where her reproductive fate was sealed the moment she'd decided to nest there. Her breeding season was over! She might have nested again had she lost only her eggs, but re-nesting never occurs when females lose their ducklings.

The following year, with a new mate in tow, Yellow Five again nested beside a wetland that couldn't support her ducklings. But this time the wetland was close enough to the food-rich tidal marsh, where the female took her brood soon after hatching. She was learning. Five of her seven ducklings survived the critical first two weeks of life and not only were they alive in October, a week before hunting season opened, they were still together.

Suitable brood rearing habitat is the first priority of a female looking for a place to breed. If she makes a poor decision she is doomed to fail, even though she hatches her brood. Older, experienced female black ducks choose locations where, if forced to leave, they have alternatives. Nesting cover and water where her mate can establish a territory are important breeding requirements, but they are not usually as critical as a place to raise her brood.

Some female black ducks never fledge any ducklings, while others are very successful. This is almost invariably a function of the way females look after their young. Most remain with their ducklings until they fledge, around seven or eight weeks of age, but others desert their ducklings after only four or five weeks. Occasionally, females desert their broods when they are only a few days old. These ducklings never survive unless they are adopted by another female who also has a brood, but this is rare. Females recognize their own ducklings and they usually drive away strangers. In general, older females are more attentive mothers. Like humans, ducks must learn to be successful mothers and, predictably, not all are good at it.

One of my students followed several marked females and their broods on a daily basis throughout the entire rearing period. Females that kept their broods close to them lost fewer ducklings to predators than did females that let their young wander. Females with broods also tended to avoid one another, except when predators were nearby. Then they often brought their broods together until the danger passed.

Two such females provided insights into the intelligence of black ducks. Both were feeding with their ducklings about 30 yards apart when they were attacked by a bald eagle. The females quickly brought their broods together, but one feigned a broken wing and flapped noisily across the water, distracting the eagle. The other female took the two broods into dense vegetation nearby. Meanwhile, the first female, flapping and flying in little hops, led the eagle half a mile away. The big, ponderous bird finally gave up the chase and continued across the marsh. The female black duck washed and preened her feathers before returning to look for her ducklings. She landed where the skirmish had begun, but they were nowhere to be seen. She swam about in tight circles, calling loudly. At that point, the other female flew to her from where she'd been hiding 200 yards away. She then slowly swam to where the ducklings were hidden. The ducklings, which were huddled together, immediately separated into their respective broods, joined their mothers and went their separate ways. Were these two females really communicating as it seemed?

Despite the next breeding season being eight months away, males are already courting females by early October. Impressing a female is serious business because with most ducks there are more males than females, sometimes two or three times as many, and most species are monogamous. This results in intense competition among males. Sex ratios at hatching are equal but females typically suffer higher mortality than males. This is probably because they are more vulnerable to shooting, but also because breeding is more stressful for them. Females put much of their body reserves into producing several large eggs and they alone incubate the eggs and raise the ducklings. I recall, for example, a female black duck hurling herself at an eagle as it flew off with her duckling. The third time she hit him he dropped the duckling, which survived. When females are attending eggs and young, males are looking out only for themselves.

Some male black ducks on my study area find a mate every year, while others never do. About 40% of females are paired by mid-October while 70% have selected mates by the end of December. All are paired by late February. Females typically choose a different mate each year, but a significant number select the same male and perhaps some of these relationships are permanent.

As the nesting season approaches, the male black duck follows his mate wherever she goes. The water nearest her nest becomes his territory. She joins him there when she leaves her nest and it is only there where she'll copulate with him. It is this anticipation of sex that keeps him on his territory. After all, he may have spent months accompanying her while waiting for her to be sexually receptive, and now he's guarding his investment. However, the male will never recognize his progeny. He deserts his mate and territory mid-way through incubation, probably because soon after she has laid her last egg the female loses interest in sex. Consequently, he loses interest in her. This is the end of the relationship, unless she loses her eggs and re-nests. Even then she may choose another male to fertilize her eggs.

Behavioral studies like mine can help managers understand why some black duck populations are declining and why blacks are rare or gone from locations where they were once abundant. I'm concerned that managers and research biologists are sometimes too focused on the habitat requirements of ducks, giving short shrift to behavioral factors that influence the distribution and abundance of populations.

In parts of Ontario, there are now mallards where once there were only black ducks. Some biologists believe the mallard has displaced, forced out, the black duck. This could theoretically happen, but has it happened? It could if the mallard, which is 20 times more abundant, genetically assimilates the black duck by inter-breeding. Mallards and blacks are genetically closely related, having evolved from common ancestral stock. Some biologists believe they are nothing more than two geographically distinct populations of the same species. At any rate, inter-breeding produces fertile hybrids that can reproduce. Although they've always overlapped in parts of their range, black ducks have predominantly occupied forested and coastal habitats of the northeast while mallards have primarily been prairie ducks. However, since about the 1950s, mallards have been expanding their range eastward into habitats that were once the exclusive domain of the black duck.

There are two ways that hybrids can be produced. Males and females of the two species can mate, forming a "mixed pair," and males of one species can rape females of the other. Mixed pairs do occur in the wild, as does rape. However, rape is rather uncommon among black ducks, and it is rare for a male black duck to rape a female mallard. On the other hand, as anyone who has observed farmyard or urban mallards can attest, rape among mallards is very common and a male mallard will rape a female black duck as readily as he will a female mallard. Interestingly, and contrary to what one might expect, it is only already paired males that rape, not males that have failed to find a partner.

But how frequently does mixed pairing and rape occur in the wild, and does this have a significant impact on black duck populations? Are blacks being assimilated by mallards? Nobody knows the answer to this, but my studies in Atlantic Canada suggest the impact is low. Attempted rape is dramatic when observed, but it almost never results in successful insemination and there are relatively few mixed pairs.

But could the virtual disappearance of black ducks in parts of Ontario be the result of mallards excluding them from breeding habitat, actually preventing them from breeding? Male mallards not only defend their territories against other mallards, but also against black ducks. This could prevent black ducks from breeding where suitable habitat is limited. However, the presence of mallards in habitat formerly occupied by black ducks is not itself evidence that mallards have displaced the black ducks. It has never been demonstrated that mallards are preventing black ducks from reproducing. For mallards to force a decline in black duck populations they'd have to be out-competing them for limited habitat. In my opinion, while mallards may be a factor, there's little evidence they've caused the decline of any black duck population. At any rate, there must be other factors involved because there have been declines where there are no mallards.

Similarly, it is unlikely that lack of breeding habitat has had a widespread impact on black duck reproduction. In fact, as early as the 1940s, duck hunters in Maritime Canada were complaining about the decline in black ducks, historically the most abundant dabbler and the "gold standard" of Atlantic Flyway hunters. Many biologists, including the well known biologist-author Bruce Wright, have stated their belief that breeding habitat in Maritime Canada is under-utilized.

The forests and coastal habitats of the northeast never produced the diversity or abundance of ducks typical of more productive prairie habitats. Although drought and lack of nesting cover are generally not the problems they are on the prairies, food is less abundant and more widely dispersed resulting in low densities. Territorial behavior has evolved to protect these scattered patches of food.

Though research hasn't shown a need, eastern managers have adopted the prairie model of habitat management. This emphasises creating or enhancing wetlands to increase production. Enhancement includes enriching wetlands with fertilizer to increase aquatic animal life, the main food of ducklings. Managers assume this will result in more ducklings fledged and ultimately more abundant populations. They point to increases in pairs and broods on managed wetlands as evidence that these projects are successful and that they are needed. Unquestionably, these projects attract breeding females, but are they really needed? Might females breed as successfully, perhaps more successfully, in unmanaged natural habitat?

My tidal marsh study area resembles a managed marsh. Nutrient-rich effluent from Antigonish's sewage treatment facility fertilizes the marsh. Permanent water, good cover and abundant food attract breeding females. In fact, the marsh supports the highest density of breeding black ducks in northern Nova Scotia. It is a great place to see ducks and other wildlife, but is it as good a place as it appears for female ducks to raise their young? Has a female perhaps been lured into making a poor choice when she breeds there?

I compared the reproductive success of black duck females that raised their young on the tidal marsh with those that bred on small (one or two acres), widely dispersed (isolated) natural wetlands where food was adequate but not abundant. Despite starting with same sized broods, females that nested on the tidal marsh fledged only about half as many ducklings as the females that nested at the dispersed sites. Also, females that nested in both habitats, but in different years, were more successful when they raised their young at the isolated sites. Predation was the probable reason for lower survival of ducklings on the marsh. Great-horned owls, foxes, skunks, raccoons, mink, otters, snapping turtles and more than a dozen bald eagles regularly forage on this marsh during the black duck brood-rearing period. Presumably, one of the attractions for predators is the high density of ducks.

I also determined the abundance, distribution and reproductive success of black ducks on four managed wetlands during the five years before and after construction of water-control structures. In addition, I did this for the dispersed wetlands in a three-mile radius around each managed site. There were significantly more black duck pairs and broods at the four managed sites after water levels were stabilized. However, there was a decrease in pairs and broods in the wetlands around these sites. Apparently, females were attracted to the managed sites from the nearby wetlands where, despite their small size, black ducks had bred successfully for years. Furthermore, there were no additional ducks produced in the general area after the four sites became managed wetlands.

These costly projects simply re-distributed pairs and broods. In my opinion, they weren't needed in this watershed where the number of breeding pairs annually varies from 75 to 115. Most years it could support 15-25% more breeding black ducks the population is below the carrying capacity of the habitat. In fact, during the 1990s, beavers created several new wetlands that were suitable for breeding ducks, a widespread phenomenon in eastern Canada. In reality, managers rarely know how many ducks their projects produce, or whether the ducks they do produce would have been produced in unmanaged, natural habitat. Attracting ducks to managed sites is appropriate only if higher recruitment rates result. This is widely assumed but rarely known. Unquestionably, the issue of carrying capacity is complex and difficult to investigate but to be accountable, managers must have a better idea of how many additional ducks their initiatives are producing.

Management initiatives may also redistribute wood ducks in the watershed. Virtually all of the nesting woodies that people see use nest boxes. They conclude from this that there are not enough natural sites for these tree-cavity nesters. Certainly, local hunters believe the boxes are necessary and that they are responsible for recent increases in the population. In reality, most female wood ducks that breed in the watershed use natural sites and they raise their broods on secluded wetlands remote from people. They also produce as many ducklings as females using nest boxes. In fact, there is enough natural habitat in the watershed to support many more wood ducks than currently breed there. Beavers have been a boon to wood ducks and green-winged teal, just as they have to black ducks.

Local wood duck production can sometimes be increased by nest boxes and this is a way of establishing breeding populations in treeless locations. However, proponents of nest box programs have unknowingly exaggerated their value as a means to increase wood duck populations. There's no evidence that maturing hardwood forest, the primary breeding habitat of the wood duck, is now or in recent years, has been limiting wood duck populations in most of central and eastern North America. Although complete removal of the virgin forest in eastern North America devastated wood duck habitat in the early 1900s, cavities and other "old-growth" characteristics have returned to much of 240 million acres of hardwoods presently standing. In fact, many bird and mammal species that use similar sized tree cavities in wood duck range have been increasing their distribution and abundance without artificial nesting aids.

Nest-box programs may actually be detrimental to wood duck recruitment. Unlike most species of ducks, wood ducks are not territorial. Pairs and broods are naturally widely dispersed because tree cavities are randomly distributed. Also, these birds are secretive and avoid one another during the breeding season. Unfortunately, boxes are often placed too close together. Consequently, females sometimes lay eggs in both their own nests and those of other females (dumpnesting), resulting in nest desertions. In fact, nesting too close together results in a range of maladaptive behaviors that reduce the reproductive success of females. Also, where wood ducks nest in high densities, predation is generally more of a problem, as is competition for food.

Research in South Carolina has shown that there is competition for natural cavities and predation is lower in well-maintained boxes. However, maintenance is generally poor across the country. The biggest criticism from a biological perspective is that there are no long-term, comprehensive studies that show wood duck nest-box programs are needed or can make a significant increase in the fall flight. Abundance and distribution of wood duck populations is likely limited as much by availability of suitable brood-rearing wetlands and hunting as it is by availability of natural nest sites.

Too often managers assume their initiatives are meeting objectives without verifying this. And managers can be resistant to change. On the other hand, a justifiable complaint of managers is that they have to manage, whereas research biologists, to whom they look to for direction, rarely need to put their theories to the test. They operate on quite different schedules. Obviously, it's impossible to achieve the ideal of doing the research to test all management initiatives before implementing them, but managers should be especially cautious about their commitment to far-reaching and costly practices and policies that haven't been adequately tested.

If competition with mallards and lack of breeding habitat don't entirely account for declines or lack of recovery of black duck populations, what other factors are involved? What about hunting? The state of Maine periodically closes the hunting season for black ducks, despite there being few alternatives for hunters; the black duck limit is rarely more than one bird. Clearly, managers there believe hunting plays a role in the population dynamics of black ducks. But determining the impact of hunting on any duck population is difficult. While results suggest that the longterm continental decline in blacks slowed after periods of restrictive harvest regulations, reducing the kill by almost 50% in the U.S. did not result in the expected increase in breeding pairs. However, about two thirds of the black ducks that winter in the Atlantic Flyway breed in the province of Québec. During a decade of severely restrictive regulations in the U.S., Québec accounted for nearly one fourth of the continental harvest, about one million black ducks over 10 years. Had Québec reduced its harvest by 50% instead of 25%, a half million birds may have survived. Would all or even most of these ducks have died before getting the opportunity, perhaps opportunities, to breed? It seems unlikely.

Managers who resist more restrictive regulations believe that duck hunting is self-regulating. The fewer ducks there are the more effort it takes to kill one. When populations are low, fewer hunters will participate so fewer ducks will therefore be killed. Advocates of this position, adapted from pheasant management philosophy, believe that during the prairie drought years, hunters were not killing enough ducks to matter, probably no more than 5% of the fall flight. Perhaps, but during 1991, the year after the lowest fall flight in history (57 million birds), sports hunters retrieved an estimated 8.1 million ducks and 2.6 million geese. How many they crippled is another issue. Unfortunately, the concept of self-regulation is another strongly defended position that has not been adequately tested, and I doubt it applies to most black duck populations. We do know that hunting is rarely curtailed once the season has begun, not least of all because estimates of how many birds are killed don't become available until after the season.

However, in some parts of their range, hunting may be having little or no effect on black duck populations. The Nova Scotia population, for example, is apparently stable, perhaps even growing, despite a four-bird limit and a three month season. Even if hunting is keeping the population from increasing more quickly, at current numbers there's no biologically based need for more restrictive regulations. This is particularly so given that duck hunters are declining in the province.

The black duck population in the Antigonish watershed increased by 12-15% during the 1990s. Although there is relatively little hunting pressure, local hunters potentially can have an impact on resident birds. Most are shot in the estuary, usually within five miles of where they were banded. About 70% of my band returns come from birds killed during the first week of the season and during the 10-day period following the general freeze-up. Predominantly naive young birds are shot in the early season, but most of the birds killed late in the season are adults. Survival after the hunting season is generally good. All but two of 32 males and 20 females that survived the hunting season, made it to the following breeding season. At least 23 of these birds were still alive three years later.

I find it much easier to constrain myself when I hunt around home. Perhaps, as Aldo Leopold observed, one takes greater responsibility for resident wildlife. I even feel differently when I hunt in neighbouring estuaries, though they're only a few miles away. Certainly, the farther away from home the less responsibility I feel toward the birds I hunt. I wonder if hunters who observe ducks during all phases of their life cycle take greater responsibility for them? Do they, in a sense, view them as their own, or at least as resident game?

In my opinion, black duck habitat management in Nova Scotia, and probably throughout most of eastern Canada, should focus on protecting existing breeding, staging and wintering habitat. Creating and enhancing breeding habitat to increase production certainly isn't cost-effective. I don't believe it significantly augments natural production. Many factors have contributed to the continental decline of black ducks and more research is needed to better understand their relative importance. Research should have a higher priority, even if funding it sometimes comes at the expense of securing habitat.

Hunting is prohibited on the marsh where I do research, and this is probably a major reason why ducks and geese remain in the area as long as they do. Cold weather in December usually locks the marsh in ice, forcing the birds onto the still open waters of the lower estuary. When this occurs, birds take a few days to find new foraging locations and the hunting then can be excellent. Three of us went out the morning after a big freeze-up. One of my friends, Will Wong, a local restaurateur, was a long-time hunting partner, but the other, Greg Hamilton, was a student of mine who we'd introduced to waterfowling earlier that autumn. It took us only 20 minutes to get to the barrier beach that keeps the sea from engulfing the estuary. But we had to wait until it was light enough to locate open water and the birds. The change in weather meant everything was different for us, too.

Dawn came slowly, revealing a stark, snow-covered landscape. The water, now absolutely calm after two days of being lashed by a driving northeasterly wind, was a sullen grey. At first we saw only three or four little bunches of common mergansers sitting behind an island where we often hunted late in the year. There were also about 20 goldeneyes in a small patch of water out from the island and another dozen among the rocks near shore. Given the conditions, there should have been more. Then I saw the black ducks, lots of them, sitting along the edge of the ice between the mainland and the island, blending almost perfectly with the rock-strewn shoreline.

We quickly launched our boat and navigated through the pans of ice toward the island. Reaching that half-acre of snow-covered rock was at that moment the most important thing in our lives. As we approached, the birds rose in a flock of a size rarely seen in Nova Scotia. We had a feeling they'd be back.

We scattered two dozen whistler decoys among the rocks along the shoreline. We put a dozen blacks in a flooded lagoon. Finally, we pulled the boat over the ice behind the island and covered it with two white sheets. We were anxious to get loaded up, but we set out eight goose decoys, just in case. Earlier in the season we'd built a drift wood blind on the island, but only the snow-encrusted skeleton remained after being buffeted by the endless winds that blow out there. We quickly brushed it in with beach heather and bayberry boughs. Soon, Will, Greg and Dee, Will's black Labrador, had a place to hide and shelter from the wind that was once again beginning to blow. I went 30 yards farther along the shoreline and settled in behind a boulder that was slowly being engulfed by the rising tide. We were ready!

The wind was soon blowing hard but it was at our backs and the decoys were in the lee of the island. The first birds to come back were the goldeneyes, normally difficult birds to decoy to the island.

We'd hunted them there many times but we usually shot only birds buzzing the decoys as they flew to or from their feeding grounds in the upper estuary. But today was different. The upper estuary was covered with ice. The birds that were now returning had been feeding on aquatic animal life when we disturbed them. Our decoys must have looked convincing because for the next half hour the unsuspecting birds came steadily to us in singles, doubles and little bunches.

Greg was just learning to wingshoot. I remember how elated he was when he killed his first whistler, a gorgeous drake. He'd missed with his right barrel but his left tumbled the bird into the water. Dee retrieved the bird as it drifted in the tide. Greg sat inspecting his trophy and chatting animatedly about his shot. "Have you ever seen anything so gorgeous," he asked, never taking his eyes off the bird! "Do you think I'll get my first black duck, too?" he wondered out loud.

Later, I "winged" a goldeneye that fell too far away to let Dee attempt to retrieve it in the ice-clogged water. While I was trying to launch the boat, a bald eagle that had been watching from atop a spruce tree on the far shore, flew to the duck. It dove repeatedly as the eagle hovered above it, but soon became fatigued. When it surfaced, the eagle snatched it from the water. The duck, which was held tightly in the eagle's talons, struggled momentarily and then went limp. The big raptor carried it back to the same tree and proceeded to pluck it. Then, methodically, it ripped the bird apart and devoured it.

The first black ducks began coming back during a lull in the whistler flight. They were wary, treating the decoys with suspicion. Most were in groups of four to a dozen, but some flocks numbered 20 or more. Greg had just reloaded after missing a black when a single bird peeled off a passing flock and decoyed. This time he made no mistake, killing the bird as it dropped its feet to pitch. "Look at the red legs and feet on this bird," he exclaimed, when Dee brought the duck to him. "This must be one of those northern blacks I've heard about." In fact, this beautiful dusky drake with the red legs and lime green bill was not a visitor from Labrador. It was a resident bird, as I discovered when I later checked my records. I'd banded it as a duckling two years earlier. He was now in full breeding plumage. "There is no unique race of northern black duck," I told Greg, "all late-season males look like this. The scientific name, *rubripes*, means red feet."

Minutes later a black duck came in on my side of the blind. I watched it land, nervously look around, and fly off in alarm. Greg asked me why I hadn't shot. I told him that I usually pass up female ducks when I recognize them. "But how can you tell the difference between male and female blacks?" he asked. "It's difficult," I told him, "but I'll help you learn what to look for." Within 20 minutes he was getting pretty good at distinguishing between males and females.

"Does it really matter though?" Greg questioned me as he passed up a female. "It probably depends on the population," I answered. "There's not likely any need when populations are stable or increasing, but protecting females can make a difference to the recovery potential of populations that are low or declining. Hunting regulations are the best way to protect females, but hunter restraint is important, too."

Greg seemed interested, so I continued. "In general, females are more valuable than males to the growth potential of populations, and older birds are more important than younger ones. Chances of survival increase with age, just as reproductive success does. Like most animals, ducks learn to do things better as they get older. In some species of birds, only a relatively few females produce most of the young. This may also be true of ducks. We do know that some female ducks are better mothers than others. These productive females may not be significant for purposes of statistical analysis, which treats all individuals the same, but they are biologically significant and protecting them is important. Unfortunately, many adult females are dying, though not all from hunters, before they reach their prime reproductive years. Indeed, in heavily hunted duck populations, hunters are probably killing a significant number of females before they've had a chance to produce any young.

Eight birds approached us from downwind and one caught my eye. It was a drake mallard. As the flock broke ranks over the decoys, each bird looking for a place to pitch, the mallard presented me with a perfect shot. Dee made the retrieve and I laid it in the snow with the black ducks. Greg, a Nova Scotian born and bred, came over to inspect the gaudy plumage of the mallard. He'd never seen one in the wild.

The honking of geese interrupted us. I didn't know where the sound was coming from but I knew it was close. I looked up to see two geese cutting across the edge of the decoys about 30 yards over the water and heading straight for Will. He shouldered his lovely little over-and-under and killed them both. We had birds to go in our limits and the flight was still in full swing, but 14 birds was enough. What a morning we'd had. The look on Greg's face said it all.

Atlantic Sea Ducks

I t doesn't take long for the sea to get into your blood. While a student in Nova Scotia I fell in love with the rugged coast with its bays, coves and estuaries. Soon after my return, I promised myself I'd learn all I could about this dynamic world where land meets sea, and about the scoters, eiders and oldsquaw-the sea ducks of the hunters - that live in this starkly beautiful setting.

It is November and with most of the fishery closed for the season, the thoughts of coastal fishermen have turned to "sea-ducking." Northern migrants have swollen the ranks of resident breeders. Names like Cape Sable, Browns-Lahave, Lercher, Anticosti, Cabot Strait and Laurentian Fan on the marine weather forecast stir the "locals," making them restless for a "shoot." Hunting sea ducks is not a casual proposition. It's dangerous and unpredictable, influenced greatly by the vagaries of weather and tide. Careful planning and reliable equipment are as critical for safety as they are for good sport.

My first hunt in Nova Scotia made me a dedicated sea duck hunter. Nova Scotia juts into the North Atlantic, taking the full brunt of winter storms that sweep down the St. Lawrence or up the American seaboard to batter its coastline. Between storms, however, safe and exciting hunting can be had on rocky ledges a mile or so offshore. We hit such a day in January. It was mild for the time of year and the wind that had blown for a week was still.

Will Wong and I made the two-hour drive from Antigonish to Whitehead on Nova Scotia's eastern shore. We kept an ear to the marine weather station and an eye on the nighttime sky. We met Pat Conrad, a coastal fisherman and a friend of Will's, sitting in his pickup truck on the government wharf, waiting for us. "You're in good time," he said, motioning for us to get into his truck. "We've got to wait for a little light. No point taking chances when you don't have to. The local fishermen have the harbor channel pretty well marked with buoys, but the tide is running and it's hard to judge where the rocks are if you get out of the channel. It can be tricky, and you wouldn't last long in that water-it's damn near frozen. The birds won't fly 'til it's light, anyway."

Before long though, we were launching Will's 17-foot big water "duck boat." The first pink glow was showing in the east. Pat took over the controls and navigated out the mile-long harbor, which was as calm as a mill pond. But once past the barrier of rocky outcrops that protects the harbor, we entered a different world, one of tossing water and white-capped surf breaking over shoals and submerged rock ledges. The sea was a wild thing everywhere we looked. The ledges where we hoped to hunt were an awesome sight. Breakers erupted over them, rocketing geysers of spray 40 feet into the air. The broken waves swirled and churned behind the ledges. The boat, big on familiar, protected waters, now seemed so fragile. This was a surreal world. Where were the waves coming from? There was no wind, yet the sound of crashing waves resembled a full blown storm. Pat surmised that the waves were coming from a storm far out at sea and many hours, perhaps days, away.

Birds flew all around us as we made for a ledge near an island where a lighthouse perched precariously on a craggy promontory, facing the open sea. Pat manoeuvered the boat into a patch of slack water about 500 feet off the ledge and signalled for me to cast the anchors. Hunting from the ledge was impossible. Once at anchor, the boat was relatively stable as it moved from trough to crest on long, gently undulating waves. Often the only visible horizon was the sky and a rim of water that completely circled the boat. While setting up, I had been watching breakers rolling in on a headland about a mile away. Twice a towering wave loomed above the others. I was scared! Were these the rogue waves I'd heard about? I mentioned my concern to Pat. He assured me we'd be safe, but he went on to say, "a couple of guys who didn't know about those waves drowned a few years ago. They should have gone out with one of the local boys." He said this in the matter-of-fact way fishermen speak of death at sea. It happens frequently, inevitably an error of judgement.

All around us birds were landing and diving for mussels and sea urchins. Oldsquaws jigged from side to side in erratic flight, just over the water. Little bunches of eiders would get up, fly a few yards, and plunge again into the surging water. The black-and-white drakes contrasted dramatically with the chocolate-brown females. White-winged and black scoters skimmed the waves in ragged lines. Surf scoters, true to their names, plunged into the breaking surf. This seemed suicidal to me. Once, two dark, small-bodied ducks pitched behind the ledge. They were rare harlequins, the so-called rock ducks, or lords and ladies, of the local fishermen. Murres, dovekies, and occasionally a puffin skimmed the boat, seemingly oblivious to us.

It didn't matter that we were off the main flight line because there were so many birds. We'd spot a line several hundred yards away as they worked toward our decoys. We'd see them, then we wouldn't, as our boat rode the waves. Suddenly, they'd be there in front of us, 200, 100, 50 feet away! We shot and shot, but hitting a bird was difficult. They flew in a straight line as sea ducks do, but the boat was constantly moving. We killed most of the birds we hit; four eiders, three oldsquaws, and eight scoters, or "coots" as the local gunners call them. We retrieved all but three or four cripples that simply outswam us.

When there was a lull in the action, we watched eiders and oldsquaws riding the waves. Occasionally an inquisitive harbor or grey seal bobbed up near the boat to look curiously at us. Patches of high, wispy cloud periodically obscured the weak sun that never got much above the horizon, reminding us that it was mid-winter. I thought about Lawrence Sargent Hall's short story, *The Ledge*, where he tells the tale of a fisherman-waterfowler whose brief lapse of vigilance cost him, his young son and his nephew their lives. Certainly our lives were in the hands of our fisherman host; we were living very much "on the edge."

I vividly remembered that hunt for days after. The sights, sounds and odors, the excitement and sense of danger all lingered. It was a powerful experience. Such encounters with the sea were almost daily fare for our fisherman friend. He admitted, however, that only "sea-ducking" could get him out there in such weather. Will and I had glimpsed a seldom-seen world. Before heading home we went to Pat's house where his wife had prepared a big lunch for us. I asked Pat if ignoring regulations was as common as it once was. "No, I wouldn't say," he replied, "but some of the boys don't pay much heed to limits or seasons. They figure they'll shoot what they want, especially if they go to the trouble of rigging up. I know one fellow who goes out for those "rock ducks" (the fully protected harlequin), but he's crazy, and he only gets a few. Most of us along this coast disagree with the renegades but we don't mess with them. Generally one or two good shoots is enough for most people."

Pat went on to say that he believed the overall kill by locals was down from what it once was. "Not many young guys are "sea-ducking" anymore," he said. "It's damn hard work. My feeling is we probably kill fewer birds than guys from the city, especially retired guys who hunt like there's no tomorrow. I hope nobody screws up our "sea-ducking." I enjoy getting out and I don't think I have much impact on the ducks. And I'd miss it. There's not much to do around here in the winter. I'll tell you though, something should be done about crippling ducks."

I encouraged Pat to continue. "You know," he said, "some guys are just out there to shoot. They don't bother chasing cripples and a lot use cheap, under-powered shells. They carry them in gallon buckets. An eider can weigh six pounds or better, you know, and their feathers are like armour. They're hard to kill."

I told Pat that I'd been on hunts where half of the birds shot at were within gunshot, but out of killing range. Some birds are obviously crippled, like those with broken wings, but how do we know how many birds are hit and fly away with shot imbedded in them? One study using a fluoroscope showed about 35% of *nesting* eiders from different regions of Atlantic Canada had lead pellets in them. Obviously these birds were survivors, but did their wounds affect how long they'd live, or their breeding success? There are few studies that investigate the sub-lethal impact of hunting. What would we find if we looked harder?

Most crippling results from hunters shooting at birds outside of lethal range, where the problems are poor pattern and loss of pellet energy. Learning what killing range is was one of my most difficult challenges, and this is probably true of most novice hunters. But this skill can be taught. Knowing and respecting killing range is part of ethical hunting, much as having a good dog and making a committed search for downed birds is.

The issue of steel shot invariably comes up in any discussion of crippling. Steel shot is less effective than lead at extreme ranges, even though the ammunition industry has improved the killing power of steel considerably. A skilled hunter can regularly kill birds at 50 to 60 yards with steel, but its effectiveness quickly diminishes beyond 30 to 40 yards. In reality, the average hunter (most of us) can't kill effectively beyond 25 yards regardless of what load he's using. Even experienced hunters may have difficulty killing birds beyond 35 yards. We should learn our personal effective killing range and concentrate on getting birds within that distance. Inevitably, crippling and imbedding birds with shot has increased with steel. Unfortunately, waterfowl hunters weren't well prepared to change from lead to steel shot. This was especially so in Canada where, it is probably safe to say, most hunters first used steel on opening day of 1998, when it became obligatory. Professional management should have done a better job of educating hunters about steel shot and about shooting skills in general. There are ways to improve shooting skills and more of professional management's time and resources should be invested in teaching these skills.

A major reason the Migratory Bird Treaty Act of 1918 was signed was to protect from over-hunting the common eider, which under the circumstances was paradoxically named. Although there's been little research on sea ducks, especially in far northern habitats, biologists have long known that they're vulnerable to over-shooting because of their modest reproductive potential; predation on eggs and ducklings is also very serious in some populations. However, it wasn't until the 1990s that managers started to get reliable information on the east coast sea duck harvest. What they discovered was cause for concern.

Sea duck numbers were lower than expected, some alarmingly so. For example, between 1950 and 1990 east coast scoters declined by 50%. Although many factors were suspected, harvest management-hunting regulations-is the only practical way of protecting these birds. Managing their vast and remote breeding habitats is entirely impractical.

For years biologists were concerned that sea-duck hunting regulations had become too liberal. For example, special extended seasons for sea ducks (only scoters, at first) began in 1938 with 16 to 30 day extensions for some states. By 1972, 13 states had special seasons which lasted up to 107 days and included bag limits of seven ducks of five species. The rationale for extensions was to reduce hunting pressure on dabbling and diving ducks, while providing increased hunting opportunities for beleaguered Atlantic Flyway waterfowlers. Sea ducks have always been heavily hunted in Atlantic Canada and states like Maine, but the 1980s saw steadily increasing pressure on sea ducks all along the coast as outfitters took advantage of liberal regulations. During the early 1990s, a record number of American duck hunters pursued sea ducks.

Armed with good data to support their concern, during the 1990s managers argued successfully for reduced limits on scoters and eiders in both the U.S. and Canada. Special seasons were also curtailed. These managers contended that hunting mortality adds to the natural mortality of sea ducks. In other words, hunting reduces their potential to sustain populations.

Attitudes toward hunting regulations vary among hunters, some wanting more restrictions and others fewer. However, it seems a growing number of duck hunters are willing to support conservative regulations. In fact, these hunters are often at the forefront of promoting conservation initiatives, but they don't always receive support from wildlife professionals.

Along a heavily gunned part of Nova Scotia's coast, a group of veteran hunters lobbied for a delay in the opening of the season. They claimed this would eventually contribute to better hunting by killing fewer local breeders. They believed females are still weak from the rigors of breeding and young birds have been flying for only a short time when the season opens. They also had concerns about "running" (chasing) birds and other unethical behavior by people who hunt only during the early season, when birds are especially vulnerable. However, their request wasn't supported by managers who felt there was no biologically-based need for more restrictive regulations. In fact, there was little biologically-based justification for either position.

In my view, regardless of biology, requests by conservation-minded hunters should be carefully considered, even if the only benefit is better relations between hunters and managers. Who, after all, is being served by an open season? It seems to me that hunters who support conservative regulations are likely more committed and responsible than those who don't. One also suspects that their concerns, especially about deterioration in the quality of hunting, are probably valid. Why not support their conservative stance on hunting regulations?

The allure of sea duck hunting is partly its dynamic, unforgiving setting. There is always something happening. A hunt on a remote island off the southwest tip of Nova Scotia is memorable because of the songbird and hawk migration that was in full career. We saw tens of thousands of birds and more than 60 species. The island is a resting area before birds strike off across the Gulf of Maine *en route* to the American coast and points south. We shot very few ducks during our week-long stay, but it was exhilarating being there during that special time.

I have vivid memories of another hunt because of the danger. I sometimes find thinking about my adventure rather sobering. The tides of the Bay of Fundy that separates Nova Scotia and New Brunswick are the highest in the world, in places rising more than 20 feet in an hour. So quickly does the tide flood the sand flats, a man cannot outrun it! The tide is always on your mind.

Hunters wait along the rocky headlands that jut into the sea, hoping to intercept passing eiders as they move along the shoreline with the rising tide. A line of a dozen decoys sometimes attracts the attention of the birds and lures them into range. But as the tide rises, the hunter is forced to retreat shoreward, moving every few minutes and pulling his string of decoys behind him. There is hardly a moment when he's not being chased from his temporary sanctuary by the relentless tide; a twisted ankle could spell doom! But the rewards are tremendous. The feeding eiders that follow the continually moving tideline offer such exciting shooting that, for some, it is worth risking limb and life. It is a heart-pounding experience.

One of my most exciting eider hunts was on the Grey Islands in the South Labrador Sea, off the northern tip of Newfoundland. It was late February and my students were heading south to party on the beach during "study" break. Unlike that of the "sun-seekers," my flight had lots of empty seats. I was going to Newfoundland to meet my friend Ian Goudie, a research biologist with the Canadian Wildlife Service. We were going to hunt eiders and collect scientific data. Ian picked me up at Deer Lake airport in mid-morning and we immediately set off along the Great Northern Peninsula for the coastal outport of Main Brook. From there we were scheduled to fly by small plane to our island destination, 12 miles offshore.

It had been snowing without let up for several days. A five-foot blanket of white covered the ground and visibility in wind-driven squalls was reduced to zero. Much of the trip was spent in a convoy of vehicles behind a snow-plough that broke trail for us. That part of the province was experiencing a record snow fall, and the banks of snow along the roadside were mountainous. Finally, late that afternoon we pulled into Main Brook, totally drained of energy. We were in no rush, we had a week. Anyway, isn't "getting there" part of the enjoyment of a trip?

Flying to the island was out of the question. Snow squalls had been making flying hazardous all week and the bush pilot, a cautious and reliable fellow, steadfastly refused to fly unless weather conditions were perfect. Besides, he never flew at night. Such prudence had probably saved his life many times.

Ian phoned a fisherman friend and arranged for us to spend the night with him and his family. Like most of the men in the community, Ian's friend passionately loved hunting. That evening after a big supper of caribou stew, he regaled us with stories of hunting sea ducks and "Turrs" (murres); this eastern-most province of Canada is the only place in North America where murres can be legally shot.

Everett's stories were always about big kills. "Back in January month," he said, "my boy-he just turned 20, you know, hit the wind and tide just right. He shot 60 eiders before the wind shifted. This is a lot of birds, I know, but the lad's still young and he hasn't had many big shoots. He wants to get his share." He looked at us as if to say, you understand, we're all part of the club. I shuddered a bit inside, remembering some of my own big shoots, though they were never on that scale! I thought about this when I went to bed. Surely it's not necessary for every new hunter to "get his share." Ethical mentors can show a better way, but it was pretty obvious that the amicable Everett was not the man to do this. Enforcement of regulations wasn't the answer to protecting the birds either. This island province, which lays claim to 10,000 miles of coastline, has fewer than a dozen game wardens.

Clearing skies overnight made for ideal flying conditions the next morning. I crawled into the back of the four-seater Cessna and stretched out on top of our gear. Ian's huge black Lab was none too happy about sharing "his space" with me, but we worked things out. The 30-minute flight to the island was otherwise uneventful, except when we saw thousands of white and brown eiders dotting the blue waters of the bay. Shortly before nine o'clock, our pilot gently set his ski-equipped plane down on a frozen bay, half a mile out to sea from the little cabin where we'd be staying. We quickly unloaded our gear and were soon waving goodbye to our pilot. Five minutes later, one of the four fishermen who'd be our hosts on the island, roared across the ice toward us on a snowmobile, pulling a freight sled. We loaded our gear and were soon at the cabin, greeting the other three fishermen.

Besides the dog and six men, the island was home to a small herd of caribou, a snowy owl and, so the fishermen believed from the tracks they saw, a polar bear that had probably drifted down from the Arctic on a pan of ice. We soon got settled in and that night as I lay in my bunk, I contemplated the discomfort and danger some people will endure for adventure. What the hell was I doing here? But so far, I was comfortable enough. I wasn't missing the television set, or anything else for that matter, and there was the prospect of some great shooting.

Next morning the sky was grey and sullen, and the northeast wind was picking up. Our hunting gear was set to go, all we had to do was eat. One of the fishermen, a veteran cook, had made a big breakfast. After eating, we split up into parties of two. I travelled by snowmobile with a fellow who, except to steam out to the Grand Banks to fish, had never been more than a few miles from where he was born. After a 10-minute run, we stopped where waves had pushed pack-ice against the shore, forming an icy point that jutted out into the sea. We used some of the smaller chunks of ice to fashion a comfortable blind that resembled an ice fortress. We secured our string of 20 decoys, converted from black ducks into eiders with a little white paint, to a rock protruding out of the ice. The ebbing tide strung them out in front of the blind. We were ready!

Lines of eiders had been moving along the shore while we were setting up. They veered well out beyond the point when they spotted us at work, but this now changed. Most of the birds came with the wind from the northeast, flying only a few feet over the water. We could see them coming for two miles or more along the coastline. Before reaching us, however, they disappeared into a big cove. A couple of minutes later, they appeared again as they rounded a headland 500 yards away. From there our decoys must have been clearly visible against the grey sea. Hugging the shore, they bore down on us. There was never any question they'd pass over our spread.

Lewis was a taciturn fellow in his early 30s. He'd never shot a bird of any kind on the wing, and he was damn sure he wasn't about to start. Nor was he sure it could be done. He wasn't too delighted when I urged him to forget about letting the birds pitch into the decoys. He looked at me and asked, "Don't we want to get as many as we can?" His question was reasonable enough given that sea birds made up a significant component of his family's winter diet. "Go ahead," he eventually said in frustration, "do what you want." He leaned his gun against the ice wall, folded his arms across his chest, and settled back to watch. His face mirrored what he was thinking.

To his utter amazement and mine, I made three consecutive triples from lines of birds that came over the decoys. I was using a Stevens pump that'd been a reliable favorite of mine for years, but I'd never come remotely close to achieving such shooting success before, and it's a good bet I never will again. We were on firm ground and, despite the cold, not too bundled up with clothing. Furthermore, come hell or high water, eiders fly in a straight line. They are a predictable if not always easy target. By mid-morning Lew and I were great buddies. He was also getting pretty good at wing-shooting. He was thrilled each time a bird crumpled at his shot. His florid face beamed in the cold air. That evening back at camp, he informed his comrades that he was going to be a wing-shooter from now on. "I can remember every bird I killed," he told the others. He dominated the conversation that evening with talk of the shots we'd made. Apparently, nobody had ever seen Lew so animated.

Ian had studied eider ecology as an M.Sc student and was now responsible for managing eiders along the Newfoundland coast. Our fishermen friends, who had made the arduous 12-mile trek from the mainland to the island by boat over a sea strewn with ice, worked for Ian when he had projects in the area. They lived along this coast and were a wealth of information about the activity and behavior of sea birds. Their theories about the birds were sometimes shaky, but their observations were reliable and provided invaluable information to office-bound managers like Ian. I was impressed with the common sense these men brought to our discussions of management issues. Ian looked at me and commented, "I go to some pains to keep in touch with these guys. They're a kind of touchstone with reality."

These fishermen hunted for something to do during the long winter, but they also shot what they needed for their families. This was not usually many birds, but the concept of a limit meant little to them. On the other hand, they were contemptuous of people who routinely killed a lot of birds and then sold them, or worse, discarded them after they'd languished in a freezer all winter. The now talkative Lew said, "I know guys who shoot as many ducks as they can, just to brag about it." "There's been a big decline in local eiders," someone said. "I guess there's other causes, but I think we're sometimes shooting too many."

I asked them about black duck hunting. One of the fellows offered the opinion that, "the arse had gone out of 'er. It's not worth going out anymore." "We locals are a big part of the problem," Lew contributed, "so it's up to us if things are going to change." Before we left the island, Ian hired one of the fishermen to be the foreman on an eider nesting study that was being supported by Ducks Unlimited and the Canadian Wildlife Service. The long term objective was to re-populate the offshore islands where "egging" and year-round gunning had wiped out breeding colonies.

Severe weather made hunting difficult. In fact, we got out only three times during our stay on the island. High winds and ice usually kept the birds well out from shore and the fishermen, all experienced men who had great respect for the forces of nature, were loath to venture onto the sea. Two 14-foot aluminum boats were all we had in camp. When the weather cooperated, we worked hard to get enough birds for our research, and for Lew's larder.

The final hunt of the trip was incredibly exciting and well worth all the effort we'd put into this island adventure. For two days the weatherman had been forecasting a northeast gale. As expected, the birds were particularly active the day before the storm struck. Flight after flight of eiders came to the cove where we'd built our blind. They were exploring the rocky shoreline for blue mussels and sea urchins, their principal food. There were about 16,000 birds wintering around the island and 2,000 were using our cove. We estimated that each day one bird ate about a pound of food. This meant they were taking a ton of animal life from the frigid waters of the cove each day. This food not only kept them alive, but their body condition at the end of the winter would determine their breeding success. Anything that kept them from feeding-bad weather or human disturbance, for example, could impact on their success.

As we travelled by snowmobile to our ice blinds in the diffuse pre-dawn light, I had a feeling we'd get some action. In fact, we began shooting as soon as we could see. It seemed there were always birds in the air somewhere, and many tolled to our decoys. We'd been shooting for about an hour when 17 birds came toward us. They were so low over the water that their wing tips brushed the mirror-flat surface. And it seemed to me their wings beat a little faster than the eiders we'd been seeing. Just before they swung over the decoys, Ian yelled out, "they're king eiders." The best opportunity had passed by the time we got squared to shoot, but we each killed a bird, and Ian's was a mature drake. The locals call these gorgeous males "bottle-nose" because of the way the base of the bill protrudes. This bulbous structure contains the salt glands which secrete salt, thus allowing them to drink seawater. Our handsome bird was quite a trophy because king eiders rarely venture close to land. Even at night, they roost far out at sea on ice beside leads of open water.

As the day wore on, the wind began blowing and slowly built to gale-force. The sea was becoming wild. The tide was beginning to flow and, backed by the now on-shore wind, driving hard against the ice-strewn point where we huddled in our ice fortress. The birds abandoned their earlier caution. Shooting was brisk as they piled into our rig. We dared not venture out to retrieve them by boat, but Ian devised a unique solution to our problem. He'd brought along a specially fashioned harness which he now put on the dog. He attached a stout hemp rope to a swivel ring over Tar's shoulders. Each time the big, muscular dog leapt from the ice ledge into the water, a vertical distance of perhaps eight feet, he paid out the rope. Tar made retrieve after retrieve, scrambling up the bank of ice into the blind. He seemed oblivious to the jagged ice. Once he completely disappeared below the surface, drawn down by an under-tow we couldn't detect. Fortunately, the harness and rope did their work.

The dog made it possible for us to continue hunting and it seemed he knew this. He sat with his head high, intently watching the coastline for birds. After each retrieve, his thick black coat took on a silver sheen as little droplets of water instantly froze to the tips of his hair in the minus 10° F air. The sea, the sky, the land were all shades of grey, and no horizon could be distinguished as the leaden water and overcast sky merged together. The strikingly beautiful drake eiders stood out dramatically against this sombre background. We shot only when birds were over the decoys, their feet extended as they looked for a place to pitch. I don't think we saw an eider any higher than 10 feet above the water during the entire hunt, and most just skimmed the surface. It was so thrilling to watch them approach knowing for several minutes we'd get a shot.

I'll never forget being in that starkly beautiful land but what motivated me to go was the prospect of a hunting adventure, and this is the only reason I'd go back, at least in February. It wasn't killing eiders that made my trip memorable. What's imprinted in my memory are the people, the birds, the landscape, the sea, the sense of adventure, the emotional intensity.

The gale eventually forced us off our icy promontory. That night it became a full-blown storm. We didn't need a crystal ball to tell us our pilot wouldn't arrive as scheduled. I had a fitful night's sleep, waking frequently as the howling wind lashed the cabin. In the morning I scratched an opening in a frost-covered window and looked out. I was greeted by a wall of swirling, blowing snow. It was impossible to see more than a few feet beyond the cabin. I gazed out in awe.

Seven days earlier our pilot had deposited us on the frozen surface of the bay, half a mile from the cabin. I wondered at the time why the two camp boats were on shore, tied to a wind-contorted spruce beside the cabin. Why hadn't they been left nearer the open water? After all, the ice of the bay was two feet thick. Now I understood. There was nothing to impede the northeast wind as it roared across the north Atlantic, building mountainous waves that now thundered into the bay. The white sheet of ice that covered the bay began to rise and fall as the water surged and fell below it. I could hear the ice creaking and groaning. I watched in amazement as it broke up. Within an hour, the tide had taken the ice out to sea. The unrestrained waves now broke against the shore with a thundering roar, sending spray against the cabin and the boats.

We spent the next three days battened down in the cabin. I

occasionally ventured forth to feel the fury of the incredible wind. Toward noon on the second day, Lew and I went by snowmobile to a little cluster of derelict houses that clung precariously to a rocky hillside. They'd been abandoned decades earlier when the provincial government embarked on a social experiment that all but destroyed Newfoundland's isolated outpost communities, and a way of life. Their inhabitants were moved to larger villages and towns where their "needs" could be better met. Instead, many believe, these self-reliant people were robbed of their dignity and identities. Lew and I stood in the kitchen of a storm battered wood-frame house trying to imagine the strength of body and spirit these people must have possessed.

The storm lasted three full days. The day after it subsided was bitterly cold, but sunny and still. Our plane approaching across the blue sea was a very welcome sight because we were running low on fuel. Later as we flew to the mainland, we saw a raft of 6,000 to 8,000 eiders in a sheltered cove where they'd ridden out the storm. This hardy race of arctic nesting eiders lives a precarious existence in the South Labrador Sea. Only a few days without feeding can result in body reserves becoming seriously depleted.

As we prepared our gear for the long drive back to Deer Lake, we learned what the storm meant to other people. While we'd been enjoying our adventure, three fishing vessels had gone down within 50 miles of where we hunted; no survivors were found.

On the flight back to Nova Scotia, I thought about what I'd seen, the people I'd met, the freedom and exhilaration I felt in this wilderness. The sense of adventure. Surely these are important reasons why people hunt....

The Prairie "Duck Factory"

Mid-October is a great time to visit Last Mountain Lake in south-central Saskatchewan. Hundreds of thousands of migrating waterfowl stage on this shallow, marshy lake and the freedom to hunt them makes this a waterfowler's paradise.

It was the mid-1970s and tundra-breeding geese had had a very successful breeding season. However, a dry spring and early summer had made it a poor year for prairie ducks. A friend and colleague, Bob Bailey, and I were staying at a former hunting lodge that had been converted to a research facility by the Canadian Wildlife Service. We spent the first day scouting fields around the lake, trying to figure out when and where the birds were feeding. In fact, we easily found the geese, but finding the owner of the field where we wanted to hunt was another story.

Our search started in a nearby town's Canadian Legion hall. After an hour or so of buying rounds for local farmers, we found someone who not only knew what fields we were talking about, but the landowner was his brother-in-law. We were in business. "Hell," our new friend exclaimed, "I'll call him for you." Twenty minutes later we were kicking tractor tires and chatting about grain prices with this friendly fellow who lived 10 miles from where he grew his crops. "Sure, hunt there in the morning, just make sure you fill in your pits before you leave." Next morning the white-fronts and snows covered us up! It was spectacular. We quickly shot our limits and left before disturbing the main flock. That afternoon we hunted Hungarian partridge and sharp-tails along the edge of the lake where we could also watch for the evening duck flight. It was one of those crystal clear October days that are so precious to prairie hunters. The azure sky was cloudless except for a ridge of billowy white cumulus tracking slowly across the northwestern horizon. Walking across the prairie was delightful, like being on a vast, grassy carpet of beautiful muted color. Ducks began flying in late afternoon. Several hundred left the lake not far from where we hunted. It didn't take long to make plans for the morning. We'd hunt ducks on the lake as they returned after feeding. We'd hunt the so-called "back flight" or "back shoot."

That night was frosty and absolutely still. The marsh near the lodge was awash with light from an almost full moon. About 10 o'clock, I went for a walk to collect my thoughts and imprint the day's events in my memory. Somewhere, tundra swans were calling. What sights and sounds they must experience *en route* to their North Carolina wintering grounds. The nighttime world was alive with activity. How little we know about what happens after the cloak of darkness descends.

The warm air from the stove felt good when I returned to the lodge. Bob was already asleep and it didn't take me long to find my bed. I drifted off to sleep thinking about the "back flight."

We awoke next morning to the rattle of long-neglected window panes, loosened by years of relentless prairie wind. It was already light when we went outside to discover that Mother Nature had provided us with all the makings of a "duck day." The sky was heavily overcast and the wind had a bite to it, but happily there was no rain. There was no rush to get to the lake, the ducks wouldn't return for a couple of hours, but we were too keyed up to eat breakfast. Besides, we wanted to watch the flocks of waterfowl as they left the lake for the fields.

Our destination was a small patch of reeds about 150 yards from the lake's marshy shore. If our earlier reconnaissance paid off, we'd be under the flight line when the birds returned, looking for a place to get out of the wind that was now gusting across the lake. Under a foot of ooze the lake bottom was hard, so getting to the reed patch wasn't particularly difficult. Typical of prairie wetlands during drought years, this shallow lake was little more than a big, muddy slough, and much of it could be traversed by a hunter wearing chest waders.

We set a dozen decoys and settled in to wait for the birds. Tundra swans crossed the lake in squadrons of a dozen or more, some so close we could see the yellow flashes at the base of their bills. The first hint that sandhill cranes were about to make an appearance was the high-pitched single-note calls that flying birds make. Finally we located them, but they weren't high in the sky as they so often are. We watched in awe as these elegant birds approached so low they had to climb to clear the reeds where we stood hidden. Flock after flock came over, fighting for every yard against a steadily-blowing wind. At that range, the birds took on gargantuan proportions and it seemed as if we could've reached up and grabbed their long legs. Perhaps 700 cranes had passed over us before we saw the first fast-moving flight of ducks on the horizon.

All morning, there'd been bluebills and redheads in range, but we were hunting dabblers and a classic prairie dabbler hunt means mallards and pintails. Before long, singles, doubles, bunches of eight to 10, and flocks of 20 or more flew across the lake, looking for somewhere to get out of the worsening weather. Most were adult drakes, and they came over our reed bed as though it were a beacon. The pintails, their white bellies dramatically contrasting against the grey sky, dropped gracefully toward us from 100 yards up. They side-slipped down on cupped wings. The mallards were much darker and chunkier and the overcast made males difficult to distinguish from females. Pintails are ordinarily cautious birds that are hard to decoy, but we were where they wanted to be, the secret of successful waterfowling. They came to our decoys without hesitation. It was beautiful to see. We were in a waterfowling mecca and we had it to ourselves. That morning it was easy to understand why hunters consider mallards and pintails "ducks of choice."

The limit was eight birds each, but we could've shot a hundred. In fact, we shot four mallards and 12 pintails, all drakes. We then stayed to watch the show. We counted more than a dozen species of ducks. Green-winged teal were particularly exciting. Unannounced, they'd be on top of us before we saw them. Like feathered rockets, they'd climb and speed away on a wind that was now blowing a gale.

The vanguard of white-fronts began returning while we were picking up our decoys. I couldn't pass up a goose that came directly over me, well behind the flock. It was probably carrying some lead. We had most of a possession limit hanging in an outbuilding back at camp, but I swung my gun and killed that bird. When I close my eyes, I can still see it falling in a long arc through the air. It was the last bird of our hunt.

Depending on habitat conditions and the size of the breeding population, half to four-fifths of the continental fall flight of ducks may come from the prairie "duck factory." This includes approximately 70% of mallards and pintails, 75% of canvasbacks, 90% of redheads and blue-winged teal, as well as other preferred species. Prairie migrants visit all four flyways and are available to more hunters than ducks from any other part of the breeding grounds. Historically, the "duck factory," 80% of which is in Canada, had the potential to annually produce 50 million or more new ducks for the fall flight. However, two main factors stand in the way of sustainably high production. Natural droughts have always periodically diminished production, but for almost a century agriculture has been transforming the prairie landscape, causing widespread, permanent loss and degradation of wildlife habitat. Now the prairie likely has the capacity to produce fewer than half the ducks it had prior to the 1930s drought. The perennial debate among waterfowl managers revolves around *how many* ducks that is.

Not surprisingly, professional waterfowl management was pioneered on the prairies and its most impressive initiatives to bolster natural production are here. However, its efforts are little more than attempts to counter the devastating effects that modern agricultural practices have had on prairie ducks. Despite successes, it has been unable to stop the decline or assist the recovery of many important species.

At one time the pintail was as numerous as the mallard. Although there have been good years for pintails, there have been few since the 1970s. Numbers dropped to historic lows in the 1980s during a protracted drought. There were only half as many pintails as mallards, which were also suffering from the ravages of a dry prairie. However, the inability of pintails to recover when water returned to the prairie in the mid-1990s has alarmed managers. Mallards staged a significant recovery but pintails remained 30% below their long term average. Kill statistics from hunter surveys indicated that age ratios were low, meaning too few young were being produced. There were now almost four times as many mallards as pintails. Why had pintails not responded to improved habitat conditions? Was their failure to recover indicative of the degraded condition of prairie habitat and an overall loss of its potential to produce ducks? Some experienced observers believe this is one factor.

The pintail is the quintessential prairie duck, wonderfully adapted to cope with the dry reality of the prairies. Although it's not the persistent re-nester the mallard is, and it tends to lay fewer eggs, females have a remarkable reproductive capacity. Indeed, when habitat conditions are good, pintail populations can recover quickly, potentially doubling in one breeding season. The big advantage pintails have over other prairie ducks is their tendency to nest early, a strategy that's evolved to take advantage of temporary water and an abundant if short-lived food supply. In good years, young pintails are on the wing well before ponds dry up and food disappears, dooming the ducklings of later nesting species.

The pintail is also mobile, pioneering new breeding habitats when the prairie is dry. However, pioneering females are rarely as successful as they would have been on a wet prairie. In fact, some females may not attempt to breed when they encounter dry conditions. In effect, they're "saving" themselves for a future breeding season, something they can do because they may live for 12 or more years. Presumably, this is an evolutionary strategy that allows pintails to *wait out drought,* which can last for years. Historically, pintail populations have tracked the wet and dry cycles of the prairies, but this wasn't the case at the end of the century.

The ability of females to fledge their young quickly is reflected in the pintail social system. Most dabbler species are seasonably monogamous, meaning that a female selects one male as her mate for the breeding season. The male then establishes a territory to protect a food supply for his female and ducklings, and to guard his mate against being raped. How successful he is determines his mate's reproductive success and his paternity. However, female pintails may need a male only for sperm. They don't need a territory because food is either so plentiful there is no competition for it, or there's so little food that they don't attempt to breed.

Nor are females usually choosy about which male she gets sperm from. Indeed, a female may benefit from having several fathers for her ducklings. This ensures the genetic diversity of her young, which in turn improves her chances of perpetuating her genes. The fact of the matter is, females may be better off without a flamboyant, colorful male hanging around and attracting the attention of predators.

This strategy liberates males to spend their time in search of females, and some males fertilize the eggs of many. Sexually motivated pursuit flights in which a dozen or more males pursue a female are common sights in the prairie sky during April and May. Unfortunately, without a mate to protect her, the breeding activities of females can be disrupted; some are even killed by persistent males during rape. Females cope with unwanted sexual overtures by being highly secretive.

As with most ducks, there are more male pintails than females, as many as three times more in some populations. This and the fact that one male can potentially fertilize several females, may have implications for setting hunting regulations. In theory, reasonable gunning pressure shouldn't unduly compromise male pintails, even in years of low production. However, one wonders what encouraged managers to allow 10 pintails in the bag when they first liberalized regulations on pintails during the 1970s. They couldn't have known what impact this would have on their recovery potential. No one will ever know if the plight of the pintail is attributable to these liberal hunting regulations.

Understanding the social system of ducks allows managers to estimate the size of their breeding population. In particular, the behavior of the mallard allows a reasonably reliable estimate of breeding pairs. Mallards are monogamous and for a period of three weeks males, which are otherwise mobile, are predictably on their territories and highly visible. Most of the population breeds at the same time so when managers fly their surveys along standardized routes, they can get reliable counts of pairs. They assume that a single male is one waiting for his mate, who would be on her nest. These pair surveys are the basis for estimating breeding populations. Surveying mallards is reasonably straightforward and statistically reliable.

On the other hand, estimating the size of the pintail breeding population is very difficult. Males are mobile because they don't stay with one female and they aren't territorial. Green-winged teal are almost impossible to survey because their behavior is similar to pintails, and their dull color and secretive nature makes these little ducks difficult to see from an aircraft. If pintails are so well adapted to the wet and dry cycles of the prairies, why didn't they respond as anticipated when the drought broke? The answer is elusive but the saga of the pintail may illustrate how the prairie has lost much of its capacity to produce ducks. It also highlights the limitations of managers to restore ducks. The problem, as some experienced field biologists see it, focuses not only on the quantity of the habitat available to nesting ducks, but also the *quality* of that habitat.

Modern farming and ranching practices have transformed the fertile soils of the prairie into an almost continuous band of cropland and rangeland. Good wildlife habitat has been relegated to isolated islands, often there only because agriculture is not possible. This is especially true of private lands. The native grasses that once provided protective cover for duck nests now occupy a mere remnant of the area they once covered, a major cause for the decline in reproductive rates of ducks.

Dabbling ducks and some divers like lesser scaup prefer to nest in the grassy uplands around wetlands. Ground-nesting is typically risky for birds, but it is especially so for prairie ducks which, to breed successfully, require about four times more nesting cover than water. Farming practices have forced ducks to nest in narrow margins of grass around sloughs and along roads and fencerows. Here they are easy picking for foxes, skunks, raccoons and crows. Alternatively, ducks are attracted to permanent cover of haylands or pastures, only to be thwarted in their nesting attempts by haying operations and intensive grazing. Pintails are particularly vulnerable because they often nest in standing stubble where they lose their nests to cultivation and seeding operations in these "nesting traps." Unfortunately, the prairie pintail population lost much of its recovery potential when southern Alberta and Saskatchewan converted from grazing to a grain economy. Even though grazing reduces nesting cover, the land is still covered with grass.

Presumably, ducks began migrating to the prairies countless generations ago to take advantage of abundant food and relatively few predators. The food situation hasn't changed, but predators of ducks, though always part of the natural ecosystem, now probably occur at much higher densities than in the past. In fact, in places predation has become the most significant factor in declining reproductive rates of ducks. This was apparent for decades but it became acute in the 1980s. Foxes, for example, destroy not only eggs and ducklings of upland nesters, but their keen sense of smell allows them to catch females on the nest, especially at night. One researcher estimated that foxes annually kill 900,000 adult ducks, mostly females. In places, mallard and pintail nest success is as low as 10%, below the 15%-20% required to sustain a population and well below the North American Waterfowl Management Plan's (NAWM Plan's) objective of 50% for key populations.

Diving ducks like canvasbacks, redheads, and sometimes scaup, nest over water in dead vegetation (cattails, bulrushes) from the previous year. This is an evolutionary adaptation to avoid predators. Although nests may be visible, foxes and skunks don't usually venture into the water. However, raccoons, a relative newcomer to parts of the prairies, have no qualms about swimming for their lunch. In some prime breeding areas the reproductive season for females is over without them ever hatching a duckling. Ironically, with the return of water to the prairie and the resulting increase in muskrats, mink have flourished. They kill a lot of ducklings even when habitat conditions are good for ducks.

Predator management has always been used by managers to improve reproductive rates and bolster natural production of ducks. This management tool involves manipulation of habitat as well as killing predators. In fact, even managers who advocate predator management, question how effective it can be if there is not adequate nesting cover and other requirements needed by breeding females. Most agree that the best way to reduce the rate of predation is to increase the amount of good quality nesting and brood-rearing cover. While they point out that prairie-wide predator control will never be realistic, they agree that selective programs may be essential where important species nest at high densities. Research has shown that predator management can produce desired results while also being cost-effective. However, it would cost many millions of dollars to do the research and implement the programs to make predator management truly effective. As it stands, this is a complex issue and managers can't reliably predict what effect predator management will have on duck production from year to year.

If increasing the amount of good quality nesting cover is the best way to reduce predation on nesting ducks, then the Conservation Reserve Program (CRP) is a U.S. federal agricultural program that does just that, though not with the intention of producing ducks. The CRP is in fact a program designed to take land out of production and conserve soil. It isn't an initiative of waterfowl management, despite being supported by a coalition of private-sector partners that includes DU. Regardless of its genesis and goals, CRP has contributed significantly to the post-drought increase in prairie ducks. Waterfowl managers and hunters have both benefitted, because without CRP the population goals of the NAWMP would not have been reached.

CRP has created 34 million acres of wildlife habitat in its first decade, land that would probably return to crop production were the program to end. Indeed, it may be that some of the best habitat for grassland-nesting ducks in the U.S. may be protected under CRP. Some researchers believe that regardless of water conditions in the Dakotas, in average years ducks may not be able to reproduce at maintenance levels without CRP. At the turn of the century, almost one third of total duck production occurred on CRP lands. Research has shown dramatically increased nesting success on unmanaged CRP lands. This is an encouraging indication that despite predators, duck production can be good where there's enough good quality natural habitat. In fact, it may be that water and prime nesting cover on CRP lands were attracting nomadic pintails and blue-winged teal that would otherwise have nested on the Canadian prairie. If so, this was probably a good thing given the shockingly degraded state of Canada's prairie habitats. In my opinion, the Canadian prairie badly needs a program like CRP because in most years there isn't enough suitable natural habitat to sustain even a modest fall flight of ducks. It is a *myth* that the Canadian prairie is still producing the bulk of the ducks that come from the "duck factory."

In the absence of an integrated land-use policy that adequately protects wildlife habitat, professional management has been using other strategies to secure relatively large tracts of unbroken land for duck production on the Canadian prairies. Managers recognize that some kind of intervention is necessary to bolster duck populations.

During the 1980s drought, I travelled to Alberta with five east coast companions to spend a week hunting and seeing first hand what professional management was doing there. Some of the exciting initiatives of the still new (1986) North American Waterfowl Management Plan were only just being implemented. Ducks Unlimited biologists had arranged our itinerary so that we would visit many different habitats *en route* from Calgary in the south to Edmonton, our point of departure in the north.

Wetlands were scarce on the drought-stricken prairie and seemingly those that did exist were there because of management's efforts. The first morning was spent visiting once prime production areas that now contributed very few ducks to the fall flight. By mid-afternoon we were travelling across the short-grass prairie where annual precipitation is rarely more than 10 inches. This is cattle country and there was widespread evidence of over-grazing. It is also a traditional pintail breeding area, but during the mid-1980s it was hard to see where there was enough vegetation for a duck to nest.

Our destination was the town of Brooks where we were to rendezvous with DU biologists who would introduce us to the ambitious initiative known as Prairie CARE (Conservation, Agriculture, Resource, Environment). This program wisely recognizes the fact that most prairie ducks are produced on private land, so it's futile to compete with agriculture for land to produce ducks. Rather, managers have adopted the integrative landscape philosophy that promotes using land in ways compatible with the needs of people and wildlife. Extension workers, many of whom live in the communities where they work, deal directly with landowners to gain their trust and respect in an effort to influence their attitudes toward wildlife and alternative farming practices. They help farmers and ranchers to see how the land-use philosophy they promote can achieve mutual benefits.

The premise of waterfowl managers is that hunters can't expect farmers, most of whom perennially face tough economic times, to produce ducks for them to shoot without something in return. Consequently, Prairie CARE provides financial incentives and technical assistance to landowners in exchange for extension workers having a say in how these landowners use their land. More fundamentally, it encourages wise stewardship of the land, a low cost educational approach to producing ducks. One of the first tasks of wildlife managers was to reclaim land that was always marginal for farming and should never have been exposed to the plow.

Extension workers have also convinced municipal and provincial authorities who control water rights to share and use water in ways that benefit many users, including farmers, municipalities and ducks. In places, this is now reflected in water-use policy. This proactive approach almost certainly results in more ducks being produced than would attempts to acquire small, isolated parcels of land.

This approach also complements management's already laudable success in conserving almost 17 million acres of wetland across Canada-DU alone has approximately 8,000 projects. Prairie CARE is an innovative and realistic way to cope with the overwhelming influence of agriculture on the prairie landscape. Otherwise, management can only react to land use practices dictated by agriculture. For example, while DU has spent about one billion dollars on wetland conservation since the 1930s, North American agriculture spends about $30 billion annually. Government subsidies to agriculture alone overwhelm any possibility of competing for land.

However, it's important not to see the farmer as the enemy. Farmers can't be expected to view ducks in the same way hunters and waterfowl managers do. In fact for them, ducks are sometimes uninvited pests, competing for their crops and costing them family income. Duck managers have a better chance of getting the results they want when they deal with the small family farmer. They are more likely to cooperate with programs like Prairie CARE than are the big corporate farmers who so often take over the land when family farms go under. During the 1990s, some 5,000 family farms were abandoned in Saskatchewan. The trend to corporate farming is a serious concern of waterfowl managers, and the crisis in the farming community should be of concern to everyone. It's also worthwhile to remember that waterfowl managers and hunters are the only ones who really care about sustaining harvestable surpluses of ducks.

The hunting community also loses in other ways when farmers leave the land. Farmers are often hunters, but even if they aren't, they tend to be supportive of hunting. The farming community in the three prairie provinces of Canada vigorously opposes the restrictive federal gun laws that so discourage boys and young men from becoming or remaining hunters. Rural dwellers see these gun laws as an infringement on their rights and freedoms, and they blame and resent urban voters for this imposition. This is another dimension of the widening gap, perhaps a rift, between urban and rural people whose perspectives and attitudes are often at odds. The issues of gun ownership and hunting highlight a fundamental difference of values.

Prairie habitats and duck populations rarely recover to former levels after serious droughts. The next prairie drought, something that is inevitable, will have the same depressing impact on populations as those of the past, regardless of management efforts. In fact, during the early 1990s the prairie was probably producing fewer ducks than at any time in history. Some biologists believe it then "bottomed-out" as a producer of ducks.

Although the prairie still produced most of the continent's ducks, during the drought years a larger component of the fall flight than previously was recruited from other regions. Habitats there are less vulnerable to climatic changes, but their wetlands are also less productive than are dynamic prairie wetlands. Although duck production is considerably lower in these habitats than it is on a wet prairie, annual production tends to be less variable. If prairie production did "bottom out," continental duck populations may not drop much lower than the record lows of the early 1990s. However, no matter how one views it, achieving and certainly sustaining the population goals of professional management is entirely unrealistic unless (or perhaps even if) the prairie continues to be a major source of duck production. The prairie must be the focus of intensive waterfowl management. Any significant shift to other habitats, like those of the tundra and boreal regions, would be a mistake.

The DU biologists were keen to show us projects and to explain how management was helping ducks cope with the drought. They were also very excited about the continental management plan. Prairie CARE, they explained, is part of a Canadian effort in conjunction with the Plan's Cooperative Prairie Joint Venture. From the beginning, DU has been heavily involved with finding the funding that makes the Plan's research and management programs a reality.

We visited research projects that showed how small, natural wetlands were being restored and managed to produce ducks. They were far more productive and cost-effective than the large projects that once were popular with managers. "Showy" projects with engineering challenges looked impressive to the uncritical eye, but they produced few ducks. We also visited "blue-chip" projects where research had shown how good quality (dense) nesting cover was not only attracting females, but hatching success was similar to what it was when large tracts of natural prairie existed. However, while it was clear that reproductive rates were higher on these projects than in natural habitat, it was interesting that nobody had any good estimate of how many additional ducks were being produced. Reasonably enough, I suppose, no one was prepared to speculate, either.

Undoubtedly, management efforts on the prairies are contributing ducks to the fall flight, and the biological knowledge and technology exist to augment natural production significantly more. But while numbers of projects and acres of habitat acquired are worthwhile measures of how much habitat is being protected, this tells us nothing about how many additional ducks are joining the fall flight.

Our tour took us to a large muddy lake that had all but dried up during the drought. The lake had earlier been the site of an outbreak of disease which had killed a quarter million ducks, including many pintails. Disease outbreaks occur naturally, usually where waterfowl concentrate on wetlands that have been flooded by a shallow layer of water after a dry period. These conditions frequently attract ducks, making them especially susceptible to diseases like avian cholera and botulism. However, while disease outbreaks are dramatic because of the numbers of birds that can die, they are usually localized and don't occur every year. When populations are healthy, disease has relatively little impact on them. It's unlikely that disease causes serious declines and only under exceptional circumstances is it likely to significantly slow population recovery. Managers could do more to reduce the risk and impact of disease on ducks, but they'd first have to be convinced it was worthwhile to put the effort and resources into doing so.

Our DU hosts had been very welcoming. They were passionate about working with wild ducks and they saw it as a privilege. They were happy men who truly believed working with DU was the best way to have a positive influence on ducks and on duck hunting. They were proud of what they were achieving on the prairie. Sure they acknowledged, there were difficulties with species like pintails and scaup, but they were convinced this would change when water returned to the prairie. Morale was good among these men who were also duck hunters.

I was impressed with what we'd seen. Certainly there was more habitat available to waterfowl because of Ducks Unlimited and the North American Plan. I also agreed with someone's comment that without DU there would be little waterfowl management on the Canadian prairies. Provincial governments, it seemed, concentrated their wildlife efforts and resources on resident birds and big game, knowing DU would take responsibility for waterfowl and their habitats. Despite this, it was difficult to shake the nagging feeling that wildlife was still losing out to agriculture. Perhaps the return of water would indeed be the hoped for miracle. Maybe ducks were poised to come back. Time would tell. I left Alberta with more questions than answers about the future of the "duck factory."

I returned to Delta many times over the years. I attended a North American Waterfowl Federation conference there in June of 1999, when the prairie was the wettest it had been in decades. I didn't see many ducks along the roadside ditch where I'd done my shoveler research; it had become clogged with vegetation and was no longer prime habitat. The one pair of shovelers I did see brought back wonderful memories. The research station itself was physically much as it always was. Some of the old buildings were gone and new ones stood in their place, but Kirchoffer Lodge was just the same. I found this comforting. The programs of the station had been rejuvenated and emphasis was once again on research and training students as waterfowl biologists. Many were busily going about their research, just like old times. The mood among the staff was also up-beat and optimistic. Positive things were happening and the place had a good "feel" about it. As a hunter, I was especially pleased to see Delta's obvious commitment to waterfowling. Its ambitious strategic plan was being amended to make specific reference to waterfowling. It was written for all to see that Delta considered hunting *an integral part of waterfowl management,* and it was prepared to be the hunter's advocate.

Delta had organized a trip to the Minnedosa pothole country to show its guests this famous breeding area where its students had a long history of field research. We visited some beautiful habitat where wetlands were surrounded by acres of upland nesting cover. We met landowners who were cooperating with waterfowl managers to raise cattle, crops and ducks. Bright, enthusiastic students were improving management's knowledge of duck biology. Both Delta and DU were obviously a positive and encouraging presence in Minnedosa.

The itinerary included the study area where I'd assisted Rodger Titman 30 years earlier. It was wonderful to be back, but I was shocked by some of what I saw. For example, where were the wetlands I remembered walking around while looking for duck nests? And what had happened to the pothole where I first met Jerry Stoudt, the quiet, knowledgeable Fish and Wildlife Service biologist who pioneered canvasback studies in Minnedosa? Unless I was mistaken, there was a tractor sitting where that pothole used to be. There was lots of cropland on our study area in the 1960s, but there was much more now. It was only a brief visit and the ducks may have been there somewhere, but neither the habitat nor the ducks were what I was expecting.

I suppose the shock of seeing our old study area so changed was intensified by the fact I'd visited all three prairie provinces that spring. Although there was more water than I'd ever seen, the lack of nesting cover was depressing. What a contrast to North Dakota! Certainly, the 1999 breeding season would tell us if water is still the best predictor of successful reproduction, and it would also reveal a good deal about the potential of the prairie to produce ducks.

The following October I was back at Delta, this time hoping to experience what was being touted as the "flight of a lifetime." We had a great visit. Rob Olson, Jim Fisher and the rest of the Delta staff couldn't have treated us better. We had some excellent shooting on the marsh and one morning we enjoyed a redhead flight that just kept coming. I'm glad I had good friends and my Lab, Calliope, to share it with me. But we never did find the mallards we were hoping for. Apparently there were good concentrations in places, but they certainly were not "everywhere" as we were led to believe they'd be.

The DU biologists who we later visited in Minnedosa were also excellent hosts who generously toured us for miles around the countryside. If anything, they were more enthusiastic about the future than their Alberta colleagues had been a decade earlier. After all, the drought was over big time. But it was more than that. Unprecedented money was going into habitat and management from both DU and the NAWMP. DU had assembled one of the most experienced and respected teams of waterfowl specialists anywhere. Research and management to improve duck production was moving ahead on many exciting fronts. Provincial governments were still not contributing in a big way, but DU was picking up the slack. Although nobody knew how many additional ducks it was producing and habitat conditions for breeding ducks were still deplorable, waterfowl management at the turn of the century was enjoying more momentum on the prairies than ever before. It was good to see, but would it translate into more ducks?

The Wintering Grounds: California Dreaming

My years at Delta taught me about more than just ducks. About three-quarters of the students there were Americans, mostly from the midwest, and so were most of the wildlife professionals who visited. The Canadian and American students were much the same-we worked and partied together-and I suppose we thought pretty much alike about most things. But I noticed one big difference. It seemed the only thing the American students ever wanted to do was get a job working with ducks. Most were pursuing degrees in wildlife ecology and management, not general biology like the Canadians, and their goal was to work with either a state or federal wildlife agency or some private-sector organization like DU. With rare exceptions, they were also duck hunters.

I was learning a lot about the biology and management of ducks on the breeding grounds, but there was a big gap in my education. I knew very little about ducks on the wintering grounds. My American friends helped to rectify this. I began visiting the wintering grounds while still a student at Delta.

It didn't take long to start distinguishing differences in the way Americans and Canadians approach waterfowling. In general, Americans take their waterfowling very seriously. Certainly they are much more into equipment and technology, and they spend more time, energy and money on their hunting. Perhaps this is because access to good quality hunting is easier for most Canadians. It was quite a shock, for example, to learn that across much of America, opportunities for public hunting are restricted. To be a duck hunter, one has to have access to private land, and this usually means being wealthy or at least well connected. There's generally considerably more competition for wild ducks in the U.S. than there is in Canada. Cruising the backroads looking for a place to hunt and then simply asking the landowner for permission is a thing of the past for most Americans.

Ever since I shot my first pintail one grey November day back on the St. Lawrence, these classy ducks have been a favorite of mine. But I never knew how truly prized they were until I started visiting the southern states. I made my first trip to Louisiana in 1971, when pintails seemed to be everywhere I went. I'd never seen flocks like those working our decoys over flooded rice fields. Pintails were 10-point birds in those days.

I kept a close eye on pintails over the years and I knew they were in trouble. However, it took a trip to California's Sacramento Valley during the prolonged drought of the 1980s for me to realize how badly populations had declined. My eyes were also opened to how serious habitat problems had become and also how few opportunities there were for duck hunting.

The valleys of California are home to large numbers of wintering waterfowl, including Pacific Flyway pintails that breed in Alaska, and Central Flyway pintails that migrate there from the Alberta and Saskatchewan prairie. However, only 7% of the wetlands that existed at the beginning of the twentieth century remain today. Of these, two-thirds are privately owned. In fact, a significant amount of the waterfowl habitat left in California is either artificially created or managed for agriculture. Waterfowl habitat in California is as vulnerable to the vagaries of agricultural markets as it is on the prairie breeding grounds.

Waterfowl hunters have an enviable history of protecting wetland habitat. For example, funds from hunters have been instrumental in the purchase of federal refuges and state management or wildlife areas, an integral part of waterfowl management in the U.S. This is also true in California, but perhaps more importantly, it may be that most of the privately owned wetlands existing there do so because of duck hunting.

California has a long tradition of club hunting. Wealthy hunters lease or buy land so they have exclusive access to high quality shooting. This land is usually managed to attract and hold birds. However, since the 1960s, there's been a decline in the number of these elite private clubs. The membership is aging and, given the decline of interest in hunting and high operating costs, clubs are having problems recruiting new members. It's uncertain whether the club tradition will continue and one wonders what will eventually happen to the waterfowl habitat that is currently protected by clubs.

Rice is an economically and politically important crop in California. In places, flooded rice fields constitute half of the wetlands available to waterfowl. Pintails, traditionally the duck of choice in California, use these fields by the hundreds of thousands. However, would landowners keep costly water on their fields for ducks after the harvest if they couldn't lease them to hunters? What are the implications of closing or significantly restricting the pintail harvest? Would pintails find alternative habitat to satisfy their needs if private lands were unavailable? There may be hidden costs to giving pintails greater protection from the gun. On the other hand, the threat that wetland habitat will be lost has frequently been used as a scare tactic by those who don't want further restrictions.

Across much of the wintering grounds, private landowners have considerable influence over waterfowl. Although the USFWS regulates hunting, it cannot, for example, force a landowner to provide water for ducks. Landowners control access to hunting-who, how many and how often people hunt, and when and where they hunt. Consequently, they have considerable control over how many birds are killed. In fact, by managing their land for waterfowl, private citizens may have more control over the waterfowl in an area than do government managers. It seems obvious that the fate of waterfowl habitat and hunting will continue to be influenced by private landowners, particularly those involved in agriculture, and this is true for both the wintering and breeding grounds.

Habitat management in Canada and the northern tier states predominantly focuses on duck production, whereas on the wintering grounds the focus is on attracting and holding ducks for hunting-consequently, killing ducks. Attitudes toward land on the breeding and wintering grounds, including gaining access for hunting, are also different. I first heard the saying, "if it pays, it stays," on a trip to Texas. We were watching ducks on a managed wetland. The landowner who had just spoken these words was explaining that the ducks were welcome so long as they paid their way. It didn't matter to him what the land was used for, but it had to make a dollar. And yes, we could hunt there for a price. Wild ducks aren't *free* across much of the wintering grounds.

Access to land for waterfowling has never been available to everyone who might wish to hunt, probably part of its allure. Similarly, the quality of one's waterfowling depends on personal circumstances, geography and many other factors. Any reasonable person knows that equitable access to waterfowling is impossible, and efforts to make it democratic are ridiculous. However, access to waterfowl hunting has become very restricted in places, no longer available to people from social and economic backgrounds who once found it feasible to hunt. Nowhere is the problem of access more acute than California, where the freedom of cruising backroads looking for a place to hunt has long been a thing of the past. Waterfowling there requires truly exceptional commitment and dedication.

Refuges and state wildlife areas provide inexpensive public

hunting, but access is very competitive and consequently unpredictable and unreliable. And certainly hunters must have realistic expectations. They may prefer pintails and mallards but they are more likely to encounter other species. Still, hunting on refuges can be satisfying and this is a good way for managers to keep hunters active. In fact, refuge hunting has become an increasingly attractive option for many American hunters and some only hunt on refuges.

In reality, Californians who want reliable hunting have to pay for it. A good many lease pits or entire fields for the day or season. This is invariably costly, especially in locations frequented by pintails and mallards. Typically, several people get together to share the costs of a lease. Guides and outfitters also provide an option, but this too is expensive.

On my trip to California during the drought, my travelling companions and I shot over leased land, but we also enjoyed the club experience. However, it was on a private ranch where habitat was intensively managed for ducks that we saw the exclusive side of waterfowling.

The setting was a series of flooded rice fields surrounding a marshland complex that was a nighttime roost for several thousand ducks and geese. In that parched region of the valley, there were few wetland alternatives available to waterfowl, but there was plenty of water on this beautiful ranch. Only a few guests occasionally hunted there, as was apparent from the behavior of the birds.

I had the pleasure of shooting with the ranch manager, Bill Moe, a personable young fellow who was good company while we watched the morning unfold in a steel-lined pit dug into a levee. Our visibility was restricted by dense ground fog, but we could hear wings and calling above us as legal shooting time approached. It had been a while since I'd heard the beautiful and stirring whistle of the drake pintail, and the lovely "whee-oo" call of the drake wigeon. We still couldn't see a thing, but "ducky" sounds were coming from everywhere in the watery world that surrounded us.

"The others in the group don't plan to shoot pintails," Bill reminded me. "It doesn't matter to me though," he continued, "you do as you please. I'll back you up but otherwise I'm not going to shoot." "I want to kill a drake pintail in California," I replied. "And, if I'm lucky, my other two birds will be drake wigeon," I told him as I pointed upwards. I had recognized about a dozen of these lovely birds as they glided through the fog, ghost-like, in the gathering light. Two or three had splashed into the outer-most decoys that were still hidden from view by fog. "Everyone will see thousands of birds this morning," Bill assured me. " You'll be able to pick the birds you want. It'll be like glimpsing the past."

The first legal birds to come in were gadwalls. I didn't intend to shoot, but I stood and swung my gun on them. Something about their flight was familiar, but I couldn't decide what. I tried vainly to pick out one bird, but they kept twisting and moving about, seemingly jostling for position. Finally it dawned on me. This was a courtship party, seven handsome males displaying to a drab female that seemed intent on avoiding their advances. None were interested in our decoys. I don't think they ever saw me standing there as they passed overhead, preoccupied as they were with each other.

It was well after shooting time before I decided to kill a duck. I had been content just to watch the birds drift through the windows of visibility that slowly opened and closed above us in the fog. The fog had also burned off enough to see the marsh about a mile away. There was continuous activity there as ragged lines of white-fronts and snow geese, and smaller groups of dabblers, lifted and flew out to feed on the flooded rice stubble.

Finally, three drake pintails that had been calling overhead, punched through the fog and dropped in on cupped wings. As they did, one veered away from the others and presented me with a perfect left-to-right shot. I squeezed the trigger and he folded up, falling dead at the edge of the decoys. Bill's black Lab seemed relieved to finally get some work. He was just getting back with my California trophy when a single drake wigeon came in, presenting me with a shot that I couldn't resist.

For the next half hour we watched ducks and geese flying everywhere. Ducks pitched into the decoys and simply swam slowly out of the rig when they spotted us 30 yards away. These birds had everything they needed on this private refuge, and they were undisturbed.

Bill and I talked about ducks and duck hunting, and we traded some of our favorite stories. He explained how he managed the ranch to attract and hold ducks. It was clear he was very knowledgeable. Bill shared my curiosity about waterfowl behavior and he told me things about wintering waterfowl I never knew. Every so often he'd look up and blow into his duck call. On one occasion, he turned a high-flying drake mallard and brought him in. I could see the sheen of his iridescent green head as he sat in the decoys, head held high, looking for the brazen hussy who'd hailed him. As we watched him swim about, Bill asked me why I wasn't using a call. "I'm useless with a call," I replied, "but I'd like to share with you some thoughts about calling."

"The expert caller makes duck "music" indistinguishable from the bird itself," I told him, "but that doesn't mean the caller knows what he's saying. I think you have to know about the behavior and social system of ducks to understand what calling means to them," I suggested. The most varied and complex calls are communications between males and females, and it is usually the female that does most of the calling. Ducks are most vocal during pairing. This may begin as early as October for some species, but it's well underway for most dabblers by December. "Look at the success you've had calling males this morning," I mentioned to Bill. "It's January and any drake mallard who hasn't found a mate is getting nervous."

"Does that mean female dabbling ducks are evaluating males as potential mates even though nesting is months away?" Bill asked me. "Female mallards and blacks," I replied, "may choose the male they intend to breed with as early as October, but most are probably testing different males before making their decision. However, once they have selected a mate, usually by early January, they don't want to be harassed by other males."

The two calls most frequently heard are the "high-ball" or "hail" (decrescendo) and the "feeding" (inciting) call of the female mallard or black duck. Other female dabblers have a variation of these calls. The "high ball" is usually heard when a female calls to her mate ("where are you, get over here, I need you"), or when an unpaired female is inviting a male's attention a "come on", as it were. For obvious reasons, this call gets the best results for hunters. Only paired females, or unpaired females who are "testing" a male as a potential mate, make the "feeding" call. It says to the male, "I'm yours, but only if you protect me by keeping other males away."

The "feeding" call is usually heard when females are interrupted by males who approach too closely, perhaps to initiate courtship. This often happens when females are feeding, hence the name. When males get really disruptive, the "feeding" call becomes more insistent. This is the "repulsion" call, a "get lost" message to unwelcome drakes.

"You'll notice that the "feeding" call is only heard when ducks are in groups," I said to Bill, "never when a female is alone or just with her mate. It happens on land, water or in flight, anytime females are approached too closely by males. It is often heard when flying birds join others already on the land or water." "You mean to say," Bill questioned me, "these inciting and repulsion calls, what hunters call the feeding call, have nothing to do with feeding?" "No," I assured him, "the female is telling other ducks that she's already chosen a mate and she doesn't want to be disturbed, much less courted."

"So," Bill said, "because it is typically males who join females, reproducing the call of males isn't usually effective, right?" I agreed, but mentioned that wigeon, pintail and gadwall males have very distinctive calls and so may be an exception. The "high ball" is really the best call because female blacks and mallards are actually calling to males, perhaps sometimes soliciting them. But a *brief* burst of any calling, so long as it's reasonably well done (not too long and not too loud), should at least get the attention of passing dabblers. Most good callers will tell you to stop calling once you've got the attention of a duck.

Diving ducks don't call much during the hunting season, so calling has limited value, but geese are very vocal throughout the year, whether sitting or flying. Geese call to keep family groups and flocks together and when greeting other geese. There is a good deal of calling when flying birds approach others already on land or water. This is mutual greeting which intensifies as the newcomers prepare to land. The sitting birds are saying, "welcome, but keep your distance," while the approaching birds are saying, "glad we've found you and the food (or safe roost) you've already discovered. We'll eat and help watch for predators, but we'll keep our distance."

Feeding geese may indeed be saying to newcomers, "there's food here, come and get it!" But they are also saying "find your own food when you join us and, if a predator attacks, I hope he gets you and not me!" The almost continual threatening and sparring one sees between family groups, especially while feeding, is for favored locations within the flock. Skill with a goose call pays off because knowledgeable hunters can actually carry on a conversation with the geese. Even birds that apparently have no intention of decoying will sometimes come in. Some callers can "talk" a flock right into the decoys. However, inexperienced callers should stop when the birds seem committed.

"Remember," Bill reminded me, "we have to leave the field by nine o'clock." We still had 20 minutes and I wanted to shoot a third duck. Just before time was up, we heard calling from behind us. I looked around and saw a female and three drake wigeon coming toward us, about 40 feet over the water. The female made a low, guttural chuckle-the repulsion call-as two males crowded her, aggressively displaying and paying no heed to her calling, or to her mate who was trying to stay between them and the female. I stood, swung my gun on one of the courting drakes, and killed him. The female wanted to get rid of these males, but I don't think she had anything so dramatic in mind! Bill's dog brought the bird in and dropped it in front of us. It was gorgeous in its nuptial finery.

We walked back along the levee to our vehicle, discussing our morning. We spent the rest of the day touring the ranch. We saw an amazing concentration of ducks, geese and wading birds, birds that were there, as were we, courtesy of the wealthy landowner.

I'd had a wonderful time with my gracious and congenial host, but even now when I think about that hunt I wonder about my reaction to it. In a way, it didn't seem like I was hunting. It certainly wasn't anything like I was used to back home. Enjoyable as the morning had been, all I did was shoot, I didn't even set a decoy. I wonder if we sometimes distort the hunting experience when we remove the uncertainty and make it predictable. Also, when we emphasize ease, comfort and convenience we may render our hunting to little more than killing.

I believe in parts of the U.S. there is a risk that duck hunting will become accessible only to the wealthy. If so, this may be perceived as economic elitism by a disapproving public that is already fed up with abuses of natural resources for the benefit of a few. A good many hunters already perceive that the working class man who once had some expectation of being a duck hunter, is increasingly being squeezed out by time and financial constraints. The argument, however true, that the wealthy hunter-landowner is protecting habitat that would not otherwise be available to wildlife, will not change this perception. In some years, professional management finds itself in the difficult position of having to ask landowners not only to shoot fewer ducks, but to provide them with habitat. Will they do so? Will the wealthy share in this way with the rest of the waterfowling community? Will they see this as their contribution to supporting waterfowl management, and perhaps a way of slowing the decline of hunters? Even the wealthy need the political support of other hunters. Many Californians have devoted a good deal of their time, energy and money to perpetuating waterfowling. They have shared in every sense. Will they continue to do so, and will the next generation of waterfowlers maintain this tradition?

This brings up the curious relationship that exists between commercial waterfowling and professional waterfowl management. Private outfitters, who indirectly kill a lot of birds, exploit a resource that is managed by government wildlife agencies on behalf of the public. Professional management is paid for by the public and by hunters who may have to compete for waterfowl with commercial interests. In a sense, the publicly supported wildlife services are assisting private enterprise in a commercial venture, often without any form of compensation. There is nothing inappropriate about this, unless commercial operators attempt to control birds and access to them. A problem arises when shooting opportunities for local hunters are restricted by commercial operators. This problem becomes acute when commercial waterfowlers also lobby government for special privileges.

Reputable outfitters can play a positive role in sustaining waterfowling, while at the same time contributing to rural economies. They may provide habitat that would not otherwise exist, a trade-off perhaps for birds killed. They can also keep hunters active, often providing superior sport. While in California, we visited a commercial operation run by a farmer who managed his land for many things, including ducks. He was in business and his land had to provide a revenue. He leased pits by the day, week, month, or season to anyone who could afford them. We were the guests of one of his customers who leased a prime pit for the entire season. He hunted almost every day, in part to justify his rent.

As we waited for shooting time on a mild, windless morning, he told us how the money and time he spent on hunting was a serious bone of contention between him and his wife. "I'm not suited to refuge hunting," he explained. "I'm not waiting in line for a chance to hunt. I want to know I can hunt when I feel like it. Shovelers, gadwalls and teal are not for me, I'm hooked on mallards and pintails."

Given his modest circumstances, this affable working class fellow was going to exceptional lengths to satisfy his passion for duck hunting. And it was costing him more than just money. It seemed pretty clear he was in over his head. I asked him his opinion about the future of waterfowl hunting in California. "I'm an extreme case, I know," he replied, "but waterfowling here is an old guys' sport. How can a young person afford to take it up? I don't know about the future."

The morning flight was a "bust" so we relaxed and chatted. David, who'd never hunted elsewhere, asked me about waterfowling in the north. I told him that to my way of thinking, the big difference was the freedom to truly hunt. For example, in the prairie provinces of Canada there are lots of birds and relatively few hunters. But the real luxury is accessibility to land where hunting opportunities are good.

There is good shooting on public lands and, except around refuges and management areas where land is frequently leased, gaining access to private land is usually as simple as asking. This has been true of the northern prairie states, but seems now to be changing.

Around eight o'clock, we had a little flurry of activity. The ducks, mostly wigeon and a few pintails, invariably approached the field well out of effective killing range. They remained high and circled repeatedly, looking over the dozen or so decoy spreads that were scattered across the field. On many occasions, they'd set their wings to come in, only to flare in obvious alarm and leave the area. These birds were recognizing and avoiding the decoys. Apparently, a good many ducks fed only at night. The best shooting on leased fields is when new birds come in or weather conditions keep birds moving.

The ducks put on a marvellous aerial show, but too often over-anxious hunters shot when decoying birds were out of range. This spoiled the shooting prospects for all of us. But everyone there was a paying customer, there to shoot a duck. I understood and even felt some empathy with these hunters, but it was a frustrating experience.

Private land that is intensively managed for hunting protects considerable waterfowl habitat on the wintering grounds, but how secure is it and does this land always provide a net benefit to waterfowl? Aldo Leopold, the guru of North American wildlife management, warned that his fellow Americans often abuse land and what's on it when they regard it only as a commodity. Some people argue that the government is a better steward of land and wildlife than is the private citizen who, particularly in the U.S., has considerable freedom to use his land as he pleases. Others argue that *enlightened* private ownership is a better way to protect land for wildlife. In fact, there are plenty of examples of misuse of land and wildlife by both governments and private citizens.

There's no question that loss and degradation of wetland habitat has reduced the capacity of the wintering grounds to support ducks. Certainly, California is a good example of this. But is there insufficient wintering habitat to support more ducks, as some people suggest? This is the rationale some managers use for easing hunting restrictions when populations increase. Like-minded managers argue that the North American Waterfowl Management Plan population goals should be reduced for species like the black duck. They claim that there isn't sufficient winter habitat to support any more birds than we currently have. This speculation is indeed depressing. If it is true, then we should forget about trying to increase populations. Professional management should then admit defeat since efforts to protect and enhance habitat have fallen short. However, many biologists believe that while lack of wintering habitat may limit the size and growth potential of some populations, this isn't so for most. There's no evidence that there was inadequate winter habitat to support the 1999 fall flight, which some managers believe was the largest since 1955.

The historic loss and degradation of natural wetlands on the wintering grounds has been enormous, but the rate of decline since the 1970s has slowed markedly. Further stemming the decline took a giant step forward with the implementation of the North American Waterfowl Management Plan. There may be a dearth of natural habitat in California, but there is considerable under-utilized natural habitat across much of the wintering grounds. State and federal wildlife services alone protect an extensive network of natural wetlands through their system of refuges and management areas, although critics take exception with the way these areas sometimes unnaturally concentrate birds. The habitat situation in California must also be seen in perspective. California itself produces many of the ducks that winter there, particularly mallards. Despite its habitat problems, California probably has sufficient habitat to produce and winter more waterfowl than it currently does. The critical issue is not so much land for ducks, but access to land for duck hunting. To paraphrase the lyrics of the 1960s song that claims there's plenty of gold in California, but it's in a bank in Beverley Hills in somebody else's name. Well, in parts of California there are plenty of ducks, but they're usually on somebody else's land and, increasingly, just as unavailable to the average hunter as that gold is. Does California provide a glimpse into the future of American duck hunting?

The Grass Roots Hunter

I enjoy hunting where strong waterfowling traditions have developed. There are many such places in Michigan, where waterfowling has always been popular; about 60,000 hunters buy duck stamps there each fall. The Atlantic and Mississippi Flyways converge in this state that is blessed with a diversity and abundance of natural habitat. It also produces many of the ducks its hunters shoot. During the fall, migrants from the prairies to the west and from Ontario to the north swell local populations. This, and ample places to hunt, have allowed people from all walks of life, rich and poor alike, to become duck hunters. In years when ducks are numerous, even hunters in the "fringe" areas enjoy good shooting. But those who can hunt the "hot spots," the areas where migrants concentrate, always have ducks, and in some years the shooting is excellent. I hunted in Michigan during most of the 1990s, a decade when some species of prairie migrants apparently experienced both their lowest and highest population levels in history.

The St. Clair River forms a sprawling delta where it flows into Lake St. Clair. The St. Clair Flats is famous for its diving ducks, especially canvasbacks and redheads, which stage there on their way to the Atlantic coast from the prairies. The public waters of the Flats are within reasonable traveling distance of several million people. It is only an hour away from the urban sprawl of Detroit. The residents of Ontario's Walpole Island and Michigan's Harsen's Island are only a stone's throw from one another across the international shipping channel. These islands are popular access points to the Flats.

Once off the 10-car ferry that links the mainland with Harsen's Island, one discovers a waterfowler's haven. Permanent homes are common but everywhere along the shore are seasonal dwellings, there to take advantage of the hunting and fishing. Most of these are modest, reflecting the working class backgrounds of their owners. A cluster of houses and stores along the main road that goes around the island, is the service center. A well-stocked general store sells just about anything the sportsman, or anyone else for that matter, could want. I remember very clearly my first visit to Harsen's Island.

My host was a state waterfowl biologist whose family had lived on Harsen's Island for three generations. Greg Soulliere had friends and family everywhere on the island. That November afternoon in the early 1990s, we found his uncle Howard in the general store discussing the decline of ducks and duck hunters with the shop-keeper and half a dozen friends. Opinions about the causes varied, but everyone agreed that the decline in both was obvious. In fact, it was obvious to everyone in this community where fewer ducks meant fewer hunters and fewer hunters meant a slower economy, with its predictable impact on the vitality of the community.

Greg's uncle Howard made the comment that while he didn't want to see anyone while he was hunting, he recognized the need for a strong, politically active and involved waterfowling community. He asked me to give the group some idea of how the number of hunters had changed over the years. I was able to tell them that based on "duck" stamp sales in the U.S. and license sales in Canada, there were minimally 2.5 million hunters in North America during the early 1950s. There was a decrease during the 1960s to about 1.5 million, but numbers again increased until in the mid-1970s they were back to the 2.5 million level. Almost certainly, more waterfowlers than ever before hunted during the years between 1970 and 1980, although part of this increase likely reflects greater compliance with licensing requirements.

However, a decline began in the 1980s that culminated in a low of 1.5 million hunters going afield during the early 1990s, when duck populations were at historic lows. Between 1978 and 1998 the number of Canadian waterfowlers declined from about 525,000 to 200,000. Nor did the ranks of Canadian duck hunters recover when duck populations increased in the mid-1990s and geese reached record highs. For example, the number of hunters in Manitoba declined from 70,000 in the 1970s to only about 15,000 in 1999. There was some recovery among American hunters when ducks increased, but at the end of the century there were fewer than 1.75 million active waterfowlers in Canada and the U.S., a decline of 30% since the 1970s, and the decline in interest was apparent across all four flyways.

Hunter numbers usually track duck populations and finding ducks was difficult during the early 1990s. Those hunters who persisted had to put more effort into being successful. But even the most dedicated hunter has to have some reasonable expectation of getting a duck. Presumably, young hunters, especially those learning to hunt without the assistance of veterans, stick with waterfowling for only a short time. When duck numbers are low, young hunters may have to wait too long between successful hunts to remain active. Interest wanes, especially if they have other hunting alternatives.

Regardless of how many ducks or places to hunt there are, boys and adolescent males are clearly less interested in hunting than they once were. Times and people have changed and the hunting fraternity is aging, one study reporting an average age of 41. This is particularly true of rural and small-town hunters who traditionally have been heavily represented in the fraternity. The decline in rural and small-town populations works strongly against hunting.

Someone asked me to expand on the decline in Manitoba hunters, so I told him about a conversation I'd had with a DU field-worker there. "The decline really started in the 1980s," he told me, "when legislation made it mandatory to get permission to hunt on farmland. How does a guy who doesn't know the area find a landowner? There are so many abandoned farms out here, and lots of farmers live in communities miles from their land. And the drought was a big factor. It took a toll on ducks, but also on hunters. Thank heavens for geese. The decline in hunters would be worse if it wasn't for them. When ducks started to come back," he continued, "some of the older guys found it just too much effort to get back into it. And everything was more expensive. Take steel shot, for example. It's hard for a young fellow to start hunting with shells so costly."

"Then there is the whole issue of restrictive gun regulations in Canada," my DU friend continued. "I don't know if there's some sinister plot to get rid of guns, but the federal government is making it very hard to own and use a gun. A person has to be 18 years old to hunt alone. Hell, I was hunting on my own at 14. Even taking out a young person who wants to try hunting is really difficult. It's getting to be just too much effort. And the loss of hunting means there is one less thing a young fellow, or anyone for that matter, can do for adventure. I hate to see us lose the opportunity to nurture young kids who have the passion to hunt. You need older guys to be mentors. They can also help younger hunters avoid the excesses of youth. You know, the tendency to *get your share*. I can tell you, rural people resent legislation that is forced on us by city people who don't understand rural life. Owning a gun is pretty much like owning a car here. It's taken for granted. Really, there are lots of reasons why duck hunting is declining. Why is there no Sunday hunting in most provinces? How many people eat wild game anymore? What do you do with the birds you shoot? Put all of this together and you can see why hunting is becoming a relic."

This had a sobering effect on the group gathered around the old pot-bellied stove in the Harsen's Island general store. The sombre mood deepened when I mentioned that the decline in the American waterfowling community, while not as acute as it is in Canada, is none-the-less a problem. Michigan, I told them, currently had about 900,000 hunters, including 750,000 deer hunters, but the 60,000 active waterfowlers was down alarmingly from the 100,000 it had been in the 1970s. Someone offered the opinion that professional management should be doing more to keep hunters active and to attract new recruits. Everyone strongly agreed but they also acknowledged that this is probably easier said than done.

Greg's uncle mentioned that the state allows hunting on a Harsen's Island wildlife area that is managed to attract and hold ducks. "This kept hunters active when ducks were low and I think it attracted new hunters, too," he told me. "I know it's been a boon to the island economy." I agreed that there are obvious benefits to refuge hunting, but I felt compelled to point out some costs. For example, to create the Harsen's Island refuge, managers drained and converted Great Lakes' coastal marsh and wet prairie to cropland. They now grow corn and buckwheat there and they flood it to attract mallards. This not only destroys natural habitat, it concentrates ducks where they're more vulnerable to hunters. And managers sometimes lose sight of the fact that their first priority should be to protect breeding stock, not make ducks available to hunters. It isn't uncommon for refuge managers to compete with one another for the biggest annual harvest, and the kill on refuges may be significantly greater than it would be if birds were more dispersed in natural habitats.

Refuge shooting may also have a greater impact than expected on important species like mallards. As many as 90% of the mallards shot in Michigan are produced either within the state or in the forested habitats of Ontario to the north, not on the prairies as many people believe. Basing Michigan hunting regulations on prairie mallard populations, as has traditionally been the case, doesn't make sense. If Michigan hunters are killing mallards from populations that state managers know very little about, perhaps regulations should be more restrictive, at least until they know more about these populations.

I told the group about personal concerns I have with refuge hunting. Apparently most hunters who go to Harsen's Island do so to shoot the refuge. They enter early-morning or mid-afternoon lotteries to select sites for their half-day hunt. However, decisions about where to hunt are not based on the usual factors that go into arranging a hunt in a natural setting. Instead, hunters consult the refuge map and tally sheet to see where most of the birds are being killed. Unfortunately, some hunters who don't get a preferred site leave without hunting, despite the vast expanses of the Flats beckoning to them.

One of the group, a man in his mid-70s, had been hunting since he was a youngster. He would continue to pole his boat on the Flats, he told us, for as long as he physically could. "Why," he asked, "do you suppose some guys hunt nothing but ducks, some don't even hunt geese?" A man in his 50s answered without hesitation. "It's the mystique," he said. "It attracts only a few of us, but we're as passionate, dedicated and committed a group of people as any you'll find. We like the rigor, the risk, the fact you can't always predict what happens, and we like the idea that we're part of a select club. Most of us don't mind going that extra bit farther, doing what it takes to get to where the birds are. I take it to heart," he said to me, "when you say refuge hunting can be too easy. I can see why some guys who don't have time to hunt the Flats, always go to the refuge. They have a better chance of getting some shooting there, and that's reasonable enough. But it can become a habit."

With that, everyone seemed to get into the conversation. "Successful waterfowling generally requires more planning and organization than other forms of hunting," said a fellow who'd been quiet until then. "It usually takes considerable time and effort to do it right. I hunt ducks because of the freedom and satisfaction I get in trying to come to terms with wild birds in their natural habitat. I feel so alive and free out there, and it's beautiful. I work hard all week at a job I don't much care for. I feel I have more control of my life when I'm on the Flats. I guess you'd say it's my escape. I love the Flats and I'd hunt if the limit was one bird! You can always find a place to rig your decoys somewhere on those marshes. Even with fewer birds, you always have a reasonable chance for some shooting. You need to plan, and you might have to shift around, but you can usually figure something out. I love it. I like to stay active and I've never been interested in sports or television, and I don't own a computer. I don't know what I'd do if I didn't have my duck hunting..."

This would have been the perfect setting for my uncle. As out of place as he would've been in a California duck club, he would've fit in perfectly with these fellows. I could imagine him embarking on one of his stories I remember so well. Two young boys about seven or eight years old came to call their grandfather to supper. He was in the middle of a story about the Flats and was in no hurry to leave, so the boys joined the group. They sat there wide-eyed and enthralled, listening to tales of waterfowling.

On my first trip to Harsen's Island I enjoyed hunting refuge mallards in the flooded corn, but it was the Flats that captured my imagination. The season was closed on 'cans and redheads so we hunted the marsh for scaup, ringnecks, goldeneyes and buffleheads - birds the "locals" once shot only out of desperation. In fact, one day we were pleased enough to shoot a couple of mergansers. We later disguised them in a stew with plenty of spices and vegetables, and a couple of scaup. The manhattans were also a big help.

Despite poor shooting, we enjoyed ourselves immensely. A wistful comment of Greg's brought home to me what the decline in diving ducks has cost duck hunters. A female 'can decided to give our decoy spread a closer look as she sped overhead. In classic fashion, she set her wings, banked, presented her grey back to us, and hooked into the wind; she sounded jet-propelled with the air rushing through her wings. At the last moment, she spotted us in the reeds. As she slipped into high gear and continued on her way, Greg, who had never hunted where canvasbacks were legal, said, "Man, I think I could get used to hunting those birds." It's hard to miss what you've never had, but on that occasion Greg came close to glimpsing what he'd never had.

The Flats had provided many memorable experiences but I was leaving without hunting divers over open water-the kind of hunting that made the Flats famous. I'd seen the family layout boat stored carefully in the rafters of an outbuilding. Apparently it was damaged and required repair, so it couldn't be used that season. I just couldn't get it out of my mind as I flew back to Nova Scotia.

Much to my delight, the following summer Greg phoned to tell me the layout boat had been refurbished and was now rigged and ready for action. I didn't hesitate when he suggested I visit to try it out. "Yes, thanks, I'll be there during the first week of November." I returned to the Harsen's Island duck camp to find the little boat sitting elegantly beside a pile of scaup and canvasback decoys. The other gear was also ready to go.

Although diving duck populations were at low levels and 'cans were protected, hunters could kill a redhead and, as Greg's dad, a retired Detroit policeman, had earlier assured me on the phone, "there'll always be bluebills." We were ready to hunt divers on the Flats and we had five days to do it.

We set up on a little island at the edge of the Flats our first morning, but we knew our hunt would be little more than reconnaissance.

We spent the stormy morning watching flocks of divers moving across the white-capped lake. Flock after flock passed lakeward of a lighthouse that was about two miles offshore. They were flying from a roosting site on the open lake to feed over shoal waters. Greg's Uncle Robert had earlier told us they'd been feeding there for about a week. One distant flock of scaup that lifted at the approach of a coast guard launch must have contained 10,000 birds.

That morning we shot a single bufflehead, but we'd already made plans to be off that lighthouse with the 10-foot layout boat as soon as the wind dropped. Hopefully, we'd learned enough during the morning to set up a successful evening shoot. The wind was still blowing hard when we returned to camp.

You can't be far from a flight line and expect good shooting when hunting divers on big water. A spread of 100 or more decoys may draw only the occasional straggler. The birds are in big "rafts" and each one knows where it wants to be. Newly arrived migrants are more easily decoyed, but they quickly learn where the roosts and feeding areas are by following experienced ducks. According to Greg's dad, the big flight of redheads and 'cans had peaked a week earlier, but there were still reasonable numbers, and the scaup flight was in full swing.

By mid-afternoon the wind back at camp had dropped enough to encourage us to venture onto the lake. We had a deep-hulled 16-foot aluminum boat for conveying and tending the layout boat, but we had to decide whether to tow the layout boat to where we wanted to hunt, or carry it across the bow. If we did the latter, we'd have a heavy lift to get it into the water and an even heavier one to get it back onto the tender after the hunt. However, by carrying the boat we could get to and from our destination much more quickly; we had a six-mile run from the camp. That first evening we carried the layout boat because we were still trying to "figure out" the birds and we needed to be mobile.

It soon became clear that we'd misjudged the strength of the wind. It was still blowing hard when we got out on the unbroken expanse of the lake. The chop kept us from going beyond the lighthouse to where we'd seen the birds that morning. Still, we felt secure enough to set up about a mile from shore. We launched the layout boat over a sandy bottom in four feet of water. We got it aligned into the wind and securely anchored before setting 60 canvasback and bluebill decoys. The bluebills were relatively new, but the Herter's 'cans had belonged to Greg's grandfather; we were especially careful with these much cherished decoys.

We set two long lines of scaup downwind from the boat so that they formed a V-shape that came together at the boat. In theory, the birds would fly along one of the lines toward the boat and spot the cluster of canvasback decoys set upwind of it. If things went according to plan, their fate would be sealed by the time they got close enough to discover our ruse. Getting everything right is difficult, particularly when it's windy, but it's frustrating when you fail to get shooting because you haven't made the effort to set up properly.

Because I was a guest, I got to shoot from the layout boat first. I went through the polite ritual of refusing Greg's offer, but in fact I could hardly wait to climb aboard the sweet little craft that was now gently rolling with the waves. I settled into the surprisingly roomy cockpit of the "pumpkin seed" and readied myself for action. We knew we were off the main flight line, but there were enough birds around to ensure some shooting. Greg motored half a mile away, anchored the tender, and found a comfortable position to watch the action we both hoped I'd get. I put two shells in the chambers of my double, then sat up and swung it to the left and right, just to get a feel for shooting from a sitting position. The boat hardly moved despite the chop. Its wide, flat bottom seemed stuck to the water. The waves gently rolled up and over the sides, and around the four inch rim of the cockpit. Being in that little boat made me feel like I was in an inverted saucer, floating in a limitless expanse of water.

The first birds to visit me were six common mergansers that pitched in downwind, about 50 feet to my right. They had followed along one of the decoy leaders according to plan. One bird, an immature male, dived a couple of times before surfacing within 10 feet of me. We were literally eye-to-eye until I sat up and galvanized him into action. His big webbed feet splashed and threw up plumes of water as he pumped his wings and fought desperately to get airborne. The others had moved farther downwind but they also took flight, reacting to his alarm but not knowing its cause. To their utter surprise, they saw me as they jumped into the wind and passed over the layout. Each one craned its long neck downward to get a better look at me. The last thing they expected was to see a hunter out there.

I'd shot a bufflehead earlier that morning, so I had two birds left to complete my 3-bird limit. I'd decided to pass up opportunities to shoot other ducks while I waited for a chance at a redhead. However, Greg was patiently waiting his turn and closing time was fast approaching. This was Michigan where closing time is sundown, not half an hour after, as it is across the Flats in Ontario.

I decided to go for two buffs, one a lovely adult male, that earlier had buzzed me and were again crossing the decoys 30 yards away. A properly set up layout boat can make a good shot out of even a mediocre marksman. I sat up, swung through the birds, and squeezed the trigger twice. Both birds were dead in the air. They splashed into the water just as eight redheads that had been coming right to me, veered off and cut across the edge of the decoys.

The wind dogged us all week, but each day we hunted the open waters of the Flats. Though tempted to try getting to the big rafts that periodically lifted en masse, creating what we called the "black cloud," we couldn't risk going the last mile that would have put us right under the main flight line. Finally, by mid-afternoon on the fourth day the wind had dropped enough for us to risk going beyond the lighthouse where a thousand or so birds were using a flight line between two feeding areas. We got the layout boat rigged in a perfect location. Again, I was first to shoot and it didn't take me long to collect my limit of bluebills.

Later, with Greg in the layout, I reclined on the floor of the tender where I could stay out of the wind but still watch the action. I could also admire the three greater scaup I'd shot. I'd laid them on the seat in front of me. Scaup are such exciting birds to hunt. They come at you with such reckless abandon! Scaup have sustained diving-duck hunting for decades, but I couldn't help wonder if their decline, now quite apparent to hunters, is partly the result of overly liberal hunting regulations. Like pintails, scaup were once 10-point birds. Managers believed populations were healthy enough to "take the heat" off other species that were allegedly more at risk of being over-shot.

I picked up each bird and smoothed its feathers, and I thought about my first bluebill shoot on the St. Lawrence, many years ago. Perhaps the scaup I hunted back then had visited the St. Clair Flats earlier that same autumn.

In a way, I found that watching the action from the tender was just as exciting as being in the layout boat. The hunter has very little room to maneuver in the single-man layout rig. Seeing anything behind you is almost impossible. Usually, birds suddenly appear in one's window of vision. Greg handles a shotgun very well. With his first two shots he killed two drake scaup from a flock of 10 that broke over the decoys. I couldn't be sure that he'd seen the birds approaching low over the water, but then I saw him suddenly sit up and point his gun. To me, the birds seemed right on top of him. His two victims crumpled and splashed into the water among the decoys. The remaining birds regrouped and continued on their way. Only then did I hear the muffled sounds of the shots he'd fired.

Part of the excitement for me was picking up the birds which, by the time I got there, were bobbing, white bellies skyward, some distance downwind from the layout boat. I returned to my post in time to see Greg's third bird, a drake redhead, approach the rig. Greg hit him hard with his first two shots. Unfortunately, the bird wasn't dead and he fell too far away for Greg to finish him with his third shot. I got underway quickly but the powerful bird dived when I got within 50 yards. It took me several minutes to subdue and kill the mortally wounded bird. I'd never have been successful were it not for the motorized tender. As Greg climbed out of the layout boat into the tender, I presented him with his trophy redhead.

We'd enjoyed a terrific hunt. We'd shot our limit of six divers and we'd seen thousands more. It took us half an hour to pick up the decoys and secure the layout boat behind the tender. We were too tired to lift it onto the bow. Darkness began to engulf us as we headed back to camp. There'd been no perceptible sunset, the sky had been overcast all day, but slowly, surprisingly, the western horizon began to glow with a reddish tinge. The glow was coming from the lights of Detroit, some 12 miles across the lake.

I sat on the bow looking back at the glow of the city lights. The layout boat rolled gently from side to side on the tender's wake. The scene reminded me of a story I'd read as a kid in some long forgotten magazine. The name of the article and the picture associated with it are still etched in my memory. "Big City Broadbills" was about hunting within sight of a city, perhaps Detroit, and the picture depicted a flock of scaup flaring above two hunters in a layout boat. The background for the picture was the glow from the city lights, silhouetting the urban skyline. I had waited 30 years to hunt "big city broadbills" from a layout boat, but now I'd done it.

It had been a long day. We had fought the wind and waves of the lake all morning and we'd spent the middle of the day visiting people around the island. The intensity of the hunt and the energy expended in setting out and picking up the rig made us more than ready for the feed of venison that Greg's dad greeted us with when we got back to camp. Greg and I both felt the effort we'd put into the hunt was part of the satisfaction we now felt, and I'm sure the intensity of the experience helped me fix it in my memory. Greg's dad made the observation that there are few opportunities today that allow men to share in activities that are physically, mentally, and emotionally demanding and rewarding. Waterfowling is one such activity that persists.

Although the distaff side of Greg's family had little interest in the Harsen's Island camp, it provided a sense of place for the men of this working-class family. I became more familiar with their diverse personalities while poking about camp, chatting, doing chores, and enjoying the camaraderie of kindred spirits. It was clear that hunting and fishing played a pivotal role in their lives.

A close family friend whose health prevented him from hunting, cooked and kept the camp in order. He re-lived his hunting days through our stories and, he confided, being there helped him endure his illness.

But the island duck camp was not everyone's idea of a haven. Though he lived nearby, the fellow who delivered my luggage (which the airline had misplaced), had never visited the island. He had no idea such a place existed, and he was anxious to get back to the "security" of Detroit city. Harsen's Island held no magic for him.

Does the Gun Really Matter?

I often thought about Al Hochbaum's admonition to give ducks a break by restraining myself, even to not going hunting when populations were low. However, my first "official" encounter with the concept of personal restraint was a couple of years later when the Manitoba government was promoting the protection of female mallards. Save Our Susies (SOS) was a well publicized initiative backed up by some of the most conservative hunting regulations in the flyway.

Later, I heard that conservation-minded managers elsewhere in the flyway were hailing this as a bold move, enlightened and far-sighted. I was surprised that this program was creating such a stir. SOS also made me more aware of how important females are to the growth potential of populations. That fall in the late 1960s was the first time I consciously avoided pulling the trigger on a female duck.

During my travels on the wintering grounds, it soon became clear that if management is serious about protecting breeding stock from the gun, then this has to happen on the southern wintering grounds. Although hunting regulations in Canada are comparatively liberal and the average Canadian shoots more ducks than his American counterpart, American hunters kill 85% of the ducks.

It also makes sense that populations are at greater risk of being over-shot when large numbers of ducks concentrate for extended periods in locations where there are lots of hunters. This would be the case in Texas, which has 110,000 duck hunters, and in Louisiana where there are 80,000. Louisiana has about the same number of duck hunters as Montana, the two Dakotas and the three prairie provinces of Canada, combined. Minnesota has 130,000 duck hunters, the highest of any state, but ducks there tend to be widely dispersed, and the hunting season is comparatively short.

The Gulf coast of Texas and Louisiana winters some of the largest concentrations of both ducks and geese on the continent. In fact, Lousiana winters more waterfowl than any other state, and they're there for three months or more. This, plus the availability of large tracts of public land mean there are better opportunities for good quality hunting in Louisiana than anywhere else on the wintering grounds. Louisiana hunters kill a lot of ducks. In fact, each year they kill about two million, more than any other state and about half a million more than are killed in the entire Atlantic Flyway. The average number of ducks killed per hunter is the highest in the United States, higher even than the Canadian average. Despite this good fortune, Louisiana hunters are infamous for abuses of waterfowl. They have an unenviable reputation for flaunting hunting regulations and for unsurpassed greed.

I'd heard little talk about declining duck populations on a trip to Louisiana in the early 1970s, but on another trip a decade later, this was the topic of conversation wherever I went. Like duck hunters elsewhere, Louisiana hunters were feeling the pinch of prairie drought. It seemed many were concerned that they were killing too many ducks. My traveling companion, George Reiger, conservation editor for *Field & Stream* magazine, was researching an article on changing hunter attitudes toward illegal shooting. We were touring the bayou parishes, meeting with hunters, outfitters, guides and wardens, but also with men who'd run afoul of the law.

I felt comfortable with the Cajuns we met. This may be because many of the people I grew up with along the St. Lawrence spoke French and a neighbouring community where I live in Nova Scotia is French-speaking. Indeed, the ancestors of these Nova Scotia Acadians fled to Louisiana after their expulsion by the British from Maritime Canada in 1755. It was in this strange but bountiful land that they found refuge from persecution and a permanent home.

One of our Cajun hosts, a man in his early 70s, had lived his entire life in the marshes. He'd rarely been inland and had ridden out many Gulf coast hurricanes. He was self-assured and certainly self-sufficient, the kind of man you could count on.

We arrived at Jesse Duet's camp early one afternoon to find him standing over a "mess" of redfish, sizzling in a huge iron skillet. His welcoming smile and friendly greeting made us feel right at home. The redfish though, were only to be a snack. Jesse's "duck supper" was already simmering on another stove inside his comfortable cabin. The pungent aroma of the fish reminded me of a gumbo made with blue goose gizzards that I'd enjoyed on a previous visit to the bayous.

We ate the redfish and talked about the changes Jesse had witnessed on the vast freshwater marshes he called home. Early in our conversation he set the record straight about something that was clearly bothering him. He didn't make excuses for having illegally killed ducks, but it irritated him when people talked about Cajuns as though they all were renegades who plundered the fish and wildlife of the marshes.

Jesse made a distinction between those people who habitually behaved irresponsibly toward wildlife and those whom he felt were legitimate subsistence hunters. This latter group, he claimed, respected the birds and appreciated how reliant they were on them. Historically, they fed their large families with whatever the bayous and marshes provided. They rarely sold the ducks they killed, despite a ready market. Bayou people killed a lot of ducks Jesse acknowledged-perhaps 200 or 300 per person, in some years-but they used them all. "And," he added, "there aren't many of us left."

"As a group," Jesse said, "Cajuns are no different than any other. You know, those recreational hunters who come out from the towns and cities, well they have a lot to answer for in Louisiana. There's never been much effective enforcement anywhere in the state," he continued, "and the courts have tended to look the other way when it comes to breaking game laws."

Getting this off his chest was obviously a great relief for Jesse, and it paved the way for us to openly discuss poaching and illegal hunting. George and I were learning a lot about the motivation and behavior of southern game violators.

Jesse confided in us that he was concerned about the duck declines he'd witnessed during the preceding decade. He acknowledged that he knew little of the world outside the marsh, but he feared that the declines, so obvious to him, must reflect what was happening elsewhere. He told us that only a few years ago he'd shot ducks with little thought of limits, but now he wondered if management could justify even the 3-bird limit that was in effect. He gestured toward one of his grandchildren who was fishing nearby and he asked, "Will there be any duck hunting for him?"

As we ate, Jesse provided information about the local habits of ducks and he was keenly interested in what George and I knew of their biology and management. All too soon, Jesse got up. "Five o'clock will come early enough," he pointed to the clock on the wall, "and it's now almost midnight." George and I were already tired from the rigors of the trip and I'd eaten three helpings of Jesse's "duck supper," appropriately washed down with a little bourbon. The idea of bed sounded good.

Jesse's rattling and banging around the kitchen as he prepared biscuits and fried another "mess" of fish roused me from a deep sleep. The aroma of coffee beckoned as I swung out of my bunk. Coffee in hand, I walked out of the cabin into the humid January air. The morning was still, but alive with a myriad of sounds I couldn't identify.

I watched Jesse grab a bag of corn from an out-building and

head for the wharf. As he went by, he impishly looked at me over his shoulder. My face must have been quite a sight in the glow from the cabin windows, because Jesse broke into gales of laughter. When he recovered, he explained that the cracked corn was for his flock of domestic ducks, not for the wild birds on the marsh. My shock was understandable though. During the trip we met people who still "set up" their hunts with bait. At one time, a good many Louisiana hunters wouldn't hunt without it.

Jesse fired up his "mudboat" with its specially designed mud-resistant shaft and propeller. Conventional outboards were useless in the muddy ooze of the bayou backwaters. George and I climbed into two of three little pirogues that were tethered in single file behind the mudboat. Jesse deftly maneuvered us into the bayou, then set off into the inky blackness of the marsh. Although I found the humid air rather stifling, I wasn't about to complain. It was a welcome change to wear light, comfortable hunting gear of a sort I hadn't worn back home since October. For the next 15 minutes, Jesse negotiated a maze of channels that seemed to be going nowhere. Then, abruptly, one widened into a amphitheatre of perhaps a dozen acres. Jesse killed the motor and, as our pirogues glided up beside him, he pointed to a dense clump of rushes in the middle of the pond. "You'll find your blind there," he told me, "but watch out for snakes. Beat around the blind with your paddle before stepping into it." I assured him I would. I'd had very little experience with poisonous snakes. I was only too happy to take his advice. "Ducks are the only source of excitement I want this morning," I told Jesse.

I found the little pirogue surprisingly stable and manoeuvrable as I paddled about, exploring. I watched squadrons of brown pelicans flying in lines, their wings remaining outstretched for several seconds before again beating in deep, graceful strokes. Glossy ibis joined the parade as did cattle egrets and a variety of herons, most of which I couldn't identify. A little flight of ducks passing over reminded me that I was also there to hunt. I set out a dozen decoys, performed my snake-proofing maneuvers, and cautiously stepped onto the platform. The blind was a piece of art, expertly woven from marsh grasses.

I was watching a distant flight of red-winged blackbirds wheeling over the marsh when my eye caught the movement of a small duck. It was coming quickly toward my decoys, just a few feet over the water. It climbed, banked and glided in, landing at the edge of the spread. It was a drake bluewing and, as he jumped, I missed him with both barrels. My next visitor was also a drake bluewing, but this time I made no mistake. I killed him as he passed 30 yards in front of the blind. He fell with a satisfying splash into the decoys. I watched a puff of feathers drift lazily down on the still air and settle on the water.

The day was warm now, far too warm for the clothes I wore. I never really made the adjustment to Louisiana weather. I shed my light sweater and stood there in my undershirt. The scene reminded me of a picture accompanying an article I'd read years ago in an outdoor magazine. It was of a fellow standing in a woven grass blind much like mine, looking at a duck he'd shot as it floated in his decoys. The sun above him was a golden orb in a blue Louisiana sky.

I shot another drake bluewing and a drake greenwing. All three birds were in exquisite breeding plumage. I laid them in the bottom of the pirogue where I could look at them. They were all I wanted to shoot, but I remember well the time when a trio of teal wouldn't have satisfied me. Ducks were still flying, but I hadn't really seen many. In fact, we hadn't seen many anywhere we'd hunted. I knew duck numbers were down, but this was Louisiana.

Jesse came for me about 10 o'clock, on his way to get George. As we approached his blind, George stood and held up three ducks; a pintail, a bluewing and a greenwing, all drakes. He was ecstatic over the morning he'd had. He talked excitedly about the early morning flight of marsh birds, rattling off a list of species, and he told us he'd experienced a good flight of ducks. I was surprised by this, but Jesse wasn't. "You're hunting," he told George, "beside a section of marsh that I lease from an oil company. I don't allow any hunting on my private sanctuary. It's for the ducks."

We took the scenic route back to Jesse's camp. This fortunate man was enjoying a wonderfully independent life in these beautiful marshes. I'm sure he'd be envied by men far wealthier than he. Back at camp, he immediately set about preparing lunch. Only after that important business had been seen to did we resume our discussion of the previous night. Inevitably, the conversation got around to the special teal season that provides southern and mid-latitude hunters with hunting prior to the regular season.

Managers argue that blue-winged teal are under-utilized because most have left the U.S. before the regular season opens. They point out that regardless of hunting, many of these long distance migrants will die before they have the opportunity to breed. While this is undoubtedly true, there was little justification for approving special seasons during the early 1990s when teal populations were well below the long-term advantage.

Ironically, the USFWS has historically recommended against special teal seasons for northern states because research showed an excessive harvest of species other than teal. Managers know from surveys that the ability of hunters to distinguish among different species of ducks is generally very poor. They also know that some hunters simply will not restrain themselves. Are we to believe that southern hunters differ in this regard from their northern counterparts? Was research done to test this assumption?

The main argument for the early season in the south is that teal arrive there well before other migrant species. In fact, even if this is generally so, there are resident (non-migratory) species, such as mottled ducks, that are vulnerable to over-shooting. When hunters are legally in the field, they're going to shoot ducks. It's difficult to believe that teal are the only birds that fall victim to the guns of southern hunters during early seasons.

Special seasons open a can of worms for management that goes beyond biological considerations. Northern states have generally been more conservation-minded about harvesting migratory waterfowl than have southern states. For example, Louisiana hunters and flyway representatives have perennially lobbied for increased opportunity to kill ducks, despite being already well served in this regard. Indeed, about one in every four ducks shot in the U.S. is shot in Louisiana or Arkansas!

It seems to me that hunters along the flyways have to perceive that management is at least attempting to provide fairness in the duck harvest. Every reasonable hunter knows and accepts that the circumstances (finances, location, contacts) of other hunters mean that many will enjoy better hunting, and management can't change this. Equality is not possible. But how do special teal seasons promote fairness? Many northern managers and hunters believe that special seasons, and other concessions that increase the kill of ducks, simply pander to the greed of southern duck hunters.

We spent the rest of the day sight-seeing and lounging around Jesse's cabin. That evening he took us to the mainland where we were to rendezvous with Dave Hall, a USFWS agent well-known by both hunters and his colleagues for his progressive approach to wildlife law enforcement. During the next few days, he would introduce us to former poachers who'd share with us their views on ducks, duck hunting, and the illegal kill.

But Dave was nowhere to be seen when we pulled up to the dock at the appointed time. "No problem," Jesse assured us, "he'll be here. I've never met a man who keeps such a hectic schedule. I don't know how he survives the pace. I couldn't do it." Twenty minutes later Dave pulled into the marina parking lot. "No time for lunch, boys," he told us during a brief introduction, "we've got to be 150 miles from here by evening."

Before we left Jesse, Dave asked him if he thought more of the bayou folk were respecting the game laws than previously. The two men were clearly fond of one another, and they just as obviously held each other's opinions in high regard. Jesse pointed a gnarled finger at Dave and replied, "Hell yes, and people respect you for helping them see why they should." George and I came to understand just what this comment meant as we continued our junket through the Louisiana back country.

As we drove, we talked about how law enforcement had been from the beginning an integral component of waterfowl management. Unfortunately, wardens generally perceive themselves more as cops than educators. Indeed, many were and still are recruited from the military or police forces. Even today, wildlife agencies may have their wardens attend the same training courses as those taken by enforcers of civil law.

Dave told us that "the system" doesn't expect its wardens to be more than enforcers. Consequently, few agents see themselves in the role of mentors; their training doesn't prepare them for this anyway. Dave was encouraged to see more biologists going into enforcement, the beginning of what he hoped would become a trend. "We don't need," he said, "the zealous policemen whose narrow interpretation of the law harasses, alienates and discourages legitimate hunters. I think this can be the "last straw" for some hunters. Many are hanging up their guns because of ridiculously detailed regulations. Mindless enforcement has restricted the freedom of hunters without doing anything significant to reduce hunting mortality and conserve wildlife populations."

It was Dave's contention that the traditional approach to enforcement has resulted in an adversarial system that pits the hunter against professional management. "How can there ever be enough policemen to protect wildlife across the vastness of North America?" he asked. Somewhere along the way wildlife law enforcement has gotten off track, because wardens once *did* believe that education was their primary responsibility.

We also discussed the contentious issue of the illegal kill's impact on duck populations. Some biologists and managers argue that the illegal kill has little significant impact, while others strongly disagree. The latter criticize management for not doing the research to determine why hunters break the law. They believe this is yet another dimension of the low priority given to important issues of harvest management. We continued on this topic as we drove, and we agreed that the fellow who occasionally takes a bird or two over his limit isn't having any effect on the population. But Dave was planning to introduce us to people who were expert at killing ducks. In fact, some had regularly killed 1,000 or more ducks a year. Furthermore, he believed there were enough people like this to matter.

Our destination lay back in the bayou country. We were going to visit the owner of a crayfish operation who was waiting to serve time for his part in the slaughter of more than 600 yellow-crowned night herons, what he called "growbecs." He and his brother had spent a night in a heronry, killing young, flightless birds. It was Friday, and we arrived toward evening to find him completing the payroll for his workers. He'd worked all day, was ready for a break, and wanted to talk.

Billy was a lean, muscular fellow of about 45, with a weatherworn face showing the stress he'd been under. He smoked one cigarette after another. "Let's go," he said gesturing toward his truck. "We can all fit in." We drove along a levee to the dock where he and his brother had launched their boat on the night they killed the herons.

He told us he was "hurting bad." "I'm depressed and discouraged," he said, "and I'm afraid of what will happen to me during three months in prison. My brother is already serving time, and I don't like the stories he tells me. Did you know there's rats in prison? I hate rats! I'm not afraid of anything in these bayous, but those rats really scare me."

"Things are changing for the worse around here," he told us. "It saddens me to see young people rejecting the old ways. They're so important to maintaining the community." We used this as our *entrée* to talk about poaching; one of the bad "old ways" Dave Hall was working hard to make sure people *did* reject.

The crayfish farmer made no excuses for what he'd done. He knew at the time what he was doing was wrong, and he confided that this wasn't an isolated case. "I'm not proud of it, that's for sure," he said, "but when I was growing up, people were never concerned about losing our resources, and nobody gave a damn about game laws. There was so much of everything. Everyone poached. Hell, poachers were local heroes. They were admired for staying ahead of the law. Even people who disagreed with poaching viewed game violations as minor infractions. No, things were different back then."

Billy stopped talking to take a long lungful of smoke. This gave Dave a chance. "When violators were apprehended," he said, "political interference and judicial indifference made a mockery of the courts and the game laws. Let me tell you, game wardens who were trying to do their job felt frustrated and most eventually ceased trying to do anything about bringing serious violators to justice. It was all very discouraging."

Billy knew he'd eventually get pinched and said he deserved to serve time. But he bitterly resented the fact that some of the people who'd bought the birds he killed were respected people in the community. "Those growbecs," he claimed, "were served at political fundraising dinners, and the people who bought them, and maybe even the guys who just ate them, yeh, them too, should do time with my brother and me. They knew they were doing wrong, too."

I was sitting next to him, and he fixed me with a gaze that made me shudder. He realized our conversation was getting "heavy" so he reached over and turned on the radio, dialing in some lively zydeco music. He started the truck and put it in gear. We drove along the levee in silence. Eventually, he informed us that we were expected to show up at his camp beside the bayou for "crawdads" and beer.

Billy had told us some incredible stories about poaching and we'd no reason not to believe him. After all, many of his stories were confirmed by Dave Hall, the federal agent who'd busted Billy and his brother.

That evening was delightful. About a dozen people, all workers in our host's crayfish operation, had gathered to meet us. They were standing around a huge pot filled with the small crustaceans that provided them with their livelihoods. Billy's mood lightened up when he saw his friends and family. He warmly introduced them to us. Everyone was hospitable and friendly, and it was obvious that they enjoyed entertaining us. These people probably lived simple lifestyles by most people's standards, rarely leaving their marshland homes, but they did so by choice.

As we chatted, I heard a phone ring in a bunkhouse farther down the levee. I was dumbfounded when, seconds later, someone called my name. How could anyone be telephoning me? Nobody back home could possibly know where I was. The caller turned out to be a fellow who I'd briefly met earlier. He was too shy to chat face-to-face with me. However, when he learned I was from Nova Scotia, he wanted to talk about his Acadian ancestors. Apparently, he was a keen history buff.

Dave again brought up the issue of game law violation. He told us that it was pretty clear to everyone that the old-style "cops and robbers" approach wasn't working in Louisiana. He and his colleagues believed that if they used the right approach, people in the bayou parishes would change their attitudes. So, they became known in the communities and eventually gained the respect of local people by being tolerant and understanding. They were fair and reasonable in dealing with violators. It was the spirit rather than the letter of the law that guided them, and they treated everyone the same; not political leverage, not social position, not money, would put a violator above the law. They focused enforcement efforts on apprehending well-known renegades, not on persecuting the occasional offender whose petty violations had no impact on the resource. To show they were serious about getting meaningful convictions though, they arranged for important cases to be tried in out-of-state federal courts.

After a few drinks, Billy wanted to talk more. He wanted us to know that he bore no grudge against Dave Hall for busting him. "In a way," he said, "I feel relieved that it happened. I knew it was just a matter of time before the law caught up with me. I respect Dave and the other wardens for their honesty and for what they're trying to achieve. It's nothing personal. I won't be looking to get back at him. Look at us now, we're friends."

He insisted that there had been genuine change in the attitudes of even seemingly inveterate poachers. "I wouldn't violate again," he told us. "And I'll make damn sure the men who work for me won't either. I know that some "reformed" poachers will go back to their old ways if ducks become abundant again, but I really think many bad-ass poachers truly changed because they knew all along what they were doing was wrong. My kids will take more responsibility for protecting the ducks and geese that I cared so little about." He stared into the velvety blackness of the bayou night and added, "I hope they get the chance..."

"You know," Dave told us, quickly changing the topic, "some of the staunchest resistance to change comes from within professional management. Agents who pioneer new approaches to enforcement are generally ignored, even resented by their colleagues. They don't get much respect or support from other sectors of professional management, either." "But why would anyone find this surprising?" George commented. "Professional management consists of autonomous parts, so integrative thinking is rare. Hardly anyone in government agencies is responsible for more than a tiny part of the system and increasingly, those "at the top" have had little experience with lower levels. Professional management has become so huge and specialized that people "do their own thing" with little understanding or even interest in what other components of management, much less individuals like Dave Hall, are trying to achieve. There's a lack of tolerance and mutual respect within the bureaucracies of professional waterfowl management. Consequently, the communication needed to make the system function properly is lacking."

Fittingly, Dave had the last "say" on the topic of enforcement. "Leaving the education of the hunter to wildlife professionals hasn't worked," he said, "and the hunting community hasn't stepped into the breach. I'm convinced that a better educated hunting fraternity would work in favor of the long-term interests of duck hunting. Hunters haven't been encouraged to think for themselves. The focus has been on enforced compliance with regulations. How can there ever be enough enforcement to truly protect wildlife? With this paternalistic approach, should there be any wonder why the relationship between hunters and law enforcement officers has become adversarial?"

We left early the next morning. As we travelled through this incredible marshland, we enjoyed more hunting and we visited reformed "poachers" who were now promoting Dave Hall's philosophy. "Having these converts spread the word in their communities is a big reason why this approach is working," Dave told us. The people we met were all fascinating characters with wonderful stories to tell, and they were more than willing to regale us with tales of their exploits. They may have been reformed, but they fondly remembered the excitement of their renegade days.

One old Spanish-speaking man of 93 had emigrated as a boy to Louisiana from the Canary Islands. His grandson translated his stories for us. The wizened veteran of a lifetime spent on the marshes had experienced hurricanes and tidal waves, and he'd been involved in the little known "trapping wars" that pitted fur trappers against one another for control of the marshes. He wanted to tell his story and we wanted to hear it.

We suspected that another fellow's outward charm only thinly masked a sinister soul. He was contemptuous of wildlife professionals and it seemed clear that he complied with regulations only when he had to and only then to stay in business. He owned a large tract of land with a palatial hunting lodge on it. He catered to corporate clients and politicians, and he complained to Dave that the three-duck limit was not enough. "How can I charge what I do and expect people to be satisfied with three ducks a day," he whined. "I put a lot of money into diking and flooding land for ducks. Look at the habitat I provide for wildlife. Why shouldn't my people get a few more ducks in return? How can a fellow run a business this way? My clients and me, we're paying our way!" He was no convert to Dave Hall's philosophy of restraint.

Ironically, I'd earlier been walking with one of this fellow's guides, when a group of 10 pintails flew over us. He looked up at them and remarked, "I haven't shot a pintail all year, and I only got a couple last year. Man, I remember when we used to shoot a pile of pintails. Where the hell did they go, anyway? At one time mallard and pintail drakes were the only birds most people were interested in shooting. I wonder if they should be completely protected?" This was a refreshing sentiment to be hearing in Louisiana, especially from a man who by his own admission had never been very concerned about "the consequences of shooting a duck."

We met the whole spectrum of waterfowlers that January in the late 1980s. One fellow, for example, always kept a cellular phone with him to remain in contact with his stock-broker. He neither knew nor cared anything about wetlands or ducks. Being in a wilderness setting meant nothing to him. He could have been anywhere. Ducks were simply targets for this man who brought a competitiveness to his hunting that was more reminiscent of a corporate board room than a duck blind. Regardless of why they hunted ducks, everyone we met bemoaned the fact they were seeing very few. George and I knew populations were at historic lows, but we, too, were surprised to see so few ducks. It seemed to me that many people were ready to support radical measures, including very restrictive hunting regulations, especially if doing this might restore duck populations. I had plenty to think about when I returned to the frozen north.

I suspect that a good many southern hunters became sincere conservationists due to the 1980s' decline in ducks. But this was certainly not true for all. While selfishness and greed are found elsewhere in the hunting fraternity, southern hunters in particular clamoured for limits "like in the old days" when duck populations began to recover in the mid-1990s. Many southern flyway council members lobbied hard for liberalized regulations, requesting seasons as long as they've been in modern times. This pressure to ease restrictions dismayed northern managers, coming as it did from states that already enjoy long seasons and the best wildfowling in the flyway. Apparently, for many southern hunters, even a modest increase in ducks meant a return to business as usual.

In general, professional management tries to manage waterfowl at the flyway (biological) or regional level, resisting pressure to manage at the state (political) level. Even though people in some states perceive themselves to be disadvantaged by this, the wildlife service really has no other choice than to consider the big picture. *Ducks have to come first!* This is ultimately in the best interests of hunters. However, keeping hunter greed at bay and doing what's right is very difficult when confronted with intense political pressure driven by parochial interests.

A closer look at the Mississippi Flyway (MF), which includes states like Minnesota and Michigan in the north and Louisiana and Mississippi in the south, reveals some interesting statistics. This flyway now accounts for the highest legal harvest of ducks on the continent, about 50% of the total. Since the beginning of the 1960s, the kill has increased by some 30%. The Mississippi Flyway kills approximately *six million ducks annually*. In contrast, the Atlantic Flyway kills *1.5 million*. But it is when one divides the American segment of the Mississippi Flyway into northern, middle and southern tiers that the disparity in the harvest becomes most obvious.

During the latter half of the 1990s, the *northern tier* states had 50% of the hunters, the *middle tier* had 20%, and the *southern tier* had 30%. However, the *northern tier states shot* 25% of the ducks, the *middle tier states* shot 15%, and the *southern tier states* shot 60%. While hunters in the northern and middle tier states annually shot an average of *seven* ducks, hunters in the southern states shot *22*.

In a sense, the disparity is even greater when one considers that about *one third* of hunters kill *no ducks* at all, and *another third* kill only *one or two*. Obviously, the remaining third kills the rest. In fact, only *one quarter* of all hunters kill *two thirds* of the ducks. Given that most ducks are killed by older, more experienced hunters, some individuals in the south must be killing a lot of ducks. This must also mean that young hunters in the northern and middle tier states get rather discouraged as they wait for their next or, in some cases, first duck.

It's interesting that the southern states produce very few ducks, and none of the species preferred by hunters, except the woodie. Not only are the migrant ducks that southern hunters kill produced in the north, they kill many more of these migrants than do northern hunters. I believe some compulsive individuals legally kill enough ducks to influence the recovery potential of depleted populations. As long as they stay legal, there are people who see nothing wrong with killing a limit every day. Take, for example, the southern hunter who in one season shot more than 500 ducks, mostly mallards. To produce that many wild mallards, it would take three to five square miles (1800 to 3000 acres) of natural prairie habitat, assuming that predation was moderate. It would take 100 square miles (64,000 acres) of natural habitat to produce that many black ducks in Nova Scotia.

Many such hunters also follow ducks along the flyways. It's hard to understand how they see nothing wrong with going to Mexico, for example, to take advantage of more generous limits. Migrant pintail populations that are in enough trouble north of the border to warrant restrictive regulations, enter a virtual free-fire zone when they go to Mexico. Would these hunters have so little concern for resident wildlife? Hunting regulations are not set with the compulsive hunter *(predator?)* in mind. There are no natural predators that kill adult ducks at this rate.

Where is the sense of fair play and sharing here? How does professional management explain the attitudes and behavior of these compulsive hunters to northern farmers whom it is encouraging to manage land for duck production? How much does it cost to protect the amount of breeding habitat required to produce the ducks they kill? What does management say to the hunter who contributes money to habitat conservation in the hope of eventually seeing more ducks? How can management encourage restraint when there are hunters who legally kill so many ducks? Certainly northern hunters and managers must feel as if they're shouldering most of the responsibility for conserving ducks. Perhaps the time has come for a return to seasonal limits on ducks-something Canada used in the early days of international waterfowl management.

Some southern states have been lobbying to extend the hunting season until the end of January. But what are the biological implications of doing this? Obviously, later seasons are designed to kill more ducks. However, there are less apparent but still important reasons not to extend the season. Late-season shooting breaks up pairs, forcing females to find new mates. Some biologists claim that this should pose no difficulty, given the disparate sex ratio. However, female ducks make quite an investment in choosing a mate, perhaps starting in September or October to test the suitability of competing males. A female mallard or black duck, for example, may reject many males before she chooses one. Although females of most species choose a different mate each breeding season, apparently some female black ducks, mallards, mottled ducks, and gadwalls repeatedly choose the same male. These males must be special.

In my own studies of wild black ducks, I've found evidence that both experienced females and those breeding for the first time tend to choose older, heavier males. Unlike females, males may not get mates in their first breeding season. There is also a hierarchy in some flocks, with clearly dominant males and females. In most animals, dominant individuals play a more important role in reproduction than do subordinates. If any male will do, why are 40% of the black ducks on my study area paired in October, six months before breeding? Why do some females remain with the same male year round, not just during the breeding season? Indeed, why are certain males apparently preferred by several females, and other males never get a mate?

One has to conclude that not all males are equal. If this is so, then breaking up pairs may have a negative impact on the female's reproductive success. Some interesting research on mallards in England suggests that females lay bigger eggs when they're mated to males they prefer. Larger, stronger ducklings are produced from these larger eggs and so are more likely to survive. Thus, hunting beyond mid-January when females of most dabbling duck species are paired, does have implications for the sustainability of populations.

When southern states began lobbying for extended seasons, part of the offered "deal" was for northern states also to get extra hunting days. Would it be wise for northern states to accept this? If they do, managers in many states would have to add days to the beginning of the season, because freezing weather usually prematurely ends their hunting seasons. Also, an earlier start to the season would result in a larger component of local breeding stock being killed. States like Michigan and Minnesota produce about a third of the ducks they shoot, and managers know that delaying the opening of the hunting season reduces the overall kill of local ducks. Without migrants to take some pressure, local breeding stock, especially female mallards, will be over-shot during early seasons.

Minnesota hunters are especially reliant on locally produced birds in years when prairie migrants are in short supply. Many middle and northern tier states in the Mississippi Flyway, including Minnesota, did not enjoy the widespread increases in hunting opportunities when big fall flights were forecast in the late 1990s. It'd be a shame to see "production" states give in to pressure by southern states and thereby squander their hard-earned and well deserved conservation gains.

It's difficult for managers and hunters to set aside parochial interests and view ducks and duck hunting from a flyway perspective. But if they do, then a philosophical question is bound to arise. Do people who legally kill large numbers of ducks have any particular obligations to their fellow hunters? It seems to me that everyone in the waterfowling community should be able to expect fair play and sharing from other hunters. What do southern hunters say to those in northern states who in some years have only a month of hunting before weather ends their season? Why should northern hunters, or their flyway representatives, support conservative regulations in order to save ducks, when they know hunters farther south are killing so many and lobbying to kill more?

Professional management can never allocate harvest equitably. But it can and should assure that gross disparities don't exist. Then there are practical considerations. What if mortality due to hunting does matter to the recovery and growth of populations, and a significant number of ducks saved from hunters' guns are likely to become future breeding stock? This may accrue benefits not only to ducks, but also to other hunters along the flyway. Hunters have to address these issues; we owe it to each other.

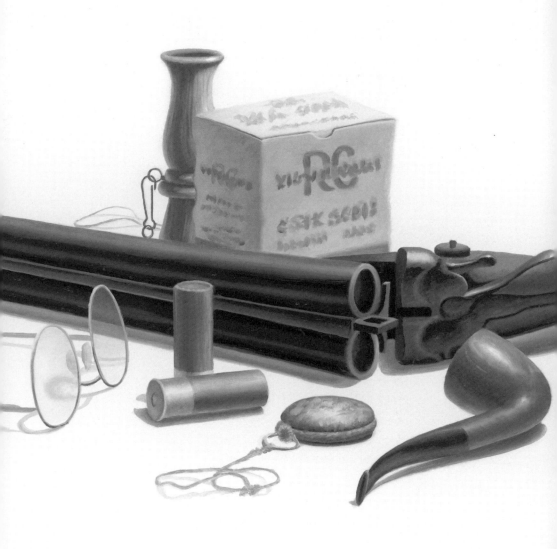

Can we Learn from the British?

Goose hunting at two o'clock on a cold February night was strange for someone familiar only with North American waterfowling. But my companion and I were gunning Scotland's Solway Firth, waiting for a shot at a pink-footed goose before it disappeared into the gloom. Several hundred of these elegant grey birds were floating on the rising tide, coming slowly closer to us as the brackish water flooded into the gully where we were crouched. They were waiting for some signal, unknown to us, to begin flying inland to feed on unharvested potatoes. Although seeing birds against a pitch-black sky is impossible, conditions this night were perfect for shooting. Birds would be silhouetted against a thin blanket of cloud that partly obscured the full moon, and thus visible for a couple of seconds.

Flashes of light followed by the muffled bark of a big gun farther along the estuary warned us that the flight was beginning. The birds before us were getting nervous and I was eager to get a shot at one. I could just make out in the wash of the moon groups of eight or 10 birds as they lifted from the main flock and flew along the tideline. My Scottish friend had taken his black Lab to another gully 50 yards away, leaving me to interpret for myself the night sounds and shadows. I would have to make my own decisions about shooting.

The first flock looked like giant moths, their whispering wings beating as if in slow motion. Two more flocks passed before my mentor joined me to ask why I wasn't shooting. "Were they in range?" I queried. His terse reply was, "If you could see them the way you just described them, then they were in range." A bit later, a single bird materialized above me. My snap shot was followed by a satisfying thud on the mudflat. I was elated when the dog came close enough for me to see the limp form of the goose in his mouth.

What a thrill to be in this "unreal" setting, excited by the sight and sounds of the geese. I was enjoying a waterfowling experience long outlawed in North America. My companion shot the only other birds killed that night. His formidable eight-gauge double boomed twice as he scored a right and left from a flock of birds that had remained after the main flock lifted with a thunderous rush of wings and flew inland. It was three o'clock in the morning but my mind raced as I tried to fathom what I'd experienced. I couldn't shake the feeling that we were breaking the law. But there would be no wardens, everything was legal and consistent with British wildfowling tradition. On that cold

February night in Scotland, only local tradition and our personal code of ethics dictated our behavior.

I was living a dream I'd harbored for almost two decades. When I was 15, I visited England with my family. My great aunt, who lived in the country and was aware of my hunting and fishing interests, had arranged for a neighbour to take me hunting wood pigeons. This introduction to country sports immediately captivated me and, ever since, I've had a love affair with the British countryside and its sporting pursuits. As luck would have it, my aunt's friend gave me a book on coastal wildfowling. What I read in Bill Powell's, *My Wild Goose Chase*, fascinated me and I promised myself that someday I'd experience British coastal wildfowling.

I visited England many times during the intervening years, but it wasn't until the mid-1980s that I was able to indulge my passion for British wildfowling. I'd taken a sabbatical leave from my university and had convinced my family it would be fun to spend a year in the south of England. I would study the behavior of waterfowl at the Wildfowl and Wetlands Trust in Slimbridge, about 30 miles from our rented accommodation near Bristol, and, with some luck, make contacts in the wildfowling community.

Soon after arrival in early August, I bought a Vauxhall station wagon so as to be mobile. The research station was the dream of Sir Peter Scott, the son of the Antarctic explorer. This world renowned naturalist was famous for his contribution to international waterfowl and wetland conservation. In 1947, he built his research facility on the Severn River estuary, an important wintering site for migrant ducks and geese. Being there reminded me of Delta. I spent three days each week at the station, observing captive waterfowl and working in the library, and much of the rest of the time I travelled the countryside. But always nagging me was my need to meet wildfowlers.

One of the first people I met was Martin Brown, the station's avian pathologist. To my delight, I discovered he hunted and fished, and he volunteered to help me in these pursuits. My first task was to purchase a shotgun so, Martin informed me, I'd have to visit my local police station where I could apply for a gun permit. I arranged to do so the next day.

The congenial desk-officer informed me that belonging to a gun club or wildfowling association would facilitate approval of my application. While I waited, he was good enough to phone a friend who belonged to a wildfowlers association in Clevedon, a coastal town only 10 miles away. Two minutes later I had the name and phone number of my contact whom I called that evening. Yes, he would sponsor me and, if I liked, he'd introduce me to the club members at their monthly meeting the following Wednesday. So far, so good!

The meeting was to be held in a seaside hotel, but Ken and I met beforehand in a nearby pub to get acquainted. I felt relaxed when we adjourned to the hotel and assembled for the meeting. I expected a casual gathering of a few fellows more interested in having a drink than discussing business, but I was mistaken. I was immediately struck by the serious nature of the meeting. There were issues to discuss and it soon became apparent that wildfowling for them was a year-round preoccupation. Thus began a new and interesting phase in my education.

Part of the business that evening was arranging for me to satisfy the clubs' membership requirements. The club is an affiliate of the British Association for Shooting and Conservation (BASC), a national umbrella organization that coordinates a network of autonomous community-based clubs; I automatically became a member when I joined the Clevedon club. Both the club and the BASC protect their reputations, and that of wildfowling, by ensuring that members are well-prepared to go hunting. This includes taking written and verbal tests on bird identification and gun handling, but hunting skills and ethics are also part of the rigorous course run by the club. Following this, candidates must prove at the club's trap and skeet facility that they can handle a gun. Only then can they go hunting. However, they are still under the guidance of a mentor, an experienced volunteer who is assigned to them. Everyone, regardless of age, background, or experience, has to go through this apprenticeship.

In due course I became a member. My mentor provided a wealth of information about wildfowling traditions and I fondly recall many evenings in a "wildfowlers pub" with him and other club members. However, it seemed strange talking about duck hunting with these working class fellows. Like most North Americans, I believed that hunting in Britain and Europe was restricted to people of privilege. These sessions opened my eyes to many misconceptions I had about British country life.

Although there are similarities between British and North American traditions, there are some remarkable differences, even, for example, in the meaning of common terms. In British terminology, hunting principally involves dogs and horses, whereas shooting involves the use of a gun. What seems less logical to the North American mind is that "game" refers not only to pheasants, partridge and grouse, but also to woodcock, snipe, hares, deer, and even salmon. Ducks and geese are not considered game. They are the British wildfowl, a term that tells us much about the evolution of British wildfowling.

Historically, the ordinary man in Britain had little opportunity to hunt or fish, primarily because there was little public land and access to private land was strictly controlled. The landowner owned the fish and wildlife on his land, and whether or not it flourished depended on how well he managed it. Wealthy landowners retained a "keeper" to manage their fish and game, and to control access to their land. Exclusion of local people from the land led to the long and, among some people, revered tradition of poaching in Britain. Poaching in North America was never so common probably because people have generally had greater access to land and wild game.

In Britain, the ordinary man who wanted to hunt had either to get permission from a landowner or poach. Getting permission was difficult and poaching was a punishable offense. However, there was another option available to people who lived near the coast. The foreshore, that part of the coast below the mean high tide line, was neither owned nor coveted by anyone. It was frequented by ducks, geese and wading birds, but few people, especially in autumn and winter. This is where the wildfowling tradition evolved and it was pursued by ordinary people who braved the elements to shoot wildfowl that belonged to no one. These wild migrants were shrouded in mystery, part of their fascination. But because nobody owned them or their habitat, nobody took responsibility for protecting them. Only the most general regulations governed their harvest. This gave the wildfowler freedom to pursue his sport, but if the birds were to be protected, the responsibility was his.

Two broad categories of wildfowler evolved; the fowler who killed for the market, and the recreational gunner. The former was similar to his North American counterpart, usually fiercely independent, a loner, someone who made his living by his wits and from his intimate knowledge of the birds and their habitats. With few exceptions, the social and economic status of the man who hunted for the market was ordinary indeed. But as with the birds they sought, there was a mystique about these men that extended beyond the wildfowling fraternity into the community. They were romanticized, revered, and by many, envied for the independent and free lives they lived. Indeed, they enjoyed a freedom rare among people of such modest economic means and social status.

These were the men who developed the technique of punt-gunning, something that lives on today, though very few people still pursue this rigorous form of wildfowling. I passionately wanted to try punt-gunning, but I had hoops to go through before someone would indulge me. First I had to find someone who would introduce me to a punt-gunner. Consequently, I made a day-long trip from the west coast of England to the east coast. Here I met a fellow who'd decide whether or not to introduce me to his punt-gunner friend. After careful scrutiny of my motives and background, I was deemed worthy of taking the next step. A meeting with the punt-gunner was set for the next night. The process was like being involved in a clandestine espionage operation, but it was an adventure.

Still, I felt some trepidation when I entered the Essex pub where I was to meet with this *bona fide* punt-gunner. I must have stood out like a sore thumb because as soon as I walked through the doorway, my host recognized me as the Canadian who wanted to go punt-gunning. He was there with a group of his wildfowling mates who were all curious, perhaps even a little suspicious, about my visit-punt-gunning is a frequent target of anti-blood sports activists. The ale relaxed us, and with each pint I could sense the initial reserve and concern of the group disappearing. Before long, we were chatting as though we'd known one another for years.

When the pub closed, we adjourned to my host's gun room to continue our discussion and view his wildfowling memorabilia. He had an amazing armory consisting of every imaginable type of wildfowling piece. I learned that punt-gunning accounts for a small fraction of the annual kill, but the potential for big kills is apparently a major reason why it's opposed by animal-rights activists. In fact, the tradition is more likely to die of attrition than closure due to public pressure. Few people will put the effort into something so rigorous, and few have the time or opportunity to learn the habits of the birds and the vagaries of weather and tide that determine both the success and safety of the punt-gunner.

Even during the halcyon days of punt-gunning, during a night's sojourn along the coast, one rarely had the opportunity to unleash the big gun. But the occasional big shot was worth enduring danger and discomfort, and the many frustrating forays when never a shot was fired.

Fate didn't hold a "big shot" in store for me either. We'd only a few nights to try our luck and the weather kept us from getting into position for a shot. But I felt no disappointment or frustration. I reassured my host, who like all good guides was disappointed for me, that I'd come for the experience, not to kill ducks. The disappearance of the punt-gunner will mark the passing of British wildfowling's elite, an elitism based only on what these men were capable of doing, not on who or what they were, and certainly not on how much money they had. Punt-gunning was a great leveller. It became the stuff of dreams for men who lived vicariously through the adventures of the punt-gunner.

The larger category of British wildfowler was the recreational hunter who pursued his sport with a shotgun, or so-called "shoulder" gun. A tradition of wildfowling developed almost everywhere birds wintered along the coast, and in each locale a code of ethics evolved to regulate the hunter's behavior. Rarely written down and never overtly enforced, the code was known by everyone and respected by most. Everyone knew what was expected of them and they also knew it was impossible to keep secrets from other wildfowlers. Local traditions were perpetuated from generation to generation, usually learned during a period of apprenticeship. Traditions two centuries old still persist today.

With few exceptions, the early wildfowlers were "locals" who lived near the coast, and the equipment and techniques they developed reflect the fact wildfowling evolved on the foreshore, the intertidal zone that is sometimes covered by the tide and at other times is exposed. Typically, offshore roosting sites of ducks and geese were inaccessible and the cropland where they foraged was privately owned. Consequently, the wildfowler had to intercept the birds along a flight-line as they flew inland or returned to the roost. This was "flight-shooting," the "pass-shooting" of the North American waterfowler. Unless weather kept the birds low, an eight-gauge, or even a six-gauge, like the one I'd earlier hefted in my friend's gun room, were used to drop high-flying birds onto the muddy foreshore. Decoys were rarely used because the birds had no intention of stopping along the foreshore. Even today, there are people who wouldn't consider using decoys and many wildfowlers disdain hunting over cropland. This is not part of their wildfowling tradition.

The social and economic environment in Britain began changing after the Second World War, when the ordinary man had more money for recreational pursuits. But because there was little wild game available, management of artificially propagated game became a way of satisfying the rapidly growing demand for shooting opportunities.

Generations of wealthy landowners had propagated game, but most new hunters either formed hunting clubs or joined commercial syndicates. However, some would-be hunters were attracted to the mystique of wild birds and the romance of coastal wildfowling. This was also more affordable than game shooting. The ranks of the wildfowling community began to swell, as they were in North America.

This influx of wildfowlers, however, created a problem for a system in which the hunter's behavior was controlled by an inter-play of tradition and his personal code of ethics. Few of the newcomers understood the wildfowling traditions, coming as most did from towns and cities, and from families and backgrounds that had little experience with hunting. Inevitably, many of these newcomers behaved irresponsibly and the problem could only worsen.

I saw an example of behavior that flew in the face of tradition while goose hunting on the Solway Firth in Scotland. Six Londoners who were staying at the "wildfowlers inn" where I was watched geese fly over them for two days, without getting a shot. They saw the birds drop into fields a mile away and correctly concluded that that was the place to kill geese. They located the landowner, paid him for access, and the next day killed 90 unsuspecting, vulnerable birds. Money had provided instant access, but it had short-circuited the local system of checks and balances that had evolved to protect wildfowl. Nothing any one did was illegal, but until then tradition had protected those birds.

The inn-keeper requested they leave but, before they went, he asked why they'd broken with tradition. In all ignorance, these men replied that they knew of no such tradition. "After all," one said, "isn't killing geese the objective of goose-shooting?" A more pertinent question to ask was why did the landowner break with tradition when he must have known it would raise a furor? Surely he wouldn't imagine the blame would fall solely on the hunters. It didn't. The incident received unfavorable coverage in both the local and regional press, not just the sporting press.

How then are wildfowl managed and harvest regulated where ill-defined and unenforced tradition has historically controlled the behavior of hunters? There is no structured system of professional wildfowl management in Britain. Nor is there a government agency like the Canadian Wildlife Service or U.S. Fish and Wildlife Service that manages wildfowl and regulates hunting. The Department of Environment in Britain has jurisdiction over migratory birds, but it does little more than designate which species can be hunted and when.

The USFWS and CWS also represent the interests of the hunting community with governments. However, in the absence of such a government agency, British wildfowlers themselves must protect their interests and promote them with government.

The Royal Society for the Protection of Birds (RSPB) and the BASC have an obvious common interest in protecting wetlands and wildfowl. These private-sector organizations act as advisors to the Department of Environment and their recommendations may become government policy. In fact, the government allocates to them responsibilities that in North America would be dealt with by the CWS and the USFWS. Consequently, the RSPB and the BASC may have considerable influence over when and where, or even if, hunting is permitted.

How wildfowling is conducted is often the result of negotiation and compromise between the RSPB and the BASC. Their philosophies are similar to the Humane Society and Ducks Unlimited, so their interests are sometimes in conflict. At times an uneasy truce exists between them. However, mutual respect is usually evident in their dealings.

In general, the RSPB prefers defined regulations that are enforced. Between this and increased competition for areas once the exclusive domain of wildfowlers, it seems inevitable that the freedoms of the wildfowling community will continue to be lost in this beautiful but over-populated land. That the wildfowling tradition still persists, should be encouraging to North American managers and waterfowlers.

The Dee Wildfowlers Club-an affiliate of the BASC-maintains the duck shooting tradition on the Dee River estuary, the border between England and north Wales. On my first visit there, I remember driving through a forest of industrial chimneys that belched smoke into the nighttime sky. Factory lights illuminated the smoke-filled sky so brightly it seemed like midday. As I drove, I thought about my first nighttime hunt in Britain.

Soon after I'd become a member of the Clevedon wildfowlers club, my mentor took me to hunt on the Severn estuary, not far from where the association holds its monthly meetings. The Severn boasts one of the highest tides on earth, something that played heavily on my mind as I sat on the foreshore watching and listening to the tide come in. My experienced companion had given me precise instructions-staying put was paramount. He would be 30 yards away and his dog would do whatever retrieving was required. That night the tide swirled around me as I watched mallards silhouetted against the glow of iron smelters in the Welsh town of Newport, across the Bristol Channel. The shooting was exciting but what made the night unforgettable was the surging tide and the dramatic eruptions from the blast furnaces. I vividly recall the fiery plumes rocketing into the sky-it was like a giant fireworks display.

My reverie was broken by a sign indicating that the next exit was mine. Before long, I found the narrow, winding road that led to the little village of Neston which I knew well from previous visits. The juxtaposition between the sleepy village and the string of industrial towns I'd come through was dramatic. Although dawn was still two hours away, when I stepped from the car I could faintly see marshland in the wash of the full moon and I heard the far-off cry of a shorebird. John Hough had given me good directions. I found him waiting for me at his home, sitting before a steaming kettle. We chatted about the day's plans over a cup of tea and he consulted his tide table, a necessity for coastal wildfowlers. He had to make absolutely certain there would be no surprises awaiting us when we were a mile out on the marsh. For my part, I could only put my faith in his judgement and experience, but his quiet self-assurance gave me the confidence I needed.

The lights of the Welsh town of Flint winked at us across the estuary as we searched for a designated access point to the marsh. John told me that the RSPB and the Dee Wildfowlers Club had agreed to impose certain restrictions on the wildfowler. For example, nighttime shooting was now prohibited, hunters had to be accompanied by a trained retriever, and the gunner had to walk to and from where he planned to shoot. Boats were not allowed.

It was dead low tide and John's yellow Lab ran ahead of us, here and there stopping to investigate a grassy hummock that might hold a snipe or redshank. Little bunches of teal jumped from the "flashes" (pools) of water that a particularly high tide had left scattered about the marsh. John stopped at one of the pools to spread cracked corn he'd been carrying in a burlap bag. This was a freedom still enjoyed by the Dee wildfowlers. "That should keep them coming back," he commented to me.

We weren't planning to hunt teal or mallards. We were going to the outer edge of the sprawling marsh to try for Eurasian wigeon and pintail. With any luck, as the tide rose the birds would move from their roost on the open estuary into the flooding marsh to feed. After an hour of heavy slogging through a muddy ooze, we found ourselves a mile from the mainland on a narrow ridge of sparsely vegetated but firm sand. John winked and touched his pocket where he kept his tide table. He assured me we'd be safe when the tide surrounded us, as it inevitably would. We'd be held captive for several hours in this watery world while we waited for the tide to recede enough to retreat to shore. In the meantime, we hoped for a memorable flight of birds.

With the first faint glow of light, we could make out birds moving along the tideline, half a mile out to sea. Curlew and teal were the first to fly onto the marsh. The curlew came in long, ragged lines while the teal flew in small groups, skimming the water's surface. Then, from a black mass on the water that I'd been studying and now realized was birds, the first bunches of wigeon and pintails began lifting and flying our way.

I loaded my newly acquired English 12-gauge double as a group of pintails looked like they'd pay a visit. They passed just out of range, but a minute later I got my first pintail from a group of eight that flew overhead. Ten minutes later, I claimed my first wigeon from a flock that sped by. John's dog was getting a workout in the flowing tide.

For the next two hours there were always birds around us. I've rarely seen such a flight of pintails. We heard only two other guns that morning, and it sounded as if they too had great shooting. When I'd shot five birds, I began thinking about how many more I'd shoot, although there was no specified limit on the marsh. John said that he'd stop at 12 birds, but I was free, he told me, to decide for myself. His rationale for shooting more than his usual "limit" of three birds was that the weather had been fine all autumn, and shooting had been exceptionally slow. I decided to shoot another three birds and then just watch the flight. My bag that day was three handsome drake wigeon and five drake pintails.

While we waited for the tide to drop and liberate us from our tiny island of sand, we discussed what a privilege it was to hunt this marsh. The quality of wildfowling in Britain is highly variable and what I experienced that morning is certainly not standard fare for most wildfowlers. It is far more difficult to be a successful wildfowler in Britain than it is in North America. For example, although access is theoretically unrestricted, in reality it is difficult to join wildfowling clubs that have access to good shooting. Club membership is usually limited and turnover is slow. Death of a member is sometimes the only way to advance on a long waiting list.

Members of the Dee Wildfowlers Club and their fortunate guests, are the only ones allowed to hunt the estuary. This is a stipulation of the local municipal council which has political jurisdiction over the area and therefore the power to decide the fate of wildfowling. This means wildfowling in an area may be one election away from oblivion.

John was very much against bag limits. "Bureaucrats and politicians shouldn't tell me how many birds I can kill," he said. "This is an ethical issue that should be left to the individual." I agreed, and commented that too often in North America getting the limit is the goal of the hunt. John acknowledged the inevitability of limits in Britain, but he felt that responsible hunters should have a sense of what is enough. John also told me that wildfowling clubs took responsibility for the behavior of their members. For example, as a club warden, he dealt with many issues involving club members, both on and off the marsh, and apparently complaints about hunter behavior were rare. This was probably due in large measure to the emphasis clubs put on education and screening candidates.

On another trip to the marsh, we were accompanied by a young fellow who was John's wildfowling apprentice. We'd been successful and as we trudged toward the seawall which protects the village from the storm-driven tides of winter, we encountered a group of birders. Our path would take us right by them. John's young friend was proudly carrying the birds he'd shot on a lanyard slung over his shoulder. His mentor asked him to put the birds in a sack so as not to offend the birders. The young fellow did so but complained that there was nothing illegal about displaying his kill. John took the opportunity to explain why it's important to show understanding toward people who don't share our love of hunting. This wasn't a lecture but a chat about responsibility and abuse of privilege.

These birders provided the young fellow with a good example of how differently people see things. An elderly lady in a finely tailored tweed suit approached us as we climbed onto the seawall. She was accompanied by a grossly overweight yellow Lab, carrying a stick. The dog immediately ran to John's lean and fit yellow Lab, whereupon they greeted each other in the ages old ritual all dogs perform. The woman admonished us in language not usually associated with old ladies in tweed suits, not so much for killing the birds she suspected we had in the sack, but for exposing John's dog to the rigors of the marsh. He was muddy and tired she pointed out, and making him work the way we obviously had, was in her words, "no way to treat a dog." I let her say her piece, but I politely asked her which of the two dogs she thought would've had the more fulfilling experience that morning. Her dog was answering its genetic predisposition to retrieve by carrying a stick. However, the admittedly tired and mud-covered dog beside us had been retrieving ducks, precisely what he was bred for and loved doing. I think the dogs would have known the answer to my query.

Accepting change has been difficult for people such as a man I know in his late 50s. His father and grandfather were Dee wildfowlers. When the municipal authority made hunting on the estuary conditional on being a club member, local wildfowlers were given the opportunity to join the club. I recall his response. "If I can't hunt when and where I please, then to hell with it." He now languishes beside some of the best duck shooting in Britain. To gain access, he'd have to place his name at the end of the club's long waiting list, something his pride would never permit him to do.

I made a pilgrimage to visit the naturalist Denys Watkins-Pitchford, then a man in his eighties, who used the *nom de plume* "BB" because it was his favorite goose load. He lived in a thirteenth century stone house beside the river Nene. It was perfectly round. This fascinating man wrote wonderfully descriptive and moving country-life literature, a popular and respected literary genre in Britain. His stories of nighttime wildfowling made me yearn for the experience. Despite his reputation, vintage and obvious knowledge of wildfowling, I discovered that he'd shot relatively few ducks and geese. "I remember a good many of them," he told me, "and I regard every one as special. There have been few days during my long life when I haven't thought about wildfowling."

My friend Martin Brown belongs to a private club of about a dozen working men who share a passion for shooting. The club leases land at the edge of the Cotswold hills. During the summer, members raise pheasants and then release them onto the "lease." With luck, they have strong, wary birds to hunt by November.

Martin invited me to join his group for their first hunt of the season. A couple of days before the big event, he briefed me on club protocol and etiquette. He told me there would be about 25 people involved, including the "beaters" whose task it was to drive the birds over the shooters. There might also be people observing the hunt, as well as an assortment of dogs. Those shooting would have to be careful. To save me possible embarrassment, Martin told me to leave my red vest and hat at home. "I know this is obligatory garb for upland hunters in much of North America," he commented, "but everyone here will be dressed in the traditional drab green of the British game shooter. But," he mused, "You'll get by with your camouflage water-fowling clothing."

Some weeks before each event, a club member is selected to be captain of the hunt. He's in charge of every aspect of the day's activities. Martin told me there'd be three, possibly four drives, and the members would alternate between shooting and driving birds. School boys would each get the equivalent of a couple of dollars for their trouble and two local farmers, whose reward would be an invitation to shoot later in the season, bolstered the ranks of the beaters. Another chap would handle the dogs and gather the downed birds. As a guest, I would be in the first group of shooters.

The captain escorted me to my stand. He'd been joking all morning, but now he was all business as he instructed me on what to do. He showed me precisely where I could shoot. He told me to remain at my stand until I heard the whistle blast that would signal the end of the drive. We'd then meet at a pre-arranged location to wait for the beaters and for the birds to be picked up. Everything was carefully organized and I felt relaxed despite being in a new setting with so many people.

I stood in a clearing midway up a hillside that was covered in 60-foot beech trees. Behind me, the hill sloped gently downward to a brook, about 300 yards away. A much steeper slope defined the other side of the valley. The hill-tops on both sides were shrouded in mist. Martin had warned me that the pheasants would break from the beechwood while still high on the hill, making for the opposite hillside. I surmised that swinging on these birds would resemble pass shooting for ducks. When I heard the captain's whistle signal the start of the drive, I loaded my 12-gauge side-by-side. I'd be ready for these artificially propagated pheasants. After all, they weren't the "wild" birds I knew back home.

We were to shoot only cocks and, as Martin had predicted, I heard the first bird break from the woods well above me. He came out of the mist, making for the hillside across the valley. While still 50 yards away, he cupped his wings protectively around his breast and began a long glide down the hill. I was apprehensive about shooting because nobody else had fired, but the moment of truth was upon me. I lifted my gun and swung through the bird as it passed directly over me, about 40 yards up. I squeezed the trigger and the bird crumpled in a puff of feathers. I watched it fall, coming to rest beside a patch of yellow gorse bushes 100 yards down the hill.

I'd only shot pheasants going away and climbing for height. I could hardly believe the speed of this bird as it passed over me. And nobody else witnessed the shot I'd made, hidden as I was from the firing line. But as the drive progressed, I was thankful I couldn't be seen. I missed the next six shots, all high birds directly overhead. My kill was only four birds.

When the drive was over, we assembled to inspect the birds before moving to another part of the lease for the next drive. One of the dead birds wore a leg marker, identifying it as a stray from the neighbouring syndicate. This generated much mirth. The members who'd already shot now became the beaters. I found this almost as exciting as shooting.

By the end of the drive, everyone was tired and ready for lunch. Martin explained that the inn where we'd eat was once a stop-over for English nobility traveling between London and their holdings in southern Wales. The pub itself was a delight.

We made another drive after lunch but that was enough for most of us. It had been a long, tiring day with lots of excitement, and besides the day wasn't finished. We were expected to join the captain and his family for an evening meal at his lovely cottage in the Cotswold hills. The food, the drink, the good company, were a wonderful way to end the day.

Without a professional waterfowl management system in Britain and the rest of Europe, there's little research being done on management issues. There's no intensive management on the breeding grounds to augment natural production and there's no standardized survey to estimate the size of breeding populations. In reality, regulating the harvest is the only effective way wildfowl are managed. Although trends in goose populations are reliably known, this isn't clear for migrant ducks. However, at the millennium, apparently duck and goose populations were stable.

In North America, most waterfowl breed, winter and migrate within the boundaries of two large and friendly nations whose people speak the same language and share the same hunting traditions. Hunting is regulated by treaties and conventions, and managed by wildlife professionals. But trying to manage hunting on a flyway basis is difficult in Europe, where waterfowl cross the borders of 20 or more countries. Their residents speak different languages, have unique waterfowling traditions, and may have different conservation values. Some countries have a deep-rooted mistrust and antipathy toward each other. Historically, northern Europeans have had a reputation for being more conservation-minded than those farther south, and sharing migratory birds has always been difficult.

However, the Europeans have an association of national hunting groups that represents most of the countries frequented by migrant waterfowl. This umbrella organization is attempting to bring flyway management to Europe. But before an integrated management plan can be implemented, the association must first get the cooperation of its member nations, and it is well aware that waterfowl management is primarily about managing people. It is first and foremost political, not scientific. The association of hunting federations has no biologists in its employ. It is, in fact, a political lobby group that represents the interests of hunters by keeping their issues and concerns before European governments. The first president was chosen for his communication skills-he fluently speaks five languages. In fact, they have their priorities straight.

The social and economic collapse of the former USSR, which is the breeding grounds for many of the waterfowl that migrate through Europe, also slows progress toward flyway-wide management in Europe. There is little money available for management there. Even monitoring breeding populations and regulating hunting is next to impossible. Waterfowl will continue to suffer from habitat destruction and increased hunting pressure, especially from foreign hunters who provide desperately needed foreign currency.

In 1983, I travelled 2,400 miles east of Moscow to Siberia in search of the Baikal teal. Even there, I encountered landscapes that were just as transformed and degraded by agriculture and forestry as the Canadian breeding grounds. It will be interesting to see if hunters in the comparatively wealthy nations of Western Europe will invest their money on the breeding grounds of other nations, much as American hunters have been doing on the Canadian prairies for decades.

The future of British wildfowling is uncertain. Not having a professional management system means the BASC has to do the job shared in North America by government wildlife services and well-funded private-sector organizations like DU. The BASC has to protect wildfowling traditions, as well as provide leadership to the wildfowling community. This enormous task is possible only because the BASC is the official representative and widely recognized advocate of the wildfowling community. This enables the BASC to speak with a strong, unified voice on behalf of wildfowlers. Meeting its challenges in difficult times is possible only because of strong administrative leadership and vision, and a singleness of purpose that everyone knows is focused on protecting the British wildfowling heritage.

I believe there's much to be learned from the British experience. I'm impressed with their emphasis on ethical behavior and personal restraint. This is taught, not left to chance. Local clubs and the BASC accept this as their responsibility. It's also obvious that the wildfowler himself has to protect wildfowling. No government agency will do this. The future of wildfowling in Britain depends on both individuals and advocacy groups, like the British Association for Shooting and Conservation.

Europe and the Anti-Hunting Movement

Whatever its immediate problems, wildfowling and indeed the future of all hunting is ultimately threatened by a loss of public support. Since the 1960s, sport hunting in Europe has come under public scrutiny of an intensity rare in North America. In response, the hunting community has either tried to convince the public of the social values of hunting, or vigorously defended its legal right to hunt. The difficulty with the latter stance is that hunting rights are rarely immutably enshrined in constitutions. In fact, they are usually dependent on the unpredictable vagaries of public attitude and politics. An experience I had in Holland one January during the 1980s provides dramatic evidence of this.

Despite being one of the most densely populated countries in Europe, Holland winters a surprising abundance of ducks and geese. Hunting is permitted but it is strictly controlled by the Ministry of Agriculture and it is used principally to control crop damage by waterfowl. Although few people hunt, most who do are from working class or farming backgrounds. Holland is also known for its militant and extreme anti-hunting activists.

My Scottish traveling companion, Colin Shedden of the BASC, and I had been invited by the Dutch Hunting Association to hunt white-fronted geese and tour the countryside. Siebren Siebenga, our host, would introduce us to a wildfowling experience long banned in North America. Siebren not only used live decoys to lure wild migrants from Siberia into shotgun range, but his decoys could fly.

Siebren had raised his five wild-stock family groups, a flock of about 30 birds, from goslings, and their dependency on him was so complete they never tried to escape. He kept his geese in an enclosure behind his village home. When he first showed us his set-up, the geese greeted him as though he was one of them, but they fell silent and held their heads high with suspicion when they spied Colin and me. Siebren knelt and affectionately stroked his geese as one would a family pet. "They'll work for us tomorrow," he assured us.

The next morning Colin and I awoke to discover four inches of snow blanketing the ground. Siebren had breakfast ready for us, but he'd already been busy putting his decoys into carrying boxes and loading them onto a trailer hitched to his car. We didn't have far to go but the slick roads made driving tricky. Our destination was a field of barley stubble where Siebren had constructed a permanent hide made of reeds. We were in no rush, but setting these decoys was more involved than merely arranging a few plastic shells or silhouettes.

Colin and I watched as Siebren and a friend who had come along to help, carried the five ganders about 30 yards in front of the blind. There they tethered them to metal pins sunk into the ground. Siebren then scattered a handful of corn for each bird. They immediately began to feed. Obviously, they knew the drill. Colin and I helped set out two dozen shell decoys. The movement of the feeding ganders made the spread appear especially realistic.

Siebren and his friend then put the females and young into the 20-foot long thatch hide that straddled one of the innumerable drainage ditches that dissect the Dutch countryside. Finally, the four of us entered the hide through a hinged door and settled in to wait for visitors. It was now light enough to see flocks of geese etched against the leaden grey sky.

The snow-covered field in front of us was indistinguishable from those stretching for miles around. What was special about our field? Siebren explained that the snow would disorient the wild geese and they would readily join birds already feeding. Maybe, I thought, but I still wondered why they'd come to us. I could see a dozen or more groups of feeding geese across the snowy landscape.

Siebren handed me a 12-gauge over-and-under and he gave Colin a side-by-side. There were no daily or seasonal limits but, Siebren explained, repeating guns were forbidden and nothing heavier than a 12-gauge and number five shot were legal. I thought this left us rather under-powered for the heavy-bodied race of whitefronts we were hunting. However, what I didn't know was that the geese would be within 25 yards of us when Siebren gave the signal to shoot. The light loads were to discourage "sky-busting" and the wisdom of this soon became clear. Even birds flying back and forth between the coastal roost and their inland foraging sites rarely flew higher than 30 or 40 yards.

As I watched the tethered birds searching for corn, a gaggle of about 20 wild birds caught my eye. They were circling a field downwind from us. Siebren had already spotted them and was now methodically slipping the mates of the tethered ganders out of the hide through an opening in the front. These birds also knew the drill perfectly. Each waddled to her mate and, despite being apart for only 15 minutes, their mutual greeting ceremony was loud and boisterous. This was enough to catch the attention of the wild birds but, while it seemed to interest them, they weren't convinced our field was where they wanted to be.

Now came the unique part of the hunt. On Siebren's earlier coaching, we each picked up a young bird, tucked its head under a wing, and rotated it in tight circles. Then, one after the other, we catapulted the disoriented birds into the air. They struggled for balance, then began climbing for 30 or 40 yards, all the time calling to their parents and grumbling loudly about being so badly used. Throughout, the adult birds beckoned to their youngsters. It sounded like every goose in Holland was in front of the hide.

We watched the young birds mill about in a loose holding pattern as they looked for their parents. Once spotted, they set their wings and glided down to them. This was all the convincing the wild birds needed. Siebren had judged the wind and arranged the decoys perfectly. The wild birds flew directly over the blind. At that range Colin and I either missed entirely or killed cleanly, and that morning we did a bit of both.

Siebren didn't shoot and Colin and I chose to shoot 12 birds that day, not the 25 our host usually shoots. Hunting in Holland ends at noon, but we were packed and gone by 10 o'clock. We would hunt again the next morning, but that day we had places to visit and things to see. It would also take a couple of hours to settle the decoys and take the dead birds to the poulterer's shop to be sold. Besides, we were well-satisfied with our dozen gorgeous white fronts.

Colin and I had come a long way to see Siebren's flying decoys betray their wild brethren. What we experienced that morning made the trip well worthwhile. Many times during the day I recalled the events of the hunt. I fell asleep that night reliving the sight of the young birds gliding in to join their parents, followed by their wild, unsuspecting cousins.

During our hunt the next morning, Siebren pointed to a parked vehicle on a nearby road. The occupants were watching us with binoculars. Hunting in Europe is sometimes a little like hunting in a fish bowl and the hunter has to be especially careful how he behaves. The occupants of the car were probably anti-hunting activists.

Not long after my exciting experience with the flying decoys, Siebren wrote requesting I send him a goose call. Why did he want a call, I wondered? After all, how could he improve on his flying decoys? I sent him an assortment of calls. A couple of weeks later, I read in his return letter that the use of live decoys was no longer legal in Holland.

What had happened?

Apparently a widely publicized slaughter of vulnerable geese had led to a public outcry and demand for more restrictions on hunters. Siebren told me later about two hunters who'd daily killed 100 or more geese during hard weather; severe conditions had concentrated the birds close to a town. What these hunters did was legal but, understandably, offensive to non-hunters who witnessed and photographed the killing and crippling of the weather-stressed geese. They asked how this greedy behavior could be called hunting or sport.

The Ministry of Agriculture requested the National Hunting Association to restrain its members. Unfortunately, some ignored the request-the association has no authority over it's members-and continued their excessive killing. As an appeasement to the public and reproach to hunters, the ministry outlawed the use of live decoys ending a tradition that had delighted generations of responsible Dutch hunters.

Interestingly, the impact of killing these geese was probably negligible at the population level, but that wasn't the issue. The issue was greed and abuse of privilege. It had nothing to do with the science of waterfowl biology. *Perceptions* do matter. They have *consequences!*

For years Europeans have artificially propagated birds, principally partridge, pheasants and mallards, to compensate for the lack of wild game. Because these birds are raised to be killed, for many people the big kill is the goal. This practice has come under the scrutiny of animal rights activists and the general public.

I'd long wanted to visit the great Hungarian plain to see the flocks of wintering ducks and geese which, in 1939, American writer Van Campen Heilner immortalized in *A Book on Duck Shooting*. One November in the early 1990s I got the opportunity but I found a very different Hungary than the one depicted by Heilner.

The ordinary Hungarian rarely gets the opportunity to hunt, especially for game like red deer and boar. These animals are reserved for the wealthy, especially western Europeans like Germans, Austrians and Italians, who inject precious foreign currency into the economy. Birds are also beyond the means of the ordinary Hungarian. Although lower status game, it is usually foreigners who hunt them. Artificially propagated birds are mass-produced to provide maximum economic return. They are shot by paying customers, but are still the property of the producer who then processes them for sale throughout Europe.

My Hungarian host, Sandor Farago, and I visited an estate where the much-hated communist leader, Kadar, once hunted red deer and boar, and lavishly entertained his guests. I met a party of 10 Germans who'd contracted with the estate managers to kill 2000 pheasants during a two-day hunt. We arrived toward the end of the first day of shooting to find 800 dead pheasants arranged in rows, males and females alternating, on the lawn of an old hunting lodge. I'd never seen so many dead birds!

The next day we visited a wooded area where a group of Italian hunters were concealed in hides around a two-acre pond. An ancient game-keeper whose stooped and crippled body must have made walking difficult, took us 300 yards from the woods to a huge pen made of poultry wire. Here he kept more than 1000 hatchery-raised mallards. He'd provided them with all the corn they could eat, but had not given them water all day.

Inside the pen was a structure resembling a ski-jumping ramp. The ducks milled around its base while the keeper urged them with a willow switch to jump onto the ramp. He was very experienced and he managed to keep a steady procession of birds walking up the inclined ramp to a platform 30 feet above the ground. Unlike a ski-jumper, these birds were going up the ramp, not down. The keeper's plan was for them to jump from the platform and fly to the pond. Several of the birds, probably experienced veterans, jumped but did not fly. Instead, they glided to the ground and waddled back to the pen. Many others, desperate for a drink, flew toward the pond. Its shining surface would have been visible through the defoliated trees. Rarely, if ever, had these birds flown, and they would have had to muster all their strength just to climb above the trees that kept them from the water. Once over the trees though, they cupped their wings and dropped toward the pond. They were greeted with a fusillade of shooting. The ducks that could not or perhaps would not fly over the trees, landed and walked to the pond, and were thus spared. But any duck that flew over that pond died.

These propagated pheasants and mallards were simply targets. In my opinion, despite these hunters being true to their traditions, and one must respect that, this was shooting and killing, not hunting.

One of the things that incensed Hungarians about the corrupt communist regime was discovering that high-ranking government and party members enjoyed exclusive access to hunting. In theory, the average Hungarian now has greater access. However, in reality, economically strapped Hungarians will probably continue for some time to be game keepers for the wealthier nations of western Europe.

Sandor and I found wild mallards in western Hungary, along with migratory pintails, wigeon, teal, pochards and geese. Three large lakes in an important wintering area provided roosts amid an expanse of cropland. The tens of thousands of geese were predominantly migrant white-fronts and bean geese, the latter so-called because of their diet. Although the less abundant resident greylag was protected, there were no bag limits and few other hunting restrictions on the migrants. These were "birds from God," wild winter visitors that few people other than Sandor felt responsibility for protecting. They arrived each autumn from the mysterious north and disappeared there again in the spring. While in Hungary, they cost nobody anything and so were an economic windfall.

We set up one morning at the edge of an estate-controlled lake near a party of Italian hunters. The previous evening had been encouraging. Good numbers of geese and ducks had been trading back and forth across the wind-swept marsh. But overnight the wind shifted and died away, leaving poor shooting conditions. Still, we hoped the geese would come close enough as they returned from the fields. Only a few stragglers cooperated.

The Italians were well positioned and managed to kill several geese. It was the last day of their trip. Over their two-week stay, they'd shot so many birds they required a refrigerated truck to haul them back to Milan. Despite these "big kills," Sandor believed hunting had relatively little impact on wild geese. For one thing, few people hunted them, in part because they were difficult. His concern was about the future. He hoped that eventually more Hungarians would have access to hunting. Many of the young men we spoke to seemed interested.

Big game in Hungary is managed and hunting is carefully regulated but this hasn't been true of waterfowl. However, recently Sandor's commitment to waterfowl conservation has resulted in the adoption of a plan similar to the North American Waterfowl Management Plan, the first of its kind in Europe. It bans hunting in certain locations, restricts the huntable species, shortens the season, and sets daily limits at four geese and eight ducks. Despite these restrictions, the hunter still enjoys considerable freedom.

Europeans are acutely aware of the need to protect their remaining habitat and wildlife, and this means hunting advocates walk a public relations tightrope. Anti-hunting activists are not only against killing animals for sport, but for many banning hunting is part of a class struggle. Unfortunately, they've drawn the public into the debate.

The hunting issue is highly politicized and it has divided urban and rural dwellers, much as it has in North America. For example, the Scottish fox hunt was legislated out of existence in 1999. However, a country-wide opinion poll revealed that approximately 70% of rural dwellers supported the hunt, while the same percentage of urban citizens did not.

In general, the global hunting community has avoided dealing with vexing issues that it perceives make it vulnerable to attack by anti-hunters. I fear this attitude will come back to haunt us. One such issue is crippling, already successfully used as the basis to ban hunting in parts of Australia. As waterfowlers, we know some crippling is inevitable. The question is, how can we reduce it to a more acceptable level? There are ways, but they involve restraint, improving shooting skills, and learning many other things that make us more responsible hunters. This can and should be taught. The problem is, who but a very few people anywhere in the waterfowling community are even talking about this, much less doing something about it. Rather, we're caught up in endless debates over new equipment and technologies (gadgetry), and about parochial issues that so often focus on killing more birds. Avoiding the truly difficult issues is what leaves us vulnerable to attack.

Too frequently in North America we rely on the courts to settle our differences. If the crippling debate goes public and anti-hunting lobbyists get this into court, the waterfowling community will lose. Opinions will be swayed and decisions made on the basis of emotion, not on the arguments and statistics of biologists. It is increasingly obvious that the American Humane Society sees the crippling issue as waterfowling's Achilles' heel. We have to better educate ourselves if we're going to successfully defend against our critics and their often valid concerns. Otherwise, we will always be caught unawares and forced to fight rear-guard actions that have low probability of success.

I believe it is essential that we proactively and skillfully engage the public, and indeed anti-hunters, in discussion about difficult issues. It is the only way that we'll have some measure of control over debates like the one we can anticipate over crippling. Recently, I introduced the topic of hunting and crippling to a gathering of naturalists who'd ask me to speak to them about waterfowl. What resulted was a discussion that I believe broadened everyone's perspective, including mine. Isn't this the essence of education. Unfortunately, those who represent the waterfowling community have not been adequately educating either hunters or the general public.

In Britain, the British Association for Shooting and Conservation adopts a moderate, tolerant approach to the anti-hunting/gun lobby, avoiding, for example, the "in your face" style of the National Rifle Association in the U.S. As the hunter's advocate, the BASC vigorously lobbies governments at all levels, and it defends the rights of hunters in the courts. However, it reduces the risk of alienating the general public by refusing to defend inappropriate issues. By avoiding extremes, it has gained the respect of the public and so continues to lobby effectively for the hunting community.

All of society loses when wild places are lost. Regardless of why we're there, everyone who loves wild places enjoys much in common. Two British authors, Ian Pitman and Richard Perry, shared with their readers what wild places meant to them. The freedom of the foreshore, that dynamic world where sea and land meet, loomed large. These naturalists shared the joy of the sunrise, while waiting for the morning flight. But only one man was a wildfowler. The other was there only to enjoy the sights, sounds, and odors of the foreshore.

Ian Pitman wrote *And Clouds Flying* from a prisoner-of-war camp in Germany. He described his memories of wildfowling on the foreshore and his dreams of going back there after the war. These dreams helped him to survive his ordeal. Richard Perry wrote about the war, vicariously experienced through the letters of a friend fighting in north Africa. His friend longed to be back on the foreshore to seek renewal of his war-ravaged spirit. Though not a wildfowler, in his book *At The Turn of the Tide,* Perry wrote that he considered wildfowling a legitimate pursuit beckoning men to wild places.

Even in the 1940s, Perry could see that wild places in England were becoming difficult to find. And the problem would get worse as people's affluence increased. Perry was also concerned that in trying to save what was left, people would "regiment" nature by confining animals to reserves with keepers to protect them. Perhaps he was anticipating the coming of wildlife theme parks. Confining wildlife in this way, he believed, would deny people "the freedom to seek the spiritual, creative and intellectual renewal that unfettered nature can provide."

Inevitably, the reserves came. But, people in Britain can still go to the foreshore and other wild places to seek spiritual renewal. The wildfowler goes during the winter when the birds are there and other people aren't. And there is still a reasonable chance he will return home with a wild *trophy*.

I'm impressed with Pitman and Perry's tolerant attitudes. They had respect for what each other considered important. Such tolerance and respect are difficult to find today on either side of the Atlantic. These men reflected the attitudes of naturalists and hunters of a generation that saw no contradiction in a person being both. Will society continue to let the wildfowler seek his renewal of spirit in the wild places that, increasingly, he must share with others?

My Wild Goose Chase

For most North American hunters, waterfowling means duck hunting. However, at the turn of the century geese were more abundant-perhaps 12 to 15 million birds, widely distributed and available to more hunters than ever before. In fact, some populations of white geese were over-abundant. Although geese will never be as numerous or widely distributed as ducks, hunters in some states once famous for ducks now shoot more geese. Some resident Canada goose flocks provide unprecedented hunting opportunities. Even dedicated duck hunters shifted to geese when ducks reached historic lows.

There are many reasons for the increase in geese, some natural and others resulting from human activity. Geese may live 20 years or more-the average is six to eight years-and they have a high reproductive potential. Their social behavior is a major reason why they're successful. For example, pairs may remain mated for life, becoming highly successful at parenting. These aggressive, large-bodied birds team-up to defend their nest and goslings against predators. In general, breeding geese are less vulnerable to predation than are ducks, particularly prairie-nesting ducks. Also, geese typically remain together in family groups until the following breeding season, increasing the survival of naive young during the critical first year of life.

Most geese breed in far northern habitats, beyond the destructive influence of agriculture, where man has minimal impact on them. Indeed, agriculture has been an almost unqualified boon to geese. Widespread planting of grain on the staging and wintering grounds provides them with abundant, high-quality food. Ironically, the same agricultural practices that have benefitted geese have devastated ducks. In particular, wetland drainage has been disastrous to ducks, which are far more dependent on water than are geese. Although water is more important during the breeding season, migrating and wintering geese may need water only for drinking and roosting.

Climatic factors are particularly important to the success of geese nesting in the far-north, and favorable conditions usually offset the risks of migration. Young geese grow quickly and adult birds recover rapidly from the stress of breeding. Food is abundant and there are relatively few predators. Breeding is often a boom or a bust, depending on whether the spring is early or late; the number of young birds in the fall flight may vary from 5% to 50% of the total. This means that even several consecutive years of breeding failures may not alarm managers. They know a couple of good years can restore populations of these long-lived birds.

Geese are more easily managed than ducks. Because they remain in distinct populations that predictably breed, stage and winter in traditional locations, it's easier for managers to detect changes in populations. Consequently, realistic hunting regulations can be set. Indeed, regulating the harvest is the primary focus of goose management. There is little attempt to intensively manage geese to increase production. This is impractical in the inaccessible habitats where most breed. Virtually all goose habitat management focuses on protecting staging and wintering habitat, and many American refuges were established with geese in mind.

Unlike the controversy over the impact of hunting on ducks, most biologists and managers believe hunting can have a significant impact on geese. They acknowledge that over-shooting, especially when reproduction has been poor, can result in several years of depressed populations. In fact, hunting is used to control over-abundant goose populations, such as urban Canada goose flocks that in some locations are doubling every five years.

Geese were rare when I was growing up on the St. Lawrence, stopping only briefly to rest. There'd be one or two nights each fall when I'd rush from the house to stare into the darkness vainly searching for the birds I could hear calling. Sometimes during the day, I would see them passing over. When I did, I always followed them until I could no longer hear or see them. I'd think about them for days after and I promised myself that one day I'd follow them along the flyways.

I remember Robin shooting his first goose, but I never did kill one on the river. Eventually though, I found myself in goose country and, with a little concentration, I suppose I can remember the first couple of dozen geese I killed. I've since shot many hundreds, but they remain special. A goose hunt is always a big event.

The Swampy Cree have lived on the shores of James Bay in northern Ontario for countless generations. Traditionally, geese were important in their diet and in their folklore. April migrants were welcome not only as harbingers of spring, but because for months the Cree would have had little fresh meat. A store of autumn-killed geese provided a hedge against the deprivations of seven months of winter. Although less dependent on geese than formerly, the subsistence goose hunt is still important.

This was a hunt I'd always wanted to experience, so I leapt at the opportunity when it came. The regional biologist in Moosonee, at the southern edge of the bay, had invited me to visit during the first week of October. This was a big week in Moosonee. The migration would be in full swing and the whole community-schools, businesses, everything-would be closed so that everyone could go goose hunting.

Three of us sat in my friend's house, talking about geese and waiting for a phone call from the "bush" pilot who was to fly us along the coast. Under the right weather conditions, a small plane could put down on a gravel bar close to where we intended to hunt. Fast moving, localized storm fronts characterize the bay's early autumn weather. We were waiting out an intense snow squall that had shut down aircraft travel. Waiting to get to the hunting grounds was agony, and it wasn't certain whether we'd get there. I had been forewarned about the vagaries of hunting James Bay. I was prepared for a long stay.

The phone call finally came and the pilot's terse message was absolutely clear. "You have 15 minutes to get to the airstrip and load your gear. I'm reluctant to go, but we'll give it a try." Five minutes later, we were at the edge of town loading our gear.

The four-seater Cessna flew us north and westward along the coastline of the bay. To my left, the vast expanse of the Hudson Bay Lowlands, a gently undulating morass of tundra muskeg, stretched as far as I could see. To my right, the sullen waters of the bay blended with the overcast sky, resulting in a disorienting greyness with no distinguishable horizon. Venturing away from the shoreline could be fatal.

Ahead of us was a mile-wide expanse of sand and mud, now exposed by a low tide and an offshore breeze. A narrow swath of bog ran inland from the bay before blending into the tundra. Every few miles, narrow gullies snaked across the tidal flats as they flowed to the bay, and everywhere I looked there were geese.

Eventually, a barely perceptible ridge of land appeared. Our taciturn pilot began a long descent toward it. I could see nothing even vaguely resembling a place to land but, to my relief, he put down on a narrow strip of well camouflaged gravel as smoothly as if it were an urban tarmac. Fifteen minutes later we stood surrounded by our gear, watching the plane disappear.

I was uneasy about the way we were rushing to set up camp. The sounds of geese flying along the tideline were tempting us to go for an evening hunt. Soon, our prospector's tent loomed above the flat terrain. We assembled our hunting gear and headed toward a little stream where we'd seen a couple of hundred birds when we flew in.

Twenty minutes out of camp the light began to fail and we realized we'd have trouble getting back in the featureless landscape. We aborted our hunt, hoping there'd be light enough to finish our chores back at camp. There wasn't, but at least we had a plan for the morning.

About three o'clock in the morning we were wishing we'd skipped the abortive hunt and taken time to secure the bulky tent. The wind had shifted and greatly increased in velocity. With it came a nasty mixture of rain, ice-pellets and snow. The tent behaved like a sail as it took the full brunt of the north wind, now roaring in, unobstructed, off James Bay. We crawled from the collapsing tent and stumbled around in the dark, doing what we should have done earlier. We only just saved the tent, the camp was in a shambles, and we were frustrated and annoyed with ourselves and with each other for letting this happen. We were utterly alone and the plane wasn't due back for five days.

We spent a miserable night waiting for enough light to resurrect the tent, and to dry our clothes and sleeping bags. What a mess! This time we did it right, despite the calling of geese. Besides, we had plenty of time for hunting, and killing a goose would be no problem.

Most of the geese had probably nested several hundred miles north and had come down along the western side of Hudson Bay to the James Bay coast. Here they fed and rested, building body reserves before striking off southwest to the edge of the prairie. Local breeders fly to the coast from their inland colonies and join the already migrating masses. There were good numbers of Canadas, but 80% of the geese were blue-phase snows. Everywhere family groups or small flocks comprised of two or three families moved along the tideline, drifting inland to feed on the sedge meadows. Rarely did they fly higher than 30 feet.

Eventually, we found ourselves trudging across a spongy-wet sedge meadow to where a creek wound its way to the bay. Overnight a flock of about 700 snows had roosted on a sand bar out from the creek mouth. We might get shooting if they flew inland to feed. I left my two companions hunkered down behind a tree stump that was so out-of-place in that treeless country. No matter its origin, it was a perfect blind. I continued on to a shallow pond beside the creek. Here I found the wispy remains of a wind-tossed blind that a Cree hunter had made from stunted willow stems. The arctic wind that had prematurely rousted us from our sleeping bags had shifted 180°, and it was now blowing an offshore gale.

We'd been in place for about an hour when the first flock of 20 birds lifted off the sandbar. They moved along the edge of the bay and then, as we'd hoped, turned inland at the creek, establishing a flight line that would bring them over us. I took two juvenile birds from the flock before I realized that every bird on the sand bar would follow the same trajectory. Shooting a limit of five birds would be easy, and the show was just beginning.

Every couple of minutes a flock or two would lift, and soon the mile-long stretch between the roost and creek was a continuous line of geese. Each flock followed the gentle contours of the ground, rarely more than 10 feet high, and most came within 100 yards of me. Every so often, a family group would pitch into my three silhouette decoys. Others simply flew by, barely reacting when they saw me. On one occasion, two juveniles that had become separated from their parents, landed and refused to leave, even when I fired at passing birds. They had no idea what I was doing in their wilderness world, but if they were going to be part of next spring's flight, they'd soon have to learn about hunters.

Every bird on the sand bar came over us. We could have killed as many as we wished, who would have known? In fact, we each shot three birds. It seemed pointless to kill more. We were enjoying the stark beauty of the land and besides, slogging back to camp would be tough enough as it was.

For some Swampy Cree, participating in the snow goose hunt is little more than being part of an age-old tradition. However, for others, geese are an important source of food. Regardless, all have the legal right to kill as many geese as they wish. Despite this, subsistence hunters consider it unethical for those who don't need the birds to kill large numbers. Certainly, the conservation officers who monitor the hunt are very much against non-native hunters killing birds beyond their personal limit, under the guise of assisting subsistence hunters.

It's a myth that all natives are inherently imbued with a conservation ethic. Ethical behavior is learned. Natives who don't pursue traditional lifestyles don't know or care about wildlife any more than non-natives, and they're just as capable of abusing wildlife. The more removed from direct contact with wildlife, the less likely they are to develop a conservation ethic, just like people everywhere. The principles of conservation may conform to common sense, but why would untrained aboriginals understand wildlife management?

Aboriginal hunting rights is a very politically sensitive issue in

Canada. The native hunt though is a reality. The question is, how should the harvest be shared between natives and recreational hunters. The formerly illegal spring kill by natives accounted for a considerable but only crudely estimated number of birds. However, amendments to the Migratory Bird Treaty Act now permit natives to hunt throughout the year. While this is unlikely to significantly increase the harvest, legalizing year-round hunting should lead to greater cooperation between natives and government wildlife agencies, resulting in more accurate harvest estimates. Southern managers need accurate estimates of the native harvest to confidently regulate the sport harvest.

Only tolerance, mutual respect, and a willingness to compromise will enable natives and government negotiators to allocate the harvest in ways that are equitable. After all, this sense of sharing is what is expected, if not always achieved, when the sport harvest is allocated between Canada and the U.S., and from region to region along the flyways. Some of the frustration experienced by aboriginal leaders must stem from the little known (they might say ignored) fact that when treaties were signed, natives didn't intend to surrender their land and its resources. Rather, they intended only to share with the new arrivals from Europe. Whatever happens, it's important for sport hunters to remember that natives take only a small component of the continental harvest, despite it being proportionately large on a *per capita* basis. During 1991, for example, natives, excluding Alaskan subsistence hunters, took 730,000 ducks and 470,000 geese, approximately 8% of the ducks and 15% of the geese harvested in North America.

Despite abuses, the native hunt is not the "unregulated slaughter" many southern hunters believe it is. If it were, the native community would be the big loser. In fact, natives generally have a socially enforced, traditional system of regulation based on hunting territories and rules. However, the native harvest *can* have a serious negative impact on specific duck and goose populations.

The Swampy Cree may be contributing to the decline of a population of Canada Geese that nests along the James Bay coast. It is estimated that a community of 3,000 Cree who live close to the primary nesting colony annually kill as many as 30,000 geese, well beyond subsistence needs, according to managers. Breeding habitat is not limiting these geese and the recreational hunt is well regulated in the states along the Mississippi River where they winter.

Not surprisingly, the Cree have little idea what happens on the wintering grounds, believing that the southern hunter is the culprit in the goose decline. Southern managers have tried to rectify this misconception by inviting Cree community leaders to the wintering grounds to see for themselves how carefully the hunt is regulated. No matter how the harvest is allocated, the first priority of both the Cree and southern managers should be to *conserve* the goose population.

Burgeoning flocks of urban Canada geese leave the impression that all Canadas are doing well. But this isn't so. The Atlantic Flyway population was the most abundant Canada goose population on the continent during the mid-1980s. It was a staple of Atlantic Flyway waterfowl hunters, and the harvest was sometimes greater than it was for ducks. During the 1990s, however, this population declined by about 30%, with an alarming 75% decrease in breeding pairs. This happened while resident (non-migratory) Canada geese were increasing rapidly. Biologists believe the decline was partially attributable to the spring subsistence hunt and egging by aboriginals, and to a much lower than usual gosling survival despite availability of suitable habitat. Almost certainly, though, an excessive sport harvest on the wintering grounds was a significant-some would say the main-contributing factor. During some years, hunters in Maryland and Delaware may have killed as many as 2,000 birds a day. Goose hunting had become big business and any attempt to close the season was resisted by commercial interests. The daily limit was eventually reduced to one bird, where it stayed for some time. In 1995, the season was closed in all states of the Atlantic Flyway. Although the temporary hunting ban and a reduction in the subsistence hunt have resulted in modest recovery, the future of this population is uncertain.

For years, few hunters knew that these geese were in trouble, but the problem was known to managers. Some critics blamed the wildlife services for not being more forceful and insistent about the closure of hunting. A few even expressed the view that senior bureaucrats should have put their jobs on the line to draw attention to the crisis. Ironically, managers once saw Atlantic Flyway Canadas as a way of keeping hunters active, while protecting declining duck populations. In parts of the Atlantic Flyway, increased numbers of once fully-protected wood ducks and common eiders are now encouraging hunters to stay active.

Back on James Bay, it was hard to believe that geese could ever be in short supply. This is always the impression hunters get when they're where waterfowl concentrate. Our pilot came just in time. The weather had worsened and snow was on the way. I later heard that only a few days after I'd left James Bay, the whole region was covered with a blanket of snow that stayed until spring.

A relatively unique situation has developed with burgeoning mid-continent lesser snow geese. They're approaching the capacity of their breeding habitat to support them. These geese winter in the gulf states and breed at northern latitudes. Traditionally, wintering geese fed in coastal wetlands, but a shift to abundant and nutritious grain crops on the wintering grounds has extended life spans and several good breeding seasons have increased reproductive rates. Individuals may now live two or three years longer than was once the case and the population is increasing annually by 5%. This has resulted in a three-fold increase since the 1970s and some colonies are so numerous that they are over-grazing slow growing vegetation on the breeding grounds.

Most biologists believe that if this trend continues, destruction of breeding habitat will cause serious problems for both the geese and other species. The question is, what, if anything, should be done? Some biologists advocate letting nature take its course. They point out that the habitat problems are relatively localized, certainly not tundra-wide as many hunters have been encouraged to believe, and they are not so immediate that there is insufficient time to fully investigate the merits of alternative solutions. But there's widespread support within professional waterfowl management to reduce the population by as many as three million birds; it numbered seven million in the late 1990s. Managers would then attempt to keep the population stable at this lower level. DU and the USFWS have aggressively promoted this position, and they've convinced legislators not only of the need to reduce numbers, but that hunting is the best way to do this. Predictably, commercial outfitters are in support of this.

However, not everyone who supports reducing numbers agrees that the spring hunt, as it is widely known by hunters, is the way to do it. Few managers disagree that hunting can be used to control goose populations, but this population may have gone beyond the point where hunting can adequately reduce it. Even the promoters of the spring hunt acknowledge this. Furthermore, how does indiscriminate killing of geese by southern hunters target the specific breeding colonies that are causing problems? Despite serious and valid concerns, the spring hunt is in place.

A more subtle concern is the behavior of hunters. For example, if killing large numbers is the objective, will hunters be concerned about killing "problem" or "nuisance" geese as quickly and humanely as possible? Will these birds be seen only as statistics and viewed with the cold, utilitarian rationalism sometimes promoted by scientists? Also, crippling may be increased. Some hunters will justify shooting into flocks of out-of-range birds because they believe "scratching down" even one goose will somehow help the population. Will hunters put the same effort into subduing a crippled bird if they see it simply as a statistic in an over-abundant population? The issue of crippling birds is *not* one the hunting community wants debated in public. At least not until we're better prepared to do so.

Professional management is sending a mixed message to hunters. That is, sportsmanship and ethical behavior depend on circumstances. Use of electronic calls, un-plugged shotguns and excessively high bag limits are sometimes unethical but not always. And, management will make the decision about appropriateness for the hunter. The rules of the spring snow goose hunt remove *accountability* from hunters. Why wouldn't this appeal to the lowest common denominator while making ethical hunters cringe?

So, what are the better alternatives? Certainly it makes sense to ease hunting restrictions within the traditional framework, but the Humane Society of the U.S., a 5.7 million-strong organization, adamantly opposes using spring hunting to reduce numbers. It does support having trained native hunters destroy eggs, goslings and moulting adults at problem colonies as a component of the subsistence hunt. Some managers claim that seeking solutions like this would be too costly. But money shouldn't be the bottom line. Somehow the money should be found. Why not find it within the funding framework of the North American Waterfowl Management Plan, if the plan is truly a blueprint for managing waterfowl. Surely after six decades of experience, professional management can find more creative ways to reduce over-abundant populations than simply taking the limits off southern hunters.

It seems strange that the USFWS is careful to conduct the tundra swan hunt in ways that minimize public concern, yet it promotes the snow goose cull. Promoting it as a conservation hunt (or harvest) seems a sop to political correctness. Why risk further alienating special interest groups like the Humane Society? The wildlife services and Ducks Unlimited may be waking a sleeping giant!

Not all lesser snow goose populations are over-abundant, and hunting can result in significant mortality. For example, banding recoveries of immature lesser snows in the Pacific Flyway suggest a mortality rate of almost 50% during the period between hatching and the next breeding season. Nearly 70% of this is attributable to hunting. Adult mortality is less than half that of immatures, but hunting still accounts for 60% of annual adult mortality.

The greater snow goose of the Atlantic Flyway is, however, another over-abundant species that concerns managers. During the 1930s, there were only about 3,000 greater snows. However, favorable conditions on their arctic breeding grounds and protection from the gun, allowed them to recover to tens of thousands within two decades. At the millennium, there were more than 600,000, and the doubling time for the population was eight years. Each year during spring and fall migration, the entire population stops along the St. Lawrence River in Québec. During the 1990s, more geese than anyone had ever seen began arriving on the river *en route* to their coastal wintering grounds from New Jersey to Chesapeake Bay.

I first began hunting greater snows during the 1970s on an island in the St. Lawrence near Québec City. The population was under 200,000 and the limit was five birds. For many years, I had a reliable outfitter who did his best to provide his customers with good hunting. But I stopped going when he died and his business was sold to an outfitter who, I discovered from experience, was interested only in making money.

Years later, a friend from Montréal with whom I had shared this bad experience, finally talked me into returning to Ile-aux-Grues. "You'll really like this outfitter," he assured me. "Say yes. And bring two friends. I'll meet you at the airstrip. You know the one. I'll arrange for the flight. We'll have a great time!" So, early one morning in mid-October three of us set off to drive the 600 miles from Nova Scotia to Québec.

As planned, my friend was waiting for us when we arrived. His first words were, "Have you heard, they had a great breeding season, we'll get some shooting, eh?" We soon got our gear aboard a heavily laden four-seater plane and set off for the island, a 15-minute flight. As we approached the island, we could see a white mass against its lee shore. It was thousands of roosting geese. Things were looking good, but it wasn't until we were met and warmly greeted by our host, a big, red-cheeked man with a friendly smile, that I began to let myself share my friend's enthusiasm.

Marcel loaded us into a beaten-up Oldsmobile that had

weathered many a winter storm on the island. I enjoyed seeing familiar sights along the two mile drive to *Auberge des Dunes,* the inn that he and his wife had operated for years. She greeted us in the same warm way. Soon we were being introduced to the guides and other hunters. Marcel told us what we'd be doing during our three-day stay, and he showed us on a big wall map details of the island's topography, including the area where we'd be hunting. Although we didn't know it at the time, Marcel was sizing us up trying to decide whether or not we were physically fit and experienced enough to hunt the tidal mud flats. The best action is usually there. This scrutiny was not something trivial; the flats were dangerous. Two years earlier, a guest of his ventured into a forbidden area and died of a heart attack when he got mired in the mud and panicked.

Later that evening, Marcel introduced us to our guide, Jean-Guy, who had lived all of his 25 years on the island. I was now forced to use what little French I possess. The good natured Jean-Guy took us over to the wall map and, to our delight, pointed to where we'd be hunting in the morning. Our pits were on the mud flats! Marcel had decided we could cope with the rigors of the mud. Marcel and Jean-Guy had a nightcap with us before they retired. As he was leaving, Jean-Guy reminded me that he'd knock on our door at 4:30 a.m. I relayed this information to my Nova Scotian friends who had even less French than me.

For the first night in quite a while I couldn't sleep. Perhaps I was over-tired from the long drive, but more likely it was because I was excited about the hunt. My insomnia would be no hardship, though. Just after two o'clock, the calling of geese stirred me. They seemed to be right outside my room. I got up, looked out the window, and saw a dozen birds in the wash of light from a beacon outside the lodge. They had swum within 60 yards of my room and were now paddling about on the mud, digging foot-deep craters with their powerful beaks as they searched for bulrush tubers. Peaceful though the scene was, it really got my heart pumping. If I needed any further convincing that we were in for a good hunt, this did it. It also dashed any hope of sleeping. I was dressed and waiting for Jean-Guy well before he arrived at the door. I skipped breakfast to instead walk along the breakwater where I knew I'd hear geese gabbling and calling in preparation for a new day.

Jean-Guy had disappeared into the gloom but he soon reappeared sitting atop an old tractor that pulled a flat-bottomed, wooden punt. He maneuvered the punt to the water's edge, where we all helped launch it and get our gear aboard. We were soon cutting across the choppy waters of the cove in front of the inn. Somehow, Jean-Guy found the channel that would take us to our destination, about two miles from the island. The river at that point was six miles wide and it seemed to me featureless in the gloom of early dawn. Despite this, Jean-Guy expertly navigated through the labyrinth of shoals and mud flats. Before long, he'd located the mud flat where earlier that summer he'd dug two pits.

We pulled the boat onto the mud. Jean-Guy quickly began fashioning decoys with sheets of unbleached newsprint, placing them in the mud around the pits. Murray Workman, with whom I've hunted for 30 years, quickly learned the technique and assisted him, while Will Wong and I bailed the timber-lined pits that had been flooded overnight by the tide. Piles of straw from the punt would provide us with a dry place to sit. Twenty minutes later, we were watching Jean-Guy's boat slicing through the rolling waves as he made his way across the channel to where a 40-foot tender lay at anchor. Here several guides had gathered to chat and play cards while keeping a watchful eye on their "sports," now scattered about the mid-river mud flats. Before leaving though, he reminded us that he'd retrieve any birds we shot. Under no circumstances were we to leave our pits. We were to signal if we wanted him.

The flats were alive with birds. Snow buntings and horned larks wheeled over the mud, settling here and there to feed. Seemingly unconcerned, they foraged right up to the edge of our pits. Twice we saw a peregrine falcon unsuccessfully attack a tightly massed flock of starlings. Black ducks, pintails and greenwings had been moving since dawn and I killed two teal that sped toward me only a few feet over the flats. The geese also began moving early, but they stayed along the tideline, still half a mile in front of us. We knew the tide was not due to turn until 8 o'clock, so it would probably be a while before the geese came near. No matter though, we were enjoying the sights and sounds of the river, and we were confident we'd get shooting. The wind that was beginning to pick up strength seemed to breathe life into our newsprint decoys.

We'd been in our pits about two hours when the first flight of geese came our way. They were working along the edge of the tide about 10 feet over the water, bucking the westerly wind that was now beating the river into a fury. We'd first seen them as a wavy line of white birds rising and falling over the white-capped waves. There was no way of knowing if they were responding to our flagging and calling, but when they got almost opposite us, they left the water's edge and cut across the mud straight for our decoys. They flared as they flew across the first pit, undoubtedly detecting some movement, but it was too late. We stood and dropped four slate-grey juveniles and one snow-white adult onto the mud. The remaining birds caught the wind and returned to the tideline. Flock after flock repeated this pattern.

The wind had become a furious thing by the time Jean-Guy picked us up. He'd waited for us to shoot our limits of five birds each, but by then the fast-flowing tide was almost upon us. We shot our last birds from a group of 10 that flew over us without any intention of stopping. One of the young birds wore a yellow neck-collar. I later learned that it had been attached that summer on Baffin island by researchers studying the social organization of snow geese. Water was already lapping over the rim of the pits when Jean-Guy signalled for us to wade the 100 feet to the boat. He'd just picked up the remaining dead birds that had been drifting away on the tide. When we were back in the punt, Jean-Guy, a truck driver when not guiding, complemented us on our hunting skills. This made me feel surprisingly good. The ride back to the inn was an adventure. Even now when I close my eyes and think about it, I can feel the wind on my face and taste the salty spray. We had worked for our birds and somehow I felt that we "deserved" them.

That night we dined on smoked sturgeon and other river delicacies. We later watched a televised hockey game with Jean-Guy and a group of locals who found the atmosphere at the inn to their liking. Talk was of hockey, a provincial passion, and goose hunting, not about weighty topics like the political difficulties between the French-speaking province of Québec and the rest of predominantly English-speaking Canada. Our stay in this unique setting was made especially enjoyable by these friendly people.

On our drive back to Nova Scotia, I savoured our adventure and thought about Aldo Leopold's brother, Frederic, who occasionally visited Delta when I was a student there. On one occasion, he was returning from a trip to the arctic. I was impressed by the way he spoke of his experiences and with his boyish enthusiasm. He was in his mid-70s, but he had a vigor and a *joie de vivre* rare in people of any age. He told me that the waterfowling he remembered best involved family excursions to their camp, and one or two such outings each season was all he needed to sustain his interest. He laughed when I admitted I thought people back then hunted every day. "No," he said, "I believe such compulsive hunting is something quite new." He reminded me that most hunters didn't have the financial means to hunt frequently, and even wealthy members of hunting clubs usually hunted only occasionally. Indeed, because of time constraints, my friend from Montréal probably wouldn't hunt again that season.

Most St. Lawrence snow goose hunters book with commercial outfitters, but a fortunate few experience a very special hunt. The Canadian Wildlife Service conducts a hunt at the Cap Tourmente Natural Wildlife Area on the north shore of the river. Most of the migrants, which begin arriving in early October, congregate first on the mud flats of the cape. Only after they've depleted the bulrush stands do they move to the mid-river islands. They remain there until late October, building body reserves in preparation for their journey to the wintering grounds. The wildlife area was formerly owned by a private hunting club. However, in acquiring this important staging habitat, the CWS agreed to maintain the hunting traditions of the club. Each autumn 1000 Canadian hunters, who've been selected in a public lottery, participate in a two-day hunt. The person drawn in the lottery can bring a companion. They hunt from noon until closing time the first day, and from opening time until noon the next.

Despite years of trying, I've never been drawn in the lottery. However, I've twice had the privilege of accompanying friends. My first trip was with Rodger Titman, with whom I'd studied at Delta. He picked me up at Dorval airport in Montréal and from there we made the three-hour drive to Cap Tourmente. We caught up on each other's news and reminisced about Delta, and we speculated about our prospects for shooting geese. It was the last week of September, rather early. Still, we couldn't pass up this opportunity.

Part of the drill at Cap Tourmente is an obligatory tour of facilities and an introductory talk. This covers regulations and protocol, and a history of both the culturally-rich area and Club de Chasse du Cap Tourmente. The two CWS personnel who spoke to us were not only knowledgeable, but they were obviously interested in their jobs. They were also hunters, so we knew they felt badly when they confirmed our fears. The birds hadn't yet arrived; there'd been only 10 birds shot all week.

Despite this, our guide took us out for the evening hunt dutifully going through the entire ritual, just as he had when he'd guided members of the old club. He did everything possible, but he couldn't *will* the birds to be there. We fired two futile shots at a green-wing teal that "buzzed" our decoys. As we walked off the mudflats at dusk, a breeze began to blow off the river. We reassured each other that our luck would be different in the morning.

Overnight a high-pressure system moved in. The wind the next morning was brisk out of the northwest. The dark sky was studded with stars as we drove to the management area from our nearby motel. We found our guide waiting for us, seated atop a mud sled harnessed to a huge Clydesdale. The horse snorted in the darkness as we approached. Perhaps the hulking animal was thinking about pulling us, along with our decoys and gear, across 200 yards of cloying mud to our pit on a sand bar beyond the mud. At least, he'd be able to rest on the firm sand before returning to shore.

While our guide set the decoys, Rodger and I took the lid off the wood-lined pit. Although it'd been covered by the tide, the uniquely designed cover had kept the inside dry. Horse, sled and guide soon were gone, leaving us to hunt on our own. Although we wouldn't see Henri again until noon, we were his responsibility and we knew he'd be keeping a watchful eye on us from a hut half a mile away.

The dawn was exquisite, but as it got light enough to see across the blue-grey waters of the river, it became obvious that the geese hadn't miraculously arrived overnight. We had mentally prepared ourselves for a hunt without any shooting, but we'd hoped to see birds. Come what may though, we were in a magnificent setting. A mile to the north, a steep escarpment festooned in autumn colors, dramatically rose 1000 feet above the river. In front of us, the river stretched for miles before meeting the south shore. Here the land, in contrast to the cliffs behind us, rose only a few feet above the river. The river's floodplain sloped gently upwards for perhaps 20 miles before reaching the hills that once formed the south shore of the archaic St. Lawrence.

Toward mid-morning we heard the high-pitched calls of snow geese. We searched the cloudless, blue sky, but it took a minute or two before we spotted them. At first there were 100s, but very soon there were 1,000s of white geese. We watched in awe as they came over the escarpment and flew to a sprawling sand bar a mile offshore. They tumbled and side-slipped like snow flakes. These mysterious birds of the north wind-truly magnificent voyageurs-were arriving from their high-arctic breeding grounds, 1,200 miles to the north. They would've stopped only once or twice to rest. Now they wanted only to sleep.

Within minutes of touching down, each bird was crouched on the mud facing into the wind with its head tucked beneath a wing. They wouldn't move from the sand bar all day. We knew there'd be no shooting for us, but tomorrow would be a different story for the hunters who'd occupy our pit. They'd be "covered up" with white geese as they searched for food.

My second trip to Cap Tourmente was different. It was in the late 1990s and greater snows were more numerous than they'd been in anyone's memory. Indeed, managers were concerned that their overgrazing of the bulrush would diminish its capacity to recover, with dire consequences for the geese and other wildlife. Bulrush is very important to the snows because there is little alternative food for them. The whole population, which stops for about a month during both fall and spring, depends on this food to complete its migration. Consequently, managers were trying to reduce numbers. They'd already increased daily limits to 12 birds, and were considering further easing restrictions.

Murray Workman learned in June that he'd been drawn in the lottery. He didn't have to ask twice if I'd care to join him. There'd be plenty of time to plan our mid-October hunt. By mid-summer, reports from the breeding grounds were predicting a bumper crop of young birds.

Eventually, the time came for us to leave for Quebéc. We took Murray's half-ton truck, which had a cap on the back. Our gear would be safe and Calliope, my black Labrador female, would be comfortable in her kennel. Along the way, we stopped to buy sturgeon from an old woman who beckoned us into the kitchen of her stone farm house. It was as if we'd stepped into a kitchen of a century ago. As she wrapped two slabs of fish in wax paper, she responded to my query about the geese. *"Oui, les oies blanches sont abondantes"* (yes, the white geese are abundant). She directed our attention to the wood stove where a snow goose gumbo simmered inside a cast-iron pot. The wonderful smelling concoction reminded me of Cajun gumbos I'd enjoyed in Louisiana.

When we arrived at the cape, there was just enough light to see skeins of geese flying to their nighttime roosts. A guide who'd come in with his party was hanging their birds in a walk-in cooler. He told us that there were about 50,000 birds where they'd been hunting, and 20,000 of them had just arrived. Approximately 35% of the flock were juveniles but, the guide smiled and pointed to the dead geese, 95% of those killed were young birds. Adults are tough to outsmart, even in Québec where greater snows first encounter sport hunters.

Our hunt the next day was spectacular. We started off in a low-water pit on the mud flats, but the tide soon forced us to retreat to a pit on the river bank. Geese were moving back and forth between the river and a barley field that the CWS had planted for their use. This would take some pressure off the bulrush. Our new location put us under the flight line. There were almost always geese flying nearby, and their calling never subsided. Once a flock of about 15,000 birds lifted in three masses. They all came over us, many in range. We just stood and watched them. Neither of us felt like shooting.

During our two-day hunt, Calli made more retrieves than most dogs do in a season. Not only did she retrieve our birds, but I took her along the shoreline to retrieve birds shot by other hunters. Surprisingly, she was the only dog in camp. Each day she got completely covered in a thick coating of grey mud. She was absolutely exhausted, but I'm sure she loved every minute of her adventure. Calli apparently formed a bond with the Belgian draft horse that pulled us back and forth across the flats. They frequently met nose to nose, giving each other what seemed to me a friendly nudge and lick!

Murray was using a 12-gauge double that'd been his father's. It took some getting used to but he was soon hitting most of his shots. We took turns shooting and backing each other up. Once we knew we could easily shoot a limit, it was hard to stay focused on killing geese. We enjoyed chatting with our guide who'd learned his English in an Alaskan mining camp. He was very experienced and we learned a lot about geese and goose hunting. Murray and I ate a big meal that first night, but Calli was too tired to eat. She curled up beside my bed and didn't move a muscle until the alarm woke us for the morning hunt.

We shot 18 geese the first day and six more the next. That was enough. It was awe inspiring to be on the mud flats with birds all around us. I'll never trade my gun for a camera, but I took several rolls of film.

On our way home, we were stopped by police for a routine auto safety inspection. On seeing the geese in the back of the truck, one policeman commented to the other, "all those birds for two guys can't be legal, can they?" He asked us to prove they were, and we did. The other policeman, himself a duck hunter, seemed unable to take his eyes off the geese. "What," he asked, "are you going to do with all those birds?" It was a good question.

Atlantic Traditions

As a kid, I remember getting off the school bus before my regular stop to visit a sporting goods shop. In the window there was always wonderful treasure to gaze upon. As the hunting season approached, there were displays of mounted birds, guns, decoys and other hunting paraphernalia. One pre-season display had as its centre piece Eugene Connett's book, *Duck Shooting Along the Atlantic Tidewater.* I coveted that book. One day my grandmother pressed some money into my hand and said, "Go and get your book dear, and perhaps a decoy, too. You won't rest until you do."

Reading the book was magical! I read it from cover to cover and in my mind travelled the coast from New Brunswick to Florida, visiting the bays, sounds and inlets whose names are synonymous with duck hunting adventure. I promised myself I'd one day hunt the places this book so vividly brought to life. If I couldn't hunt, I'd at least go to "breathe the air."

My dream began in earnest when I moved to Nova Scotia. Now I could begin my tidewater exploration. The sea, the coastal estuaries, and the brackish marshes of northeastern Nova Scotia became my home waters.

I enjoy early season hunts, but it is when winter storms sweep down from the north, blanketing the landscape with snow and sealing the marshes and shallow waters with ice, that my spirits soar. This is the time of year to hunt goldeneyes, the whistler of the hunter and the wariest of diving ducks. Those who don't know the bird may find it strange that it is a favorite of mine, but I love their looks, the sound of them, and their wild haunts.

I have many memories of these ducks. I watched them during winter on the St. Lawrence when I was a kid. In the spring, I'd sneak onto forbidden land downstream from the huge power dam that held back the waters of Lake St. Lawrence. I'd crawl to the crest of a hill overlooking a small cove and spend hours observing their mating rituals. The drakes were resplendent with snow-white breasts and flanks, black backs and sterns, yellow feet and bottle-green heads with small white moons between black bill and golden eye. They'd fly in short hops, land and skitter across the surface, dive and bob up beside a smaller, brown-headed, gray-bodied female. Their flashy posturings and guttural squawks were designed by evolution to attract her attention. The first whistlers I ever held were killed by Mr. Smith, who one day gave five to my father. At the time, I was home from elementary school recovering from pneumonia. I spent more time in the garage gazing at the ducks hanging from a rafter than I did in my sick bed.

Goldeneyes are at home in ice and snow. These hardy birds migrate southward from northern forests only after cold weather has set in and most other ducks have fled southward to warmer climes. They can be found in the north country in winter on big waters and along fast-flowing rivers, wherever they can find open water and food. They often feed near shore, unlike other diving ducks which tend to raft far out on open waters. This usually makes them more accessible to hunters.

The most exciting time to hunt goldeneyes is when skies are gray and blustery, such as when a nor'east gale is lashing the landscape. There isn't much competition for good gunning points then. The opening-day crowds have retreated to the warmth of their homes and the hunters you occasionally run into are almost always skilled, dedicated waterfowlers who rarely interfere with your gunning and often provide good company.

The flight of the goldeneye is fast and acrobatic and the whistling of their wings can be heard at a great distance, alerting you to possible action. They rarely gather in large flocks, so a realistic gunning rig might consist of only a dozen or so decoys. They are heavily feathered and hard to bring down. A cripple will put the best dog through its paces. I also find them reasonable table fare, especially in a stew.

Goldeneyes, particularly mature drakes, can match wits with the most crafty waterfowler. Males that have survived a gunning season or two are very difficult to decoy. In fact, I view goldeneyes as the most intelligent of all diving ducks. This statement deserves a fuller explanation because measuring the intelligence of animals is difficult. But if how quickly an animal learns to avoid danger is a reasonable measure, then we may be able to say something about how smart a duck is by its response to hunting. By this standard, I agree with most waterfowlers that dabbling ducks are smarter than divers. Among diving ducks, canvasbacks and redheads seem particularly dim. Even heavy shooting in favorite feeding areas sometimes fails to keep them out of the decoys. Setting up where they want to be is more important than the detail of your decoys and the way they're rigged. Whistlers on the other hand usually respond only to whistler decoys, and the rig has to be set just right.

I recall a hunt that embodies all the elements of whistler

shooting and also demonstrates the bird's intelligence. For a couple of weeks, three of us had been hunting hard on a Nova Scotia estuary that held about 400 whistlers. My daily surveys revealed these birds had been in the area for more than a month. From experience, I knew they were exceedingly wary. Then a two-day northeast blow brought in about 200 new birds. They arrived toward evening and roosted that night in a location rarely used by "resident" whistlers. We made plans to greet them at dawn.

During the night the snow had stopped falling. It lay knee-deep on the ground and clung to the branches of the spruce trees. The clouds had cleared but the wind was still blowing. The temperature was about 20 degrees F. In the dark, it was slow, tedious work to push our boat through the snow to the water's edge. We didn't want to work up a sweat and then have to sit for hours in the cold wind. It took more than 30 minutes to launch the boat, but well before shooting time we had two dozen whistler decoys rigged off the craggy end of a small island. It was a favorite feeding area for whistlers, but "resident" birds had learned to avoid it when decoys bobbed on the water.

That morning, flock after flock of "resident" birds came in from their ocean roost, only to flare from our rig. However, the new birds, which had spent the night on the estuary near the island, came readily to our decoys. They were looking for company and a place to feed. We killed our limits, but only four of the 18 birds were adult drakes, even though nearly two-thirds of the new ducks were mature males.

During the morning, the newcomers investigated nearby waters but they didn't encounter the "residents," which had continued several miles up the estuary. Late that afternoon the "residents" gathered in a loose-knit raft after feeding. They then flew *en masse* to their roost, a mile out at sea. As they passed overhead, the newcomers lifted and joined them. The next morning we set up in the same place, but the newcomers remained with the "residents." They passed by our island and continued up the estuary. We shot only five immature birds. It had taken the new ducks only one day to learn the drill. Had we been hunting newly arrived bluebills, we'd probably have had three or four days of good shooting.

Most people hunt common goldeneyes, but the Barrow's goldeneye, a first cousin of the common, is rarely shot. It's hard to distinguish between the brown-headed females and immatures of the two species, but one can readily tell the difference between mature drakes. Unlike the common with its green head and round, white patch, the

Barrow's drake has a purple head with a white crescent between bill and eye. Both are very handsome in their winter finery.

Barrow's tend to keep to themselves and don't mix with other species, even commons. The estimated wintering population of Barrow's along the Atlantic Coast may total only 4,000 to 5,000 birds. They arrive on their wintering grounds in late season. Most make the long flight from Labrador and the lava flows of Iceland where they nest, to specific wintering sites along the St. Lawrence River and the New Brunswick coast. The first challenge facing a hunter who wants to add a Barrow's to his life-list is to find them.

Will Wong, my Antigonish restaurateur friend, and I once spent 12 hours driving through a blizzard to hunt Barrow's along the St. Lawrence River in eastern Québec. Treacherous road conditions had forced police to temporarily close the highway to traffic, putting us well behind schedule. But Pierre Dupuis, a Canadian Wildlife Service biologist, had phoned to say he'd located a large concentration of Barrow's, and we were determined to hunt them. When we finally walked into the restaurant where we'd arranged to meet, I was relieved to see Pierre waving a greeting from a back table. It'd been a nerve-wracking drive. We had a couple of drinks to relax and we enjoyed a leisurely meal before heading to our motel. It didn't take us long to fall asleep.

Four hours of sleep was not nearly enough, but our drowsiness vanished during breakfast when Pierre announced that wind and tide conditions were perfect for gunning. And it was much milder. He'd been observing an accessible flock for several days and he had a plan.

Eventually, we found ourselves picking our way across a boulder-strewn beach to a rocky outcrop that jutted into the river. The tide was still going out, but it was due to turn within the hour. After rigging the decoys, Pierre said, "Find a comfortable place to hide behind a big rock. The birds will fly along the shoreline and cut across this point."

Shooting light came slowly, delayed by fog and an overcast sky. When I could finally see along the shoreline, the sand, stones and rocky outcroppings, worn smooth by centuries of wave erosion, appeared black. Waves materialized out of the fog and broke against the rocks. The dawning landscape was monochrome. Everything that wasn't black, was gray. Will and I ignored an early flight of black ducks and then wondered if we'd made a mistake. "Don't worry," Pierre reassured us. "The goldeneyes will fly when the tide starts to come in. Trust me, this is the place to be today."

He was right. Soon after his reassuring words, six drake Barrows came out of the fog and swung over the decoys. I had killed a few Barrow's, but the first one of this trip fell to my second barrel as it sped from the decoys. It was about 50 yards out when Dixie, the black Lab Pierre had borrowed from a friend, gathered it in. I smoothed the bird's feathers and laid it on a rock. The snow white breast contrasted sharply against the black stones.

For the next two hours the whistlers came steadily, but there were flurries of intense action when birds seemed to be all around us. I watched Will and Pierre shoot birds that had flown inland behind me. Their white bodies and flashing wings stood out dramatically against the dark, sombre hillsides. We hunted until 11 a.m., when the flooding tide had almost peaked and waves were breaking against my legs. Rain had started, so Pierre's suggestion to quit for a meal and afternoon nap sounded good. Our morning's bag was 16 Barrow's and two commons, all but four were males.

Later that afternoon, we drove along the river to sight-see. The wind had died, making it easy to see flocks of resting goldeneyes a quarter mile offshore. There were several hundred Barrow's scattered among flocks of common goldeneyes, scoters, eiders and oldsquaws.

We awoke the next morning to a steady rain and no wind. We set our decoys but no flight developed. Through binoculars, we could see ducks a mile offshore. We killed only four goldeneyes, but we'd had our *trophy* hunt the day before. We quit early and, over lunch, decided we wouldn't hunt the next day. The weather forecast was again calling for a drop in temperature and freezing rain. If we left early, perhaps we could avoid these dangerous conditions. So we bid Pierre *adieu* and began the long drive back to Nova Scotia. Thankfully, the trip was uneventful.

The overnight change in our gunning fortunes is typical of goldeneye hunting. It can be fabulous one day and disappointing the next. This is only part of the reason I am drawn to hunting these birds. I enjoy shooting under rugged conditions in beautiful parts of the country for ducks that are the epitome of wariness. Few hunters are willing to face the often raw elements to pursue these exciting ducks. I think a limit of *mature* drake goldeneyes is one of the most difficult accomplishments facing eastern wildfowlers.

Many hunters believe that if they work a little harder or go a little farther they will find ducks. For most in the Atlantic Flyway this has not been true for some time. Atlantic Flyway hunters have had to set aside their preferences and adjust their attitudes, or hang up their guns. Lack of ducks and places to hunt make it difficult to maintain enthusiasm for duck hunting. Only those with exceptional dedication and commitment persist.

For years I could see this happening along the St. Lawrence. When I returned there with my family during the summer, Robin would give me the grand tour. Riverside real estate had become an expensive commodity, and it had been transformed by cottages and the trappings of summer living. The pasture where I found my first teal nest was someone's manicured back yard. Places once the domain of ducks, and later in the season of duck hunters, had been invaded by a generation of people who weren't even aware of what had happened. Indeed, my parents had "up-graded" our cottage to a year-round dwelling. In so doing, they'd contributed to the suburbanization of the countryside. I still love the setting, but the "new" house has never held the charm of the cottage where I used to clean my fish and ducks in the kitchen sink. I loved listening to the autumn wind rattle the windows of the none-too-tightly sealed cottage.

Perhaps the most dramatic change though, was in the people and their lifestyles. Because of pollution, health officials recommended against eating pike, muskie and walleye. Even the much loved yellow perch, always a high-priced local delicacy, was a risk to health. This was disheartening for the recreational fishermen, but it was more serious for the Mohawks whose traditional way of life was tied to fishing. Some people believe that the deterioration of the fishery contributed to the unsavoury things that happened within the native community. By the late 1980s, running contraband cigarettes was a lucrative cross-border trade that replaced fishing and guiding as a popular livelihood. In the bars and hotels along the river, talk of fishing and duck hunting took a back seat to more exciting stories of smuggling. Hunters and fishermen thought seriously before venturing out onto the river, especially at night.

Hunting had changed too. In part, this reflected inevitable changes in technology and the seemingly inherent striving of people everywhere to be more efficient, more successful, and generally better at whatever they do. This is true also of duck hunters. The human male's psyche may still be partly entrenched in his evolutionary past, hence perhaps his motivation to hunt, but the technology he brings to hunting has become space-age. Robin once reminded me that back in the 1960s we'd anticipated most of the changes that had come to pass, and we knew then that we too were contributing. For example, our bigger, faster boats could quickly get to places where ducks once found sanctuary. What we didn't see as inexperienced young men was that we were also eroding the mystique of waterfowling.

Many people of my generation hung up their guns when they were faced with fewer ducks and increased competition for places to hunt. They could not accept losing their freedom to hunt whenever and wherever they wished. Robin told me that many hunters he knew quit because they were simply unwilling to do things differently. For example, some were unprepared to pay for modestly priced daily or seasonal permits to hunt on Indian land where they once hunted for nothing. They would quit before doing that.

Seeing good numbers of ducks certainly helps maintain interest in hunting. However, most of the Atlantic Flyway never had either the diversity or the abundance seen in the other flyways. Only about 10% of prairie-produced ducks migrate to the east coast, and most of these winter from coastal New York southward; less than 5% of the ducks shot in more northerly states and Maritime Canada are from the prairies. Despite this, at one time opening day anywhere along the flyway meant getting at least some shooting, with the prospect of better to come. Increasingly, ducks are found in small, isolated and sporadic concentrations.

The decline of ducks in this flyway is real. Indeed, some Atlantic states formerly wintered impressive concentrations of ducks. South Carolina, for example, was once an important state for mallards. However, it now winters about one-twentieth of the mallards it did in the 1950s, a far cry from the "legions" and "myriads" of ducks ("black ducks and mallards outnumbering all the rest") that Archibald Rutledge, the poet *laureate* of South Carolina outdoor writers, wrote about. Nobody knows why mallards decreased. Perhaps they are "short-stopped" farther north by changes in land-use or weather, but there is plenty of suitable habitat for them in South Carolina. On the other hand, mallard populations that traditionally migrate there, may have declined more than managers realize. Ironically, were it not for the once protected wood duck, South Carolina duck hunters would be poorly off indeed.

For years, Atlantic Flyway managers have tried to compensate for declines in wild ducks by propagating and releasing wild-strain mallards. This practice is controversial because of concerns that mallards will hybridize with black ducks and also spread disease. However, these risks have not been conclusively demonstrated and some biologists believe they are inflated. Restoring wild populations should be management's first priority, but we know that carefully reared mallards will behave like wild birds. These are not the mallards I saw in Hungary, nor are they the game farm birds sometimes encountered in North America. Although it is well documented that even large-scale stocking of mallards does not significantly augment wild stocks, released mallards can improve local hunting. They may even provide some relief for wild birds. In South Carolina where traditional duck hunting is threatened, I believe the benefits of released mallards outweigh the risks.

The issue of releasing propagated mallards, which is opposed by the USFWS, highlights a dilemma for professional waterfowl management. Encouraging involvement by hunters inevitably means giving up some control. Common sense is needed here because sometimes wildlife professionals block attempts by responsible citizens to get involved in waterfowl management. It seems to me that the professionals need all the help they can get. They can't manage waterfowl entirely on their own. And who, after all, are waterfowl being managed for, if not for citizens like hunters?

From an early age, I'd wanted to hunt Chesapeake Bay, especially for the canvasbacks and redheads that made it so famous in waterfowling lore. I read everything I could about the bay and the colorful people who live along its shores in villages and towns that are steeped in waterfowling tradition. But by the early 1960s, sporting magazines were reporting serious declines in 'cans, and intense competition for places to hunt.

By the time I got to hunt Chesapeake Bay, there was no open season on canvasbacks and redheads. However, my interest was piqued when my friend George Reiger mentioned he might be able to arrange a hunt for brant. These northern nesters had had a successful breeding season and the USFWS had recommended to legislators the opening of a limited season. Grayson Chesser, a friend of George's, was to be our guide. His family has lived on Virginia's eastern shore for three generations. Grayson is also a highly regarded decoy-maker in this area that boasts an illustrious history of decoy-making. We would use his works of art when we hunted for brant and greater snow geese on the outer banks of the bay.

George and I found Grayson waiting in his workshop. We got acquainted over a cup of coffee and we chatted about our prospects. "There was a hard frost overnight," Grayson told us. "The birds will be on the move looking for new feeding areas, so we'll see plenty of birds. With any luck we'll get some shooting."

An hour later, we were launching Grayson's boat in the half light of a January morning that had all the makings of a "duck day." Grayson mulled over his game plan. "I know where we'll set up," he finally announced. Black ducks jumped from the reeds as we headed for the main channel, pulling a skiff filled with decoys and gear. Out on the bay, we saw skeins of geese, mostly snows but also a few Canadas, etched against the pink glow of the eastern sky. We still had a mile to go when we saw the first brant. A flock of about 300 rose and labored into the wind as we motored across the bay where they'd roosted overnight.

While George and I watched them, Grayson was reconsidering his plan. He threw the outboard into neutral, letting us drift with the tide. "We'll set up on that point of land," he said, pointing across the bay. "It divides the bay into two small coves. I built a blind there earlier this fall." We were still unloading our gear when a flock of eight birds flew over us, about 30 yards up. I had seen very few brant in the wild. I watched their buoyant flight as they continued along the shoreline. Grayson sct 15 floaters in front of the blind, while George and I put a dozen full-bodied, standing birds in a tide pool 60 yards behind the blind. By now little gaggles of brant were moving back and forth across the bay. Many approached quite near before veering off. Things looked good.

Grayson hid the boats 200 yards away from the blind. He'd watch us from there and hopefully he'd have birds to retrieve. The decoys looked incredibly lifelike on the choppy water. Grayson later told us how satisfying it was to watch us hunting over his decoys. Making them had been a labor of love and now they were being appreciated by someone else. A skipjack heading to the oyster beds put up a flock of several hundred brant. They settled again after the boat passed, except for about 50 that drifted our way. Most passed well in front of us, but 14 broke away and made for the decoys, only 20 yards above the water.

As the flock scattered to pitch, George gave the signal to shoot. He stood and killed his two-bird limit. I must have been mesmerized by them because I didn't manage a shot. As I watched them reassemble and escape downwind, I spotted a straggler approaching the decoys. It stayed high, with no intention of stopping, but it passed directly overhead. I stood, swung and fired. There was a perceptible delay before I saw it crumple. The wind carried it to the pool behind the blind. It splashed among the decoys and lay dead. I was on my way to get my first brant when George warned that there were more birds heading our way. Minutes later, I shot my second brant, only this bird came from behind. I dropped it among the floating decoys. As Grayson picked up the three birds that were drifting away on the ebbing tide, I retrieved my first brant. What a handsome, sleek little goose, and what a trophy. Despite our efforts, these were the only brant we shot during the trip.

I'd had a wonderful Chesapeake adventure but now the fun was over. George drove me to Washington, D.C., where I was scheduled to talk about black duck biology at the Wildlife Management Institute. On the way, we drove through the flat farmland of Maryland. There seemed to be Canada geese everywhere. Eventually, the rural countryside gave way to suburban sprawl and industrial development. In the press of traffic and the blare of horns, I soon forgot the geese. I'd forgotten we'd been hunting within a three-hour drive of 20 million people. It took a while to adjust to the dramatic juxtaposition between rural and urban America. I wondered as I looked into the faces of people on the streets, if there was anything in their lives that gave them the kind of pleasure I'd experienced on the Chesapeake? I hope so, but I wonder... The windswept point where I shot my first brant was physically not so far away but, in another sense, it was worlds away from Washington. It seemed strange to be going to the city to talk about wild ducks, but that was where the decision-makers were.

I enjoy hunting alone, but sharing the experience with others is better. In recent years, I've spent more time with students and young colleagues, and I'm surprised how much I've enjoyed this. I think I'm getting more than ever from hunting. Apparently, these fellows have the same sleepless nights I once did and they feel the same excitement as I still do when ducks come in.

I was with Daryl Ingram, a colleague of mine, when he killed his first black duck on the wing and later when he shot his first whistler. He was elated! Calli made both retrieves. As we walked to our truck after the season's last hunt, he was philosophical. "I only shot a few birds this year," he said, "but it was a great year. Somehow the days without birds made the days when we connected even better. Man, I look forward to getting out. I get excited just walking to the blind, don't you? I can't explain it but I think I'm a better person, certainly a happier one, because of hunting. I think society would lose something important if there was no hunting." I couldn't explain it any better but I knew what he meant.

Over the years, my two nephews, Kyle and Craig Abraham, regularly visited us in Nova Scotia. They accompanied me when I was doing my research and we hunted feral pigeons near home. They got to be decent wing shots. However, it was difficult for them to hunt when they were back home in Ottawa. One evening my sister, Celia, phoned with an interesting proposal. Craig had promised to improve his performance in school if he could spend a week hunting with his uncle in Nova Scotia. This made me think of my own school days and how important hunting with my uncle Lal had been to me. "Why not," I responded to Celia, "I think it's a great idea."

I picked Craig up at Halifax airport the day before the season "opener." During the two hour drive to Antigonish, we planned the hunt. Craig knew the venue because he'd helped me build blinds there during the summer. That evening we dropped by Will Wong's restaurant to finalize plans for the morning. Craig was getting excited but so was I. Not only was my nephew going to be hunting with me, but this would be Calliope's first real hunt. My nine-month-old Labrador had been retrieving pigeons for three months, but the moment of truth had arrived for her, and for me. Would she retrieve ducks?

Next morning, Will's duck-boat sent water spraying as it sliced through white-capped waves that were being driven by a southwest wind. Periodically, squalls of rain pelted us. At the end of our three-mile run up the estuary, Will cut the motor. We were approaching the half-acre lagoon where we'd built a blind. As the boat glided to the beach, we heard quacking and the rush of wings above the sound of the wind. These birds had probably spent the night there. "Some should come back," I assured Craig.

Our blind was located close to a row of 30-foot spruce trees. They would shelter us from the weather and hide us from birds approaching from behind. However, most of the ducks would probably come across the water in front of us, or across a hayfield to our left. We tossed out a dozen black duck decoys and made adjustments to our woven-reed blind. All this time Calli was rushing about, exploring the area. Every so often, she'd return to inspect what we were doing. She'd sit watching us, head tilted to one side. She sensed something exciting was about to happen. Shooting time couldn't arrive fast enough for Craig. He desperately wanted to kill his first duck. I was in no rush, though. I was savouring the anticipation of the morning flight.

A few minutes before shooting time, Craig loaded the 20-gauge pump he'd used for pigeons during the summer. I put a leash on Calli and snubbed it to a sturdy poplar branch we'd incorporated into the blind for that purpose. I felt sure she'd retrieve, but I wasn't convinced she'd wait until I sent her. I loaded my 12-gauge double and reminded Craig that I'd back him up. I'd also call the shots, at least initially.

Gunshots from Will and Allen MacMullin half a mile away, greeted the morning flight and the new season. Three blacks climbed above a dark ridge of spruce trees that was between us and the cove where they were set up. After a moments hesitation, they headed our way. Two kept going but the third veered toward our decoys. It cupped its wings and dropped toward the lagoon. At my signal, Craig stood and fired twice. He watched the frightened bird flare over the lagoon and continue on its way. In his excitement he hadn't swung through the bird. No problem though, there'd be more.

Craig missed a couple more shots before a black came from behind us, saw the decoys and put on the brakes. She banked, dropped and came over the lagoon. I didn't say a word. Craig timed everything perfectly. He stood and shot. The bird was dead in the air. I released Calli who took the shortest route to the duck-straight through the front of the blind. However, the rest of the retrieve was perfect. She quickly returned with Craig's trophy.

About 20 minutes later, Craig winged a black that fell across the lagoon. It immediately dived and was gone by the time Calli got there. I waded to where I was convinced I'd find the duck hiding in the exposed roots of a wind-tossed spruce. Calli wanted to go into the hayfield, but each time I called her back. She eventually slipped away when I became engrossed in my search. According to Craig, who could see everything from where he sat in the blind, Calli hightailed it across the field. A couple of minutes later, I saw her coming toward me. She was carrying the still-live duck as she hurried past, heading for the lagoon. I watched her swim to the blind where she presented the bird to Craig. She had held her head high and looked straight ahead when she passed me. She was having nothing to do with anyone who had so little faith in her. When I returned to the blind, I realized that the band we discovered on its leg had been put on by me the previous July, when it was still a duckling.

Shooting the duck was one thing, but Craig wasn't comfortable with dispatching it. I showed him how to do it quickly. He knew he'd eventually have to do this himself, just as he'd have to learn to prepare ducks for the pot. But we'd have plenty of opportunity to discuss this. Craig had questions about everything. I found myself re-living those delightful days with my uncle when I too asked questions endlessly, and "hung" on his every word.

I was showing Craig how to determine the sex and age of the birds we'd shot when the drone of an outboard motor interrupted us. Will and Allen had decided it was time to quit. Although Craig would have stayed all day, he reluctantly agreed that our six teal and three black ducks, while short of the limit, were enough. Besides, it was past mid-morning and Will had to get back to his restaurant for the lunchtime trade. I hadn't mentioned it to Craig, but when the rain stopped and the first blue sky appeared, I decided to take him to some of my favorite ruffed grouse coverts. Grouse were in an abundant phase of their population cycle and I knew Craig would enjoy hunting these woodland "rockets." October in Nova Scotia is a fantastic month for the outdoorsman. We don't have the abundance of waterfowl other places have, but we do enjoy a mixed-bag of outdoor activities. Waterfowl, grouse, woodcock, snipe and, when the water is right, Atlantic salmon, are all options.

What a morning it had been. Everyone had shot birds, Craig and I had shared time together, and I now knew I had a good dog in the making. The waterfowling community also had a new hunter who was starting off on the right foot.

Living a Dream

Waterfowl Conservation at the Millennium

For almost seven decades, the North American waterfowl hunter has been served by a model and unparalleled system of waterfowl management. Although the primary responsibility of the federal government wildlife services (USFWS and CWS) is to conserve populations, maintaining them at harvestable levels has always been a major objective. In theory, this is straightforward. Populations are monitored to estimate abundance and determine trends, research establishes safe harvest levels, and hunting regulations limit the kill to protect breeding stock. In addition, management attempts to augment natural production by securing and enhancing habitat, and by increasing reproductive success through intensive management. From the beginning, the wildlife services have been complemented by an active private-sector and this unique partnership has unquestionably benefitted the waterfowling community.

The abundance of ducks fluctuates annually due to natural and human factors but, at the millennium, the wildlife services claimed there were as many breeding ducks as in 1955, when it became possible to reliably estimate populations. The 1999 continental fall flight, they believed, reached record abundance. Geese too were at historic highs. From this, one might assume that waterfowl management has been highly successful. That "great American experiment," as Albert M. Day (then Director of the USFWS) called it in his authoritative 1949 book, *North American Waterfowl,* is a success. But has it been an unqualified success? Might habitat, waterfowl, and hunters be better off had professional management done some things differently? How well has it protected habitat and breeding stock, and sustained preferred species at harvestable levels? How well has it served the interests of waterfowlers, without whom there'd be no need for fall flights of 100 million ducks, or for the habitat to support them? Without hunting would there be any need for the NAWMP or for the large, costly and complex system waterfowl management has become?

Let's consider habitat, the importance of which is undeniable and the battle to protect it never over. Despite continued loss and degradation, federal, state and provincial wildlife services have protected impressive amounts of wintering and breeding habitat, particularly wetlands that would otherwise be permanently lost. Conserving habitat, however, is where the private-sector comes to the fore.

Ducks Unlimited (DU Inc. and DU Canada) has long been

the continental leader in wetland conservation. Originally, DU Inc. built its reputation by raising money from American hunters to secure breeding habitat on the Canadian prairies. In addition, state-based waterfowl organizations like members of the North American Waterfowl Federation (NAWF), have for decades protected habitat. However, the implementation of the NAWMP in 1986 put habitat conservation into high gear and the future has never looked better. The Plan illustrates how successful partnerships can be forged between Americans and Canadians, and between governments and the private-sector. DU was a major force behind the NAWMP's conception, implementation and expansion, and it is a driving force behind its funding.

Widespread loss of habitat (the contiguous 48 states lost half their wetlands during the 1900s) has diminished the capacity of the wintering grounds to support ducks. There will never again be ducks in places where they were once plentiful, especially along the two coastal flyways. But in general, the wintering grounds could support significantly more ducks and geese than its diverse habitats currently do.

On the other hand, there is little doubt that the lack of good quality breeding habitat sometimes limits the size and growth potential of duck populations. The breeding grounds comprise a vast area of different habitats where management has to carefully consider how, when and where to invest its resources. In fact, trying to secure significant amounts of habitat is simply not practical across most of the northern breeding grounds. Ducks there are too widely dispersed to make this economically feasible. Government and private-sector managers have wisely concentrated their efforts on the prairies, where breeding ducks occur in the highest densities on the continent. Here securing and intensively managing habitat to augment natural production can be worthwhile. Despite the fact that agriculture has destroyed much of the land's potential to produce ducks, professional management has achieved laudable successes, especially with implementation of the NAWMP and initiatives like Prairie CARE. Research has shown that intensive management, such as enhancing nesting cover and predator management, can produce more ducks than are produced on unmanaged land.

However, some perspective is needed. Management's capacity to augment natural production will always be constrained by economics. Only a small fraction of the prairie habitat already protected will ever be intensively managed. And professional management can only protect a small amount of prairie for duck production so long as there are no land use policies that specifically address this issue. Will duck production ever be important to anyone but hunters and waterfowl managers? Agriculture is driven by markets that can quickly and radically change farming practices wiping out years of conservation effort. Patterns of land use and climatic factors that affect habitat conditions will always be the most critical factors determining whether or not there will be enough ducks to shoot. It will always be the sheer size of the northern breeding grounds, and not intensive management, that accounts for most of annual duck production and the size of the fall flight.

Above average precipitation in the latter half of the 1990s increased the number of ponds and produced high quality upland nesting cover, particularly on Conservation Reserve Program lands on the northern prairie. This was responsible for the increase in prairie ducks that occurred then. Little of the increase was directly attributable to waterfowl management. To be sure, the NAWMP made a contribution-its 1.5 billion dollar expenditure had conserved five million acres of wetland habitat and upland cover-but the CRP, for example, was protecting seven times (34 million acres) as much wildlife habitat. There was no significant increase in habitat during the years leading up to the increase in prairie ducks. Production from existing projects and programs hadn't stemmed the decline in prairie ducks prior to the return of water. In a sense, it was water and a U.S. federal government policy that gave professional waterfowl management a reprieve. Certainly the degraded Canadian prairie, increasingly a waterfowl desert, was playing less of a role in producing ducks than ever before.

Despite laudable efforts, professional management has had only a modest impact on continental duck production, and this is unlikely to change significantly. Most ducks are produced on unmanaged public or private lands. All of management's habitat initiatives probably account for no more than 5-10% of the prairie ducks that enter the fall flight. The continental figure is closer to 5%. Intensive management in eastern forests accounts for no significant additional black ducks or green-winged teal. Indeed, this is true for all species important to Atlantic Flyway hunters. A significant percentage of Pacific Flyway pintails are produced in unmanaged, probably unmanageable, Alaskan habitats. Even much hailed wood duck nest-box programs probably produce few ducks that would not otherwise be produced in natural habitat. Intensive management of species like greater scaup in northern tundra and boreal forest habitats is entirely impractical.

In reality, *nobody* has good estimates of how many additional ducks enter the fall flight as a result of management's efforts.

Even with stepped-up management, there are too many physical, biological and social factors beyond management's control to ensure harvestable surpluses of all species. For example, if research reveals that contaminants on the wintering grounds are reducing the reproductive potential of scaup, what can management do about it? Not much. Similarly, even with a major infusion of money for intensive management on the prairies, significantly increasing pintail reproduction is a daunting challenge.

However, despite the diminished capacity of the prairie to produce ducks, habitat conditions during the spring of 1999 must have been adequate to produce the biggest fall flight since 1955. There must have been enough habitat to accommodate the record population of breeding ducks that was detected during the spring survey. Mallards, which are used as an indicator of what is happening with ducks in general, were apparently never more abundant. Does this mean that the widely acknowledged habitat difficulties on the prairie have been exaggerated? I suspect not. The problems are only too real, *especially* in Canada.

So what about professional management's claim that, in general, prairie ducks were back, with some species at record levels? Is it possible there weren't as many ducks as managers believed there were? Could it be that managers cannot reliably compare changes in the size of the breeding population that have occurred since 1955? Undoubtedly prairie ducks had recovered from the drought-ravaged levels of the 1980s and early 1990s, once again showing their resiliency. But were they back to levels of the 1970s, 1960s, or 1950s? How confident were managers when they said prairie duck populations were back to robust levels, as promised, when water returned? What do managers say to veteran hunters and experienced field biologist-hunters who doubt whether the ducks were back? Many say the flight, particularly mallards, was not what they remember from the past, much less a record. Hunters have selective memories, remembering the good times when they saw lots of ducks. This is why managers rely on scientific data when it exists. But *might* it be that the record estimates at the turn of the century partially reflect the way breeding pair surveys have changed since 1955?

The annual spring breeding pair survey (index) is perhaps the most extensive and accurate wildlife survey in the world, an enviable achievement of North American waterfowl management. The survey is designed for prairie mallards, but it also provides long-term trends for nine other species of ducks. Although the aerial survey includes habitats north to Alaska, efforts are concentrated on the prairie "duck factory." However, changes in these aerial surveys, including improved techniques and a more systematic approach to surveys (looking harder), may be finding more ducks than formerly. And, it may be that statisticians can't make the data comparable from year to year.

Perhaps estimating the numbers for the fall flight from the size of the breeding population no longer enables a reliable yearly comparison. Biologists must consider not only the number of breeding pairs, but also the quality of the habitat when they estimate the breeding success of the population. However, experienced field biologists have been warning for decades that degraded prairie habitats cannot produce the ducks they once did. Even if one assumes that the breeding pair index is reliable and comparable with the past, how can biologists make adjustments for the diminished capacity of the habitat to produce ducks? Because degraded habitats of today produce fewer ducks than formerly, managers may be unknowingly inflating their estimate of the size of the fall flight.

In theory, the fall flight forecast has always provided a continental perspective. However, in reality, little attention was paid to regions other than the prairies. Surveys of eastern habitats for species like black ducks, wood ducks, and green-winged teal, for example, have only been standardized since the mid-1980s, and managers there are still wrestling with reliability. The fall flight estimates for many species are little more than vague approximations and they may not be reliable indicators of population trends.

In fact, most biologists are uncomfortable with pre-season predictions of the fall flight. They point out that the annual spring breeding survey is the only reliable indicator of abundance and health of populations. Good numbers of breeding birds and favorable habitat conditions should result in an abundant fall flight, but that's as far as they want to commit. Rightly so, they want only to discuss trends (up, down, stable), not actual numbers. They know it's impossible to estimate precisely, such as 83, or 87 or 105 million ducks, from the crude estimates derived from breeding pair surveys. One never sees ranges or margins of error for fall flight estimates which may be 20% or more.

Biologists also know that many factors can confound the reliability of the breeding pair survey. For example, although experienced female ducks tend to return to where they've nested previously, and young females return to where they were hatched, some species are mobile, pioneering new locations and even new habitats in search of better breeding conditions. Consequently, birds may move into or out of the traditional survey area, thereby distorting population estimates.

Given the difficulties with surveying ducks, the wildlife service began a risky practice in 1970 when it acquiesced to pressure from hunter groups and members of the outdoor media and issued the first official fall flight forecast. It has been locked into doing so every year since, risking embarrassment and having its credibility challenged. Predicting the size of the fall flight is at best an *educated guess*. The fall flight forecast has led to confusion. Predictions of big flights have also been the rationale to lobby for liberalized hunting regulations. Restraint and caution have always been hard concepts to sell to some, but this is especially tough when the message implies that the "good old days" were never better.

Reasonably enough, government and private-sector bureaucrats want to report good news, and what better news is there than ducks have surpassed the 100 million continental objective of the NAWMP. What a way to enter the new millennium, and what a vote of confidence for waterfowl management, especially for those within management who perceive themselves as *being in the business of producing ducks*. But has professional management been over-zealous in spreading the good news? Is the news as good as it seems? Have promoters of big flights failed to exercise adequate caution? And why have they continued to enthusiastically make these predictions when previous flights had fallen short of expectation?

The fact that not all species are back as expected should temper enthusiasm. Indeed, the species composition of the fall flight has changed remarkably over the years. It now shows big increases in shovelers and gadwalls, species not traditionally favored by hunters. However, scaup and pintails, species that have been heavily hunted are at worrisome low levels. I find it surprising that even after duck populations had reportedly recovered, in many states the green-winged teal continued to be the number one bird in the hunter's bag. This included states like Texas, where greenwings are not preferred.

Predictably enough, the media picks up on the enthusiasm over big fall flights and tells hunters to prepare themselves for record numbers of ducks. This is a recipe for widespread disappointment and disillusionment. Part of the difficulty with the media hype is that although it reaches hunters everywhere, prairie ducks do not migrate to all parts of the continent. Predictably, many hunters will be disappointed even when prairie ducks are abundant. No matter how one does the arithmetic, across much of the continent fall flights at the end of the century fell short of expectation.

Minnesota hunters must find these predictions particularly confusing. Prairie ducks migrate through that state but, in 1999 for example, Minnesotans had their poorest duck hunting season in history! And what does the 2000 fall flight (down 15 million) say of management's ability to sustain large flights? One wonders what hunters who never experienced a noticeable increase in ducks will think when they are told that ducks are again declining. These hunters become the skeptics and critics of management.

Are the ducks actually out there somewhere? Are hunters just not seeing them? Changes in weather patterns and habitat availability are perennially invoked to explain why ducks stop short of traditional destinations or are delayed getting there. But eventually they have to show up somewhere. Mid-winter counts on the wintering grounds have not been locating the ducks. It is true that ducks are mobile. For example, a component of the canvasback population that once wintered on the Chesapeake Bay may now migrate to the Gulf of Mexico, probably in response to changes in food availability. However, ducks are generally faithful to traditional migration patterns, predictably using the same staging and wintering locations. There is no doubt that changes in weather patterns during the 1990s have been responsible for shifts in the timing of migration for some duck and goose populations. Most prairie ducks, for example, make their exodus from the breeding grounds some time during October, certainly by early November. From year-to-year, the timing of the big push may vary by a week, 10 days, maybe two weeks, but if ducks haven't arrived at locations along their traditional route within a couple of weeks of their usual arrival time, it's a good bet they aren't coming. And it's also a good bet they aren't somewhere else. Hunters lose faith in waterfowl managers who simply say the ducks are out there somewhere.

It seems safe to say that hunters want to see more ducks, but has the prairie "duck factory" reached its capacity to produce ducks? Or, despite degraded conditions, could it produce more if there were more breeding pairs? Even with low individual reproductive rates, more pairs would result in more ducklings being hatched. As a consequence, the fall flight would be bigger. With more pairs breeding, presumably populations recover quicker and become more abundant. Had there been more breeding females, would pintail and scaup populations have recovered as did other depleted species? Pintail habitat didn't decline as quickly or dramatically as their numbers did, and northern habitats where many scaup breed have been relatively stable during their decline. The point is, lack of good quality habitat does not alone explain why some species have remained low.

No reasonable person doubts the critical importance of good quality habitat to reproductive success, but does professional management put too much faith in the belief that more and better habitat will inevitably result in more ducks? Has it relied too much on the miracle of water to bring back prairie ducks? Even if the 1999 fall flight was a record, achieving it required a record wet year that was disastrous to many small farmers. Can management's habitat and population objectives be achieved *only* under such exceptional and rare circumstances?

I believe the visionary men who conceived the North American Waterfowl Management Plan expected it would guide waterfowl management and safeguard the future of waterfowling. Why would there be a need for a fall flight of 100 million ducks if not to sustain harvestable surpluses? However, it seems to me that the Plan has been side-tracked. It has become almost exclusively a habitat plan, not a waterfowl management plan. There is a step-by-step implementation strategy to reach habitat goals, but no such strategy to achieve population goals. Apparently, the assumption is that more and better habitat eventually will translate into more ducks. This is based more on faith than on science. *There are other factors involved.*

The Plan's overwhelming emphasis on habitat was probably inevitable given DU's habitat focus and its pivotal role in the conception and operation of the Plan. But certainly it has gone well beyond its original focus on waterfowl. For example, the 1998 update broadened its scope to include non-game birds and their habitats. The Plan's holistic emphasis on landscapes and its diversity of special interest partners suggest it has evolved into a more broadly-based initiative than ever imagined by its originators. The NAWMP is the most exciting habitat conservation initiative ever implemented by management, and there are benefits to waterfowl and waterfowlers, but it's hard to argue that its primary objective is to manage waterfowl and perpetuate waterfowl hunting.

If having a larger breeding population can increase production and consequently the size of the fall flight, then what's standing in the way of achieving this? One possibility is that we're shooting too many ducks. In fact, concern about over-shooting had begun to build before 1900 when hunters perceived a deterioration in the quality of hunting. Nearly all species were in decline before spring shooting was closed. The Migratory Bird Treaty Act (1918), which provided uniformity in hunting regulations and set federal bag limits and seasons in Canada and the U.S., pointed to a decimation in numbers that had occurred well before the 1930s prairie drought. Both the convention and the establishment of government and private-sector professional waterfowl management were responses to what had become intolerable hunting pressure on waterfowl populations. Since early last century, conservation-minded hunters and writers repeatedly expressed the view that once ducks can fly, the *most serious* predator they have is man.

Managers acknowledge that hunting is the only principal source of mortality that realistically can be controlled, and research has shown that mortality is reduced with lower bag limits and particularly with shorter seasons. However, with few exceptions, there has been little serious relief from the gun for waterfowl. In 1935, Miles Pirnie, Michigan's respected waterfowl manager, criticized the almost five months of hunting pressure (September to mid-January) along the flyways as too much for some duck populations. But what has changed in this regard? Instead, a contentious debate rages over whether or not hunting matters to the stability and growth of populations. It focuses on whether or not ducks can be stock-piled. In other words, will some of the ducks that are saved from the gun survive to breed?

That ducks can be saved for future breeding stock is implicit in the use of hunting regulations that are designed to limit the kill. Presumably, there is a point, a threshold, where any additional mortality from whatever source (predation, disease, hunting, etc.), compromises the recovery potential of the population. But influential biologists have convinced both hunters and managers that ducks can't be stock-piled. They claim that severely restrictive regulations, even closure, would not significantly increase the size of the following year's breeding population. They argue that hunting does not add to natural mortality of ducks and they support their position with complex statistical analyses. It is interesting that many of these same biologists promote hunting as a way of reducing goose populations.

Despite wide acceptance of this aggressively promoted position which is evident in liberal hunting regulations, the stock-piling issue has not been resolved to everyone's satisfaction. While hunting is unlikely to be the *primary cause* of declines, it may be a *contributing* factor. Almost certainly it *slows* or *prevents* the recovery of badly depleted populations. And there is statistical evidence to support this position. This is also common sense. An increasing number of biologists support restrictive regulations as a way of protecting breeding stock. *They believe stock-piling should be given a chance!*

The Adaptive Harvest Management (AHM) strategy assists managers in setting hunting regulations for some species. It is based on the estimated size of the breeding population and its projected reproductive success. Regulations range from liberal to very restrictive, with provisions for closure. Here too, it's assumed that saving ducks from the gun matters, and some level of stock-piling is not only possible, but expected. While the AHM's first responsibility is to protect breeding stock, managers have attempted to maximize the harvest within its framework. The reason for this is that managers believe hunter satisfaction, hence participation, will decline (along with revenues) if regulations are too restrictive. The trouble is, managers understand very little about hunter satisfaction; it has never been determined what "too restrictive" is. Furthermore, managers don't know what responsible hunters will agree to in order to protect duck hunting. I believe that what they want is to see more ducks, not to kill the maximum number of ducks that management deems allowable, especially if the latter comes at the expense of the former. I also believe that they will support restrictive regulations if this could result in more ducks.

The politics of duck hunting make closing the season unlikely. But managers don't need closure to better understand the impact of hunting on duck populations. This can be done by stabilizing regulations-keeping limits and season lengths constant throughout the flyways regardless of breeding conditions. This experiment has never been tried for long enough to be conclusive. When tried formerly, it was abandoned because regulations were set too liberally for current habitat conditions, the result of negotiators scrambling to protect parochial interests. Management should try this again, but with conservative regulations. I believe hunters-we may be down to the "hard core"- would support this. Management needs to know more about the impact of hunting on ducks, despite its being difficult scientifically and politically to do so.

In fairness, too often when managers recommend restrictive hunting regulations, they're modified by politicians to comply with demands of an irresponsible and powerful hunting lobby.

Consequently, the published regulations may be quite different from those recommended by managers and they may not be in the interests of waterfowl conservation. Many of the factors involved in setting regulations have nothing to do with science, and these may distort biological considerations. This is a concern of and frustration for managers who try to do the best they can for the long term interests of waterfowl and, ultimately, for hunters.

Highly detailed hunting regulations give the impression that managers understand precisely the population dynamics of all duck species. In fact, there is a good deal known about prairie-nesting mallards, but there's relatively little known about other mallard populations and about many other species, even important ones like pintail and scaup. Managers know little about green-winged teal, ring necks, goldeneyes, and other species important to "have-not" regions like the Atlantic Flyway. Frequently they are forced by lack of data to make decisions about a species based on what is known about prairie mallards; the biology and habitat of the species in question may bear little resemblance to mallards or to prairie habitats. With few exceptions, the best managers can say about the impact of hunting on many species of ducks, is that it varies with different populations; it probably has little or no impact on some, but significant impact on others.

The prevailing philosophy is to promote liberalizing hunting regulations *whenever* there is a predicted increase in ducks, however modest. The rationale frequently heard is that science hasn't proven that legal hunting has resulted in an overharvest for any duck population. But nor has science proven that hunting isn't preventing the recovery of some depressed populations. Proponents of the former position know that the hunting issue, and many others in waterfowl management, are unlikely ever to be settled by research, at least not until this becomes a priority with senior bureaucrats. In the meantime, hunting regulations should be more conservative, especially in regions where there is high hunting mortality.

Managers have known about the decline in scaup for almost two decades. Yet, serious research to investigate this decline began only after populations dropped to historic lows. Even then, this research focused heavily on issues related to habitat and reproduction, with little attention hunting mortality. Furthermore, hunting regulations for scaup have remained relatively liberal during their decline. The story is similar for pintails. Despite a severe prairie drought in 1933 and 1934, the usually progressive state of Michigan allowed a daily limit of 12 pintails, but it restricted the limit for teal and most diving ducks to five birds. During the 1970s, the point system allowed hunters to shoot additional birds of species that presumably could absorb increased pressure. Even after pintail populations began to decline, they received virtually no special protection. Pintails of *both* sexes fell victim to heavy shooting. The point system almost certainly compounded the negative effect that the 1980s drought had on population recruitment. This could be one reason, perhaps a very important one, why pintail populations have not recovered despite improved habitat conditions. Who will ever know?

Unfortunately, the acrimonious and divisive debate over the impact of hunting on ducks has damaged management's credibility, and it has confused and disillusioned hunters. This issue has also been a source of irritation between DU and the government wildlife services. The USFWS has to resist a vigorous hunter lobby and political interference when it recommends conservative hunting regulations. Unfortunately it does this without the support of DU, which could carry considerable weight.

Historically, DU has avoided issues related to hunting, reiterating always that its focus and contribution to waterfowl hunting is habitat conservation and management. The ducks will come back, DU says, if there is adequate habitat. But in fact, DU has tacitly supported *liberal* hunting regulations by refusing to implicate hunting as a potentially significant mortality factor. When pressed on this, the response has been that hunting, (at current harvest rates, whatever they are) doesn't add to natural mortality and it doesn't significantly affect the recovery potential of populations. Historically, DU has not supported, much less promoted, restrictive hunting regulations, and it has done little research on this. Instead, it typically recommends voluntary restraint by hunters when populations are low. One suspects that DU's unwavering focus on the "motherhood" issue of habitat-who can argue against protecting habitat?-has sometimes been to the detriment of waterfowl conservation, and ultimately to waterfowling. Securing habitat is *not always* the best expenditure of conservation dollars especially if one of the objectives is perpetuating waterfowl hunting.

Telling the hunter that killing ducks does not matter, plays into the hands of a small but powerful component of the waterfowling community that is motivated by greed and selfishness. These people apparently have difficulty viewing duck hunting from a flyway perspective, much less a continental one. Rather, their parochial view seems to be that if they don't get their share, then someone else will. Restraint is a foreign concept.

It's important to be honest about who the hunter is. As a group, we truly have been conservationists and we've paid our way, indeed far more than any other outdoor group. Who but hunters would have started an organization like DU, and where would DU be today were it not for hunters? Because of us, there is more wetland and other habitat available to wildlife and everyone benefits from what we've protected. But we've sometimes idealized the hunter, making him something he isn't. As individuals, hunters span the spectrum. I believe most are unselfish and ethical people who derive important benefits from hunting. But there are those who are irresponsible, selfish, and motivated by greed. These people sully the image of all hunters and the waterfowl community would be better off without them.

Would management have closed hunting for beleaguered species like pintails had the prairie drought continued? How far would it have let them and other troubled species decline? Although this was a period of more restrictive regulations, why weren't pintail regulations standardized at *very restrictive (low limits and short seasons)* to see if this would help their recovery? *If ever a duck needed a break, it's the pintail!* I believe hunters had become accustomed to conservative regulations and would have continued to support them, especially if they were told this might result in obvious increases.

While at Delta in the 1960s, I remember conservation-minded biologists saying that 10 million mallards should be the benchmark for the breeding population. Below that, they believed, the population was out of its "comfort zone" and restrictive regulations should then be considered. They were concerned that management was adjusting population goals downward to conform with reality, and they predicted that five million would become the new "magic" number. Perhaps they were unnecessarily cautious, but population figures for mallards have been in this "comfort zone" only three times since 1955. Even when mallards declined to under five million (1985), many managers were still saying that the current rate of hunting mortality would not have a significant effect on populations.

In general, management attempts to base its decisions and policies on the best available scientific information. However, sometimes important decisions must be made on inconclusive data, or worse, on no information at all. Unfortunately, precise estimates of the fall flight and detailed hunting regulations give the mistaken impression that the harvest can be precisely predicted and controlled. Research may eventually provide managers with predictive harvest models for all important species, but this is a long way off. In reality, managers may never know enough about some species to develop reliable models. Waterfowl management is not and probably never will be the precise application of scientific principles that the profession would like it to be.

Decisions based on untested assumptions or inadequate information are often little more than educated guesses. At such times, decision-makers should err, if indeed they err, on the side of caution. Management should acknowledge its limitations and that these limitations frequently thwart its efforts to manage effectively. It may also be wrong about even long standing practices and policies. It should be prepared to have its assumptions challenged, especially when they fly in the face of common sense, such as when experienced hunters and biologists are skeptical about the reported size of the fall flight. The observations of responsible people cannot be simply dismissed as anecdotal, and therefore of little value. To remain credible, professional waterfowl management has to be honest and straightforward about what it can do.

Waterfowl management is as much an art as it is a science. The science is usually most apparent in the management of populations, while the art, the much harder part, is in managing people. In fact, wildlife management has long been recognized as primarily the management of people. Why would ducks need to be managed if it weren't for hunting? It may be that waterfowl management will always be first and foremost political, not scientific. The science is usually straightforward and readily understandable by most people, if properly explained. It is not "rocket science" and it usually conforms to common sense. The trouble is that professional waterfowl management has lost touch with the hunter, its "client," its original and arguably still its main reason for existing. Indeed, management seems to know very little about the behavior, motivation and expectations of hunters. And management has not been educating hunters and keeping them accurately and honestly informed about what is happening with ducks and duck hunting.

For some people, the fact we still have harvestable "surpluses" of ducks in North America is proof that waterfowl are being managed successfully. However, Europe has nothing like our professional management system yet, at the millennium, apparently it too was enjoying abundant waterfowl populations.

It seems to me that there are two legitimate concerns about the performance of professional waterfowl management. After seven decades, DU, the continent's leader in wetland conservation and premier manager of ducks, still can't estimate reliably how many additional ducks it puts into the fall flight from all of its intensive management and acres of protected habitat. And the government wildlife services, whose responsibility it is to protect and conserve breeding stock, still don't know reliably what impact hunting has on the recovery potential of duck populations. By fostering the notion that it is in the business of producing ducks, and by promising hunters more than it can realistically be expected to deliver, professional waterfowl management leaves itself open to constant criticism.

Waterfowling Tomorrow?

During the prairie drought of the 1980s and early 1990s, there was a predictable decline in both ducks and hunters, but the number of active hunters has always tracked the fall flight forecast. Bad news about ducks keeps hunters home. So what was happening when duck populations began to increase in the latter half of the 1990s, culminating in the much anticipated and widely publicized record flight of ducks and geese at the turn of the century? There was an increase in American duck hunters, though not what was expected, but the Canadian waterfowling community, which had fallen to an historic low, continued to decline. For example, in the prairie province of Manitoba, where hunting regulations were liberal and opportunities excellent, there were only about 20% of the hunters there'd been in the 1970s. Almost as many Americans as Canadians bought licenses to hunt in Manitoba. The decline was incremental and insidious, attributable to many things, but it has resulted in a crisis. How could the waterfowling community have let this happen, and what are the implications for the future of duck hunting in North America?

Waterfowl hunting has always required exceptional dedication and commitment. It usually takes more time, energy and planning than other type of hunting, and it may require considerable financial outlay for equipment and access. It never attracted more than a small proportion of total hunters. However, this is only one reason why veteran hunters have been hanging up their guns and the waterfowling community is failing to attract new recruits.

Waterfowlers fall into two broad categories, those who are concerned about the future of the tradition and those, probably the majority, who give this little thought. Buying a license and complying with regulations are the only responsibilities the latter acknowledge. I fell into that category for far too long. Those who care about the future get involved in the many ways necessary to support and protect the tradition. Perhaps these hunters more fully appreciate the benefits they derive from hunting, and therefore feel they owe it something in return.

Indeed, the origins of professional waterfowl management can be traced to concerned hunters who in the 1930s recognized the need for a system to protect waterfowl and waterfowling. The partnership that developed between professional management and hunters was a mutual dependency and, for the system to work effectively, hunters had to be involved in the management process. However, it seems from early on, the essential nature of the partnership slowly began to erode. Hunters began taking the system for granted, expecting that it would always protect their interests, whether they got involved or not. This prompted Edward C. Janes to write in his 1954 book, *Hunting Ducks and Geese,* that the future of waterfowl hunting was in jeopardy because of "apathy, greed and complacency of sportsmen." It seems that having a professional system to look out for them made some hunters "smug and self-satisfied."

On the other hand, professional management began to grow and diversify, becoming less responsive and accessible to hunters. In fact, for many hunters the face of government management was that of the law enforcement officer who, especially in the U.S., was there only to enforce laws and, too often it seemed, harass hunters and infringe on their freedom. They were not there to conserve the resource by informing and educating hunters. As for private-sector management, the fundraiser was usually it's only contact with hunters. While professional management was becoming increasingly bureaucratic and aloof, the hunter was withdrawing and, though not exactly adversaries, the partnership was under stress and an estrangement was developing. The critical-minded hunter was losing respect for both his fellow hunters who took advantage of the system, and for professional management.

The estrangement could be seen in the way hunters who wanted to get involved were denied the opportunity to participate. Professional management was becoming secretive, uncommunicative, and sometimes patronizing, telling the hunter only what it decided he needed to know. Seemingly, it did not respect the average hunter's intelligence and willingness to act responsibly when provided with guidance and leadership. Professional management was becoming dismissive of hunters and unwilling to listen to their concerns. Waterfowl management was becoming the domain of the professional.

For most of their existence, the USFWS and CWS were almost exclusively in the business of waterfowl management. However, during the 1980s this began to change. Largely as a result of increased demand from other interest groups, the federal wildlife services began shifting their priorities away from waterfowl and their habitats, to other wildlife and habitats. This meant less effort and fewer resources were going into sustaining duck hunting, the beginning of a trend that increasingly puts the onus to protect its interests back on the waterfowling community.

Presumably, the CWS and USFWS will always have the ultimate responsibility for managing migratory birds; it is their legal mandate. However, the focus of federal, state and provincial wildlife services will shift more and more to harvest management (regulating hunting), with much less effort and resources going into production management (intensive management of habitat and populations). This has been happening for some time on the Canadian prairies where, for example, the provincial wildlife services have essentially left waterfowl and wetland management to DU, while they attend to resident (non-migratory) wildlife and their habitats. This division of labor between governments and the private-sector has always existed, but it will become more pronounced and obvious. Indeed, there is speculation that the management of geese will be shifted from the federal government to the states and provinces, and DU will become the "official" manager of the continent's ducks.

The composition of the wildlife services is also changing. At one time, most waterfowl professionals came from a hunting background. Those who didn't, usually saw hunting as consistent with their view of conservation. They also recognized the contribution hunters were making to habitat conservation, and they acknowledged the partnership between professional management and hunters. The concept of a partnership has largely disappeared and some professionals don't know it once existed. The problem is compounded by many of the new generation of managers being chosen for the wrong reasons, those reflecting political correctness and bureaucratic willingness, not interest in or knowledge of wildlife and its management. Indeed, some people within the wildlife services are philosophically opposed to hunting. This means there is now much less personal commitment to waterfowl hunting and less institutional interest in perpetuating it. The fact that waterfowlers have played an important role in wetland conservation will not protect the hunting tradition. The bottom line is the federal wildlife services will not be looking out for the waterfowl hunter as they once did.

Surely the private-sector will step into the breach...? In the hunter's eyes, DU, the continent's biggest and most influential waterfowling association, has historically had a higher profile than the government wildlife services as the molder of attitudes and the defender of the waterfowling tradition. Indeed, this has sometimes been a source of competitive tension between them. DU undoubtedly continues to serve the hunter, but the waterfowling community is a declining market. On the other hand, habitat conservation has developed into a lucrative business that has the potential to grow enormously. DU has always been a survivor, slowly shifting its original focus from ducks for hunters, to wetlands for ducks and conservationists, to landscapes for wildlife and indeed, for everyone. Arguably, these changes in focus are good for wildlife conservation, and in some ways good for ducks too, *but they also make economic sense.* Whatever it was in the beginning, DU has become a business and its policies and decisions increasingly reflect this reality. DU will survive whether or not there are duck hunters, perhaps with a new name that isn't so confining and doesn't carry unwanted baggage. It seems to me this line of thinking requires further investigation.

At one time, DU was obviously a duck hunter's organization -unquestionably the waterfowling community's advocate-and everyone knew it. The decade of the 1980s saw unprecedented membership growth, mostly non-hunters. This trend in membership has continued, especially since implementation of the NAWMP, creating something of an identity crisis for DU. Currently DU is serving two masters, which have decidedly different and sometimes conflicting expectations of it, and they may be on a collision course. DU is trying to reconcile the demands of both constituencies while trying to satisfy its dual objectives-habitat for non-hunters, ducks for hunters, DU may be able to continue serving these two masters, but if some day it has to make a choice between them, I fear that hunters will lose out.

In the meantime, DU is characteristically trying to avoid controversy. It is being politically correct in a social environment that frowns on hunting. Ironically, at a time when DU's stepped-up management efforts (on the Canadian prairie, for example) are benefitting hunters, it is withdrawing from the hunter, albeit perhaps reluctantly. Where, for example, was DU while the bottom was falling out of the Canadian waterfowling community, something that didn't happen over-night? It was promoting itself as a "conservation company."

DU is publicly committed to basing its management decisions on the best scientific information available. Research has shown predator management to be an effective way of increasing duck production, and this is beneficial to hunters. Yet, DU has withdrawn its support for predator management, saying that its policy, indeed its mission, is to secure, conserve and manage habitat. DU believes that ducks are more likely to breed successfully as a consequence of its habitat initiatives. It will not kill a predator to save a duck for a hunter to shoot. Perhaps its scientists have decided there isn't enough scientific evidence to support predator management. But might its unwillingness to support this management tool be coming from its policy makers? Administrators who don't want to risk offending the non-hunting membership (in places, more than half of its supporters). I fear DU will be forced to decide between its two constituencies. The pressure to do so will probably come from corporate sponsors whose support for DU is their way of promoting a responsible image with a public that is becoming less supportive of hunting. If this is true, do duck hunters want DU to be the "official" manager of the continent's ducks?

DU is not prepared to publicly declare its support for hunting, much less promote it. Critics say that this should not be surprising given that DU has rarely lobbied on tough, controversial issues of any kind. This is an interesting criticism. While DU supports hunting through its Green Wing program and its magazine, its promotion of itself through advertising to the general public in newspapers, radio and T.V., studiously avoids *any* reference to hunting. To the public, DU is simply a habitat conservation organization.

This drifting apart of professional management and the waterfowling community comes at a pivotal juncture in waterfowling's history. Two major problems threaten its future. By far the bigger and more immediate problem is the loss of interest in waterfowl hunting, part of a more general decline in hunting interest. The second problem is a decline in public support for hunting. These problems may be linked and rooted in increasing urbanization and changing social attitudes. Whatever the underlying causes, if the waterfowling community is to have a future, it will have to find ways to convince both potential hunters and the public of the individual and societal values of waterfowling. Unfortunately, the waterfowling community has not been doing this. The failure to recruit youth is only partly attributable to the anti-hunting lobby, increased public concern over killing animals, and issues of gun ownership. More importantly, I don't believe duck hunting is any longer viewed by young people as satisfying. If the waterfowling community can't convince young people of the value of hunting-for example, what it meant to me when I was growing up -then it will wither and die.

So who is responsible for promoting the individual and social values of hunting, for recruiting new hunters and educating the public about hunting? Although government and private-sector management have traditionally done this, they haven't been effective. In many ways, the independent outdoor media have done more to keep hunters and the public informed about wildlife and its management issues, including hunting. At the same time, the media have been critics of professional management; watchdogs that held it accountable for its policies, programs, practices, and its claims. It applauded what was positive and panned what wasn't. The outdoor media have always been an essential communication link between the professional and the hunter. Historically, it was through the independent media that hunters learned about the partnership between managers and hunters.

At one time, the outdoor media wrote for a diverse readership, but this is no longer so. It still has considerable influence over the attitudes and behavior of hunters, but it has lost much of its former ability to keep hunting issues before the public. Increasingly, it has been writing only for hunters and fishermen. And even then the emphasis has been on how, where and when to hunt or fish, only rarely on ethics, philosophy, and issues of conservation. This criticism seems especially true of outdoor television, much of which is highly commercialized. Both the waterfowling community and professional management need the independent outdoor media to provide a reasonable, fair and accurate voice that is committed to truly communicating and educating hunters and the public. If it is to re-capture its traditional role of educator, the media has to be well informed. Unfortunately, this is not always the case.

To be informed the media have to communicate with professional management. That this is rare shouldn't be surprising. There is little meaningful communication within professional management. The researchers, managers, wardens, administrators, and others go their separate ways, rarely getting together to discuss fundamental issues. The meaningful communication needed to make the system work as effectively as it could is lacking.

Few professionals consider it their responsibility to communicate with the hunter, the public, or the media. In fact, most *shun* this contact. Valid complaints go both ways, but in general, the media criticize professional management for being unresponsive and inaccessible, as well as secretive, defensive and unwilling to be self-critical. The media point out that they put their reputations and sometimes their jobs on the line every time they communicate with the public, but wildlife professionals rarely allow themselves to be in this situation.

This lack of communication reflects a poor understanding and respect for the role others play in waterfowl management. The independent outdoor media are an essential liaison between professional management and the hunter. Hunters need a well-informed media to help them cope with the social, economic, political and biological realities that affect them. The problems confronting the Canadian waterfowling community would be less acute had there been a more vigorous and influential outdoor media.

I believe the spring snow goose hunt provides an example of poor communication. There isn't strong support for it within the waterfowling community, and many respected people in the outdoor media warn against it. They're concerned about greed, lack of sportsmanship and devaluation of the birds, as well as commercialization of the hunt. Indeed, some American outfitters see goose hunting possibilities in Canada as a free-trade issue. This is a sensitive issue that risks squandering the goodwill that exists between American and Canadian hunters. However, government wildlife services and most private-sector waterfowl associations promote the spring snow goose hunt.

The problem with taking restrictions off hunters is that people don't see degraded habitat in the remote north, they see dead geese close to home, and for most, these geese are not simply statistics-birds to be culled. The public sees hunters killing large numbers of geese without the usual sporting restraints, and this introduces the question of hunting ethics. There are right and wrong ways to kill, and how hunters do their killing matters to the public and to other hunters. Unrestricted shooting of snow geese risks over-stepping people's sense of fair play. A comment of a friend who'd returned from the spring hunt in Québec summed it up for me: *"It's not hunting."*

Most people don't care one way or the other about hunting. They tolerate it and probably will continue to do so if they believe hunters are truly hunting and not merely killing. Professional management has the legal right to use the "conservation hunt" to control snow goose populations. However, the waterfowling community, already small and declining, may lose credibility. Few people think about hunting unless some issue gets their attention. The snow goose cull could be an issue that forces them to take sides.

Hunting ethics should be an essential part of hunter education; stressed as much as safety, the usual and sometimes only focus. But whose responsibility is it to teach this? Some say the issue of ethics is personal, and teaching ethical behavior isn't the responsibility or indeed the business of government wildlife agencies. In my opinion, this is their obligation. It's a dimension of management's challenge to both serve and lead the hunter-part of the *art* of management. However, there can be no question that representatives of the hunting community-the clubs, associations, etc., must accept this as a fundamental responsibility. Traditionally, the outdoor media have had a strong presence in this regard-some might even consider the media to be the ethical conscience of the waterfowling community. Whatever the case, leaving hunter education to wildlife professionals has not worked, and the hunting fraternity has not compensated. It seems that if individuals don't consider teaching ethical behavior their responsibility, then it doesn't happen.

It also seems inevitable that the waterfowling community itself will have to take greater responsibility for protecting its interests and future. I suspect that most waterfowlers look to DU to do this, and there is no question that it could be much more effective than it is. DU has a continental presence, a positive image with hunters, managers, governments and the public, and it has decades of experience in waterfowl management. It also has an excellent team of management and research professionals. Because of them, we know considerably more about waterfowl and wetlands, and about their management, than would otherwise be the case. Perhaps things would be different if these people were more influential within the DU hierarchy and were more involved with determining policy, but they aren't. In truth, unless DU continues to secure and manage habitat, do research, and manage ducks for hunters, the future of North American waterfowl hunting will be substantially compromised. Unfortunately, I don't believe that DU has a strategy to protect waterfowling. And what if it is becoming less involved with duck hunting? What if it really is, as I suspect, unwilling to promote the values of hunting and to be waterfowling's unabashed advocate? Instead of focusing almost exclusively on fundraising, DU could be taking advantage of its widespread presence in communities not only to organize hunters, but to educate both them and the public. Would this, for example, have helped prevent the crisis in Canadian waterfowling?

We know that community-based waterfowl associations can effectively promote hunting. For example, the South Carolina Waterfowl Association annually brings 8,000 to 9,000 kids to its education center to mingle with biologists, landowners and hunters. The Wetland Habitat Alliance of Texas (WHAT) influences the attitude of landowners toward wildlife and public hunting. It works with the

U.S. Department of Agriculture and the Forest Service to encourage rural kids (4H and Future Farmers of America) to develop a broadly based land ethic which includes hunting. The hook for getting participation is summed up by the motto "learn by doing." WHAT also takes its message to urban kids. During the 1990s, its volunteer-based Wildlife Clinics introduced 128,000 school children to its land-use philosophy. It is at the community level where one encounters the committed volunteer who is a valuable resource for professional management and the waterfowling community.

State waterfowl associations have established strong community support through their chapters and they've strengthened relationships with other organizations that share common goals. For example, the Minnesota Waterfowl Association (MWA), whose motto is "We don't duck waterfowl issues," protected hunting as part of a coalition dedicated to safeguarding many aspects of Minnesota's outdoor heritage. A recent constitutional amendment to protect the privilege to hunt, fish and trap, received 77% of the popular vote. MWA also provided leadership when it established the Coalition of Minnesota Conservation Organizations. It also used government legislation to obtain major funding increases for the state's Department of Natural Resources. Lack of participation in the political process has been a serious failure of Canadian waterfowl hunters.

The prairie drought of the 1930s was obviously a crisis that threatened ducks and duck hunting. It was also obvious to everyone that more control over ducks and hunters was needed. Both had to be managed. The ambitious system of government and private-sector professional management that resulted, recognized that hunter satisfaction is linked to having plenty of ducks. Consequently, management's primary objective and challenge was to conserve adequate habitat and breeding stock to achieve this. Hunters now had a professional system to protect their interests and future.

I suppose it was inevitable that government wildlife services would become big, impersonal bureaucracies, just as it was inevitable for DU to become primarily a business. But was it inevitable that both would become so distanced from their roots, the duck hunter? This has left the waterfowling community without a well thought-out and carefully planned strategy to protect its future. In my opinion, there is a leadership void in the continent's waterfowling community and it won't be filled by the government wildlife services or the NAWMP. Who then does the hunter turn to for support? Who is the waterfowler's advocate?

What's happened in Canada should have a sobering influence on the entire North American waterfowling community. I think it less likely that such a decline in hunters will occur in the U.S., where hunters have always been more politically active and involved with management. But there are disturbing things happening in the U.S. and hunters there will have to be vigilant to avoid going down the same road as the Canadian waterfowling community. It won't be anti-hunting legislation that ends waterfowl hunting in Canada and the U.S., it will be hunter apathy, compounded by greed.

And lest American hunters think that the decline in Canadian waterfowlers will not jeopardize the future of their waterfowl hunting, consider this. Who except Canadian waterfowl hunters will lobby for changes in land use policies that benefit ducks? Who but hunters will lobby for other things important to sustaining waterfowling along the flyways? Without a strong, politically active hunting constituency in Canada, there will be little government interest in sustaining harvestable surpluses of ducks, especially for Americans to shoot. Only hunters are truly interested in protecting and perpetuating the waterfowling tradition. What has happened in Canada is bound to have negative repercussions for American hunters.

The North American waterfowling community needs strong leadership to unify and to provide direction. If not DU, then who else can and will do this? Will one of the state associations like that of California, South Carolina or Minnesota step up and do so? The Delta Waterfowl Foundation is each year expanding its membership and influence. Can it meet the challenge and become a continental presence? Somebody has to do this soon.

During the last October of the millennium, my boyhood friend Robin Casgrain visited me in Nova Scotia to hunt and visit with his son Peter, who was studying at the university where I teach. Early one frosty morning, Peter and Robin were huddled in a blind at the edge of a tidal marsh. I'd been saving this favorite spot for such an occasion. The wind was blowing hard against their backs and the tide was rising. There was also a good flight of birds coming to the cove to feed. Everything was unfolding as planned.

I was nearby with Calli, watching and hoping the ducks would decoy to Robin and Peter. Robin and I had grown up hunting black ducks, but Peter had only seen the odd one on the St. Lawrence. He was hoping to shoot his first black duck, and the birds cooperated. His first black was in fact one of a double. A pair flew into the cove and immediately locked up on the half dozen decoys bobbing in the choppy water in front of the blind. As they hovered in the wind looking for a place to pitch, Peter stood and killed the drake with his first shot. He missed the hen with his second, but killed her as she climbed into the wind.

Calli made the retrieves and the three of us admired the birds and savoured the moment. Robin's face beamed with pride. The flight was in full tilt by the time we settled back into our blinds. Robin and Peter shot another four blacks, and Robin got a couple of the Nova Scotia greenwings he'd hoped to shoot.

We must have seen at least 200 birds during the morning, and many showed sufficient interest in our decoys to keep us continually excited. While Calli and I watched the show, I wondered what the future would hold for Peter. How many more generations of hunters will thrill to a morning flight of wild ducks coming to a secluded marsh? I knew I couldn't think of anywhere I'd rather be, and I was pretty sure Peter, Robin, and Calli felt the same way.

Epilogue

Edward C. Janes had it right in 1954 when he warned that the future of waterfowl hunting was in jeopardy because of the apathy and greed of sportsmen. There have always been people who work tirelessly for waterfowling, but Jane's observation unfortunately applies to a large component of the waterfowling community, and it is probably timeless.

In my opinion, North American waterfowling's future is uncertain. Although having a professional waterfowl management system provides some security, there have been troubling changes in both the government wildlife services and the waterfowling community's private-sector representatives. These changes should make waterfowlers pause and think hard about their future. Are waterfowling's traditional advocates as dedicated to perpetuating its future as they once were? Are they doing everything that's needed to protect it? The decline in the Canadian waterfowling community is an obvious indication that all is not well.

Janes puts the responsibility for protecting the future squarely on the shoulders of the hunter. And when you think about it, who else can address the issues of greed and apathy? However, the waterfowling community also needs strong, visionary leadership. The time is right for a renewed vision of the future. We have to keep what is good of tradition and change what needs to be changed. Surely the waterfowling community is in dire straits if during this time of unprecedented personal and corporate prosperity, money is standing in the way of making these changes.

If this book has raised questions, as I hope it has, raise them in turn with other hunters and with government and private-sector professionals. And insist on answers that make sense, because they should make sense if they're good answers. Take responsibility for making change happen. Don't leave what must be done to someone else.

Bibliography

Adaptive Harvest Management and Considerations for the 1995-96 Duck Season. Office of Migratory Bird Management (USFWS). Arlington, VA.

Anderson, D.R. and K.P. Burnham. 1976. "Population ecology of the mallard VI. The effect of exploitation on survival." USFWS Resource Publication 128.

Ankney, C.D. and R.C. Bailey. 1989. "Increasing mallards, decreasing American black ducks - no evidence for cause and effect: a reply." Journal Wildlife Management. 53: 1072-1075.

Beckford, P. 1926. *Thoughts on Hunting.* New York: Alfred A. Knopf.

Begbie, E. (ed.). 1989. *The New Wildfowler.* 3rd ed. London: Stanley Paul,

Bélanger, L. and J. Bédard. 1989. "Responses of staging greater snow geese to human disturbance." Journal Wildlife Management. 53: 713-719.

Bellrose, F.C. 1980. *Ducks, Geese and Swans of North America.* Harrisburg: Stackpole Books.

Berkes, F. 1982. *Waterfowl management and northern native peoples with reference to Cree hunters of James Bay.* Musk Ox 30: 23: 35.

Boyd, H. and G.H. Finney (eds.). 1978. "Migratory game bird hunters and hunting in Canada." Canadian Wildlife Service Rep. Series No. 43:

Boyd, H. and C. Hyslop. 1986. "Effects of hunting on survival of American black ducks: a response." Wildlife Society Bulliten 14: 328-329.

Burnham, K.P. and D.R. Anderson. 1984. "Estimating the effect of hunting on annual survival rates of adult mallards." Journal Wildlife Management. 48: 350-361.

Burns, M. 1996. *The Private Eye: Observing Snow Geese.* Vancouver: UBC Press.

Camp, R.R. 1952. *Duck Boats: Blinds: Decoys and Eastern Seaboard Wildfowling.* A.A. New York: Knopf.

Cartmill, M.A. 1993. *A View to a Death in the Morning: Hunting and Nature Through History.* Cambridge: Harvard University . Press.

Connett, E.V. 1947. *Duck Shooting Along the Atlantic Tidewater.* New York: Bonanza Books.

Cooch, E.G., D.B. Lank, R.F. Rockwell, and F. Corke. 1989. "Long term decline in fecundity in a snow goose population: evidence for density dependence?" Journal Animal Ecology. 58: 711-726.

Cooke, F., R. Rockwell, and D. Lank. 1995. *The Snow Geese of La Pérouse Bay: A Study of Natural Selection in the Wild.* New York: Oxford Univ. Press.

Cooke, F. and D.S. Sulzbach. 1978. "Mortality, emigration and separation of mated snow geese." Journal Wildlife Management. 42: 271-280.

Conroy, M.J. and D.G. Krementz. 1986. "Incorrect inferences regarding the effects of hunting on survival rates of American black ducks." Wildlife Society Bulletin. 14: 326-328.

Conroy, M.J., G.G. Burnes, R.W. Bethke, and T.D. Nudds. 1989. "Increasing mallards, decreasing American black ducks - no evidence for cause and effect: a comment." Journal Wildlife Management. 53: 1065-1071.

Conroy, M.J. and D.G. Krementz. 1986. "Incorrect inferences regarding the effects of hunting on survival rates of American black ducks." Wildlife Society Bulletin. 14: 326-328.

Cowardin, L.M. and D.H. Johnson. 1979. "Mathematics and mallard management." Journal Wildlife Management. 43: 18-35.

Day, A.M. 1949. *North American Waterfowl.* New York and Harrisburg: Stackpole and Heck, Inc.

Decker, D.J., T.C. Brown, and R.J. Gutierrez. 1980. "Further insights into the multiple satisfactions approach to hunter management." Wildlife Society Bulletin. 8: 323-331.

Decker, D.J., J.W. Enck, and T.L. Brown. 1993. "The future of hunting - will we pass on the heritage?" In: Proc. 2nd Governor's Symp. on North America's Hunting Heritage. Pierre, S.D.

Enck, J.W., B.L. Swift, and D.J. Decker. 1993. "Reasons for decline in duck hunting: insights from New York." Wildlife Society Bulletin. 21: 10-21.

Evrard, J.O. 1970. "Assessing and improving the ability of hunters to identify flying waterfowl." Journal Wildlife Management. 34: 114-126.

Farrington, S.K. Jr. 1945. *The Ducks Came Back: the Story of Ducks Unlimited.* New York: Coward-McCann.

Feierabend, J.S. "The black duck: an international resource on trial in the United States." Wildlife Society Bulletin 12: 128-134.

Francis, C.M. and F. Cook. 1992. "Sexual differences in survival and recovery rates of lesser snow geese." Journal Wildlife. Management. 56: 287-296.

Francis, C.M., M.H. Richards, F. Cooke, and R. Rockwell. 1992. "Long term changes in survival rates of lesser snow geese." *Ecology 73:* 1346-62.

Frederickson, L.H. et al. (eds.). 1990. "Proceedings 1988 North American Wood Duck Symposium." University. Missouri, Columbia.

Furtman, M. 1991. *On the Wings of a North Wind.* Harrisburg: Stackpole,

Grandy, J.W. 1983. "The North American Black Duck (Anas rubripes): A Case Study of 28 Years of Failure in American Wildlife Management." International Journal for the Study of Animal Problems. Vol. 4, 35 pp.

Gray, B.T. and R.M. Kaminski. 1989. "Illegal harvest of waterfowl - what do we know?" Trans North American Wildlife and Natural Resource Conference. 53: 333-340.

Gray, B.T. and R.M. Kaminski. 1993. "Assessing a mail survey to estimate illegal waterfowl hunting." Wildlife Society Bulletin 21: 188-193.

Grinnell, G.B. 1901. "American Duck Shooting." *Forest and Stream Publ.,* New York.

Hanson, H.C. 1965. *The Giant Canada Goose.* Carbondale and Edwardsville: Southern Illinois University Press.

Hargrove, E.C. 1989. *Foundations of Environmental Ethics.* Englewood Cliffs, NJ: Prentice Hall.

Hawley, A.W.L. (ed.) 1993. "Commercialization and Wildlife Management: Dancing with the Devil." Krieger Pub. Co., Malabar, FA.

Heilner, V.C. 1939. *A Book on Duck Shooting.* New York: Alfred A. Knopf.

Hestbeck, J.B., D.H. Rusch, and R.A. Malecki. 1990. "Estimating population parameters for geese from band-recovery and mark-recapture data." Trans North American Wildlife and Natural Resource Conference 55: 350-373.

Hestbeck, J.B. 1993. "Survival of northern pintails banded during winter in North America." Journal Wildlife Management. 57: 590-597.

Hestbeck, J.B. 1994. "Survival of Canada geese banded in winter in the Atlantic Flyway." Journal Wildlife Management. 58: 748-756.

Hochbaum, H.A. 1944. *The Canvasback on a Prairie Marsh.* Harrisburg: Stackpole. and New York: Wildlife Management. Institute

Jackson, R., R. Norton, and R. Anderson. 1979. "Improving ethical behavior in hunters." Trans North American Wildlife and Natural Resource Conference 44: 306-318.

Janes, E.C. 1954. *Hunting Ducks and Geese.* Harrisburg: Stackpole Co.

Johnson, F.A., B.K. Williams, J.D. Nichols, J.E. Hines, W.L. Kendall, G.W. Smith, and D.F. Caithamer. 1993. "Developing and adaptive management strategy for harvesting waterfowl in North America." Trans North American Wildlife and Natural Resource Conference 58: 565-583.

Johnsgard, P.A. 1974. *Song of the North Wind.* Anchor Press/Doubleday. New York.

Kimball, C.F. 1970. "Hunter party violation rates during special teal and regular hunting seasons 1965-1969." USFWS Migr. Bird Population Stn. Admin. Rept. No. 196, 8pp.

Kortright, F.H. 1942. *The Ducks, Geese and Swans of North America.* Washington, DC: American Wildlife Institute.

Leitch, W.G. 1978. *Ducks and Men: Forty Years of Co-operation in Conservation.* Ducks Unlimited (Canada). Winnipeg.

Leopold, A. 1933. *Game Management.* New York: Charles Scribner's Sons.

Leopold, A. 1966. *A Sand County Almanac.* New York: Oxford University Press.

Linduska, J.P. (ed.). 1964. *Waterfowl Tomorrow.* U.S. Printing Office, Washington, DC.

Lynch, J. 1984. "Escape from mediocrity: a new approach to American waterfowl hunting regulations." *Wildfowl* 35: 5-13.

MacNab, J. 1983. "Wildlife management as scientific experimentation." Wildlife Society Bulletin 11: 397-401.

Marchington, J. 1980. *The History of Wildfowling*. London: A and C Black,

Matthews, G.V.T. 1990. "Managing Waterfowl Populations." IWRB Special Public. No. 12. Slimbridge, UK.

Migoya, R. and G.A. Baldassarre. 1995. "Winter survival of female northern pintails in Sinaloa, Mexico." Journal Wildlife. Management. 59: 16-22.

Nelson, L. Jr. and J.B. Low. 1977. "Acceptance of the 1970-71 point system season by hunters." Wildlife Society Bulletin 5: 52-55.

Nichols, J.D., M.J. Conroy, D.R. Anderson, and K.P. Burnham. 1984. "Compensatory mortality in waterfowl populations: a review of the evidence and implications of research and management." Trans North American Wildlife and Natural Resource Conference 49: 535-554.

Ogilvie, M.A. 1978. *Wild Geese*. Vermillion, SD, 1996: Buteo Books.

Ortega y Gasset, J. 1972. *Meditations on Hunting*. New York: Charles Scribner's Sons.

Perry, R. 1943. *At the Turn of the Tide*. London: Lindsay Drummond.

Phillips, J.C. and F.C. Lincoln. 1930. *American Waterfowl: Their Present Situation and the Outlook for Their Future*. Boston and New York: Houghton Mifflin

Pirnie, M.D. 1935. *Michigan Waterfowl Management*. Lansing: Dept. of Conservation.

Pitman, I. 1947. *And Clouds Flying*. London: Faber and Faber.

Raveling, D.G. and M.E. Heitmeyer. 1989. "Relationships of population size and recruitment of pintails to habitat conditions and harvest." Journal Wildlife Management. 53: 1088-1103.

Reiger, J.F. 1975. *American Sportsmen and the Origins of Conservation*. New York: Winchester Press.

Reiger, G. 1980. *The Wings of Dawn*. New York: Stein and Day.

Reynolds, R.E., B.G. Peterjohn, J.R. Sauer, and T.L. Shaffer. 1994. "Conservation Reserve Program: benefit for grassland birds in the northern plains." Trans North American Wildlife and Natural Resource Conference. 59: 328-336.

Ringelman, J.K. 1997. "Effects of Regulations and Duck Abundance on Hunter Participation and Satisfaction." Trans North American Wildlife and Natural Resource Conference. 62: 361-376.

Romesburg, H.C. 1981. "Wildlife science: gaining reliable knowledge." Journal Wildlife Management. 45: 293-313.

Scheffer, V.B. 1974. *A Voice for Wildlife: A Call for a New Ethic in Conservation.* New York: Charles Scribner's Sons.

Scott, P. 1936. "Morning Flight." *Country Life,* London.

Seymour, N.R. and W. Jackson. 1996. "Habitat-related variation in movements and fledging success of American black duck broods in northeastern Nova Scotia." Can. Jour. Zoology. 74: 1158-1164.

Sheaffer, S.E. and R.A. Malecki. 1995. "Waterfowl management: recovery rates, reporting rates, reality check!" Wildlife Society Bulletin. 23: 437-440.

Skutch, A.F. *The Minds of Birds.* College Station: Texas A&M University Press.

Sowls, L.K. 1955. *Prairie Ducks.* University. Nebraska Press, Lincoln.

Smith, R.I. and R.J. Roberts. 1976. "The waterfowl hunter's perceptions of the waterfowl resource." Trans North American Wildlife and Natural Resource Conference. 41: 188-193.

Sparrowe, R.D. and K.M. Babcock. 1989. "A turning point for duck harvest management." Trans North American Wildlife and Natural Resource Conference. 54: 493-495.

Trefethen, J.R. 1975. *An American Crusade for Wildlife.* New York: Winchester Press.

"Waterfowl Population Status. 1996." Canadian Wildlife Service and U.S. Fish and Wildlife Service.

Williams, B.K. and F.A. Johnson. 1995. "Adaptive management and the regulation of waterfowl harvests." Wildlife Society Bulletin 23: 430-436.

Wright, B.S. 1954. *High Tide and an East Wind: The Story of the Black Duck.* New York: Stackpole, Harrisburg and Wildlife Management Institute